The Mayor's Game

THE
MAYOR'S
GAME

*Richard Lee of New Haven
and the Politics of Change*

by Allan R. Talbot

HARPER & ROW, PUBLISHERS

New York, Evanston, and London

FIRST EDITION

LIBRARY OF CONGRESS CATALOG CARD NUMBER: 67-11346

To Elizabeth

Contents

REPRISE

Illustrations follow page 116

Preface

"There is no denying that the government of the cities is the one conspicuous failure of the United States." Such was the indictment in 1888 of an Englishman, James Bryce, whose book, *The American Commonwealth,* remains a landmark in the study of American politics, especially as a starting point for studies suggesting that city government has remained in the doldrums while the problems of the cities are approaching the point of being beyond hope of repair.

"Who the hell is James Bryce?" was a recent question of Richard Charles Lee, Mayor of New Haven, Connecticut. With that question Lee inadvertently, yet succinctly, noted an essential difference between the scholar and the practitioner. Thirteen years ago Lee, ignoring landmark scholarship and the dire warnings of contemporary critics, set out to rebuild a city not knowing how serious some of the problems were or that others even existed. His successes and failures and those of the people who helped him are the subjects of this story.

The lessons of New Haven's experience are not to be learned through Lee's style of leadership or through his administration's specific approach to the problems of urban blight and poverty. Lee is an unusual politician, and New Haven is but a village compared to major U.S. cities where the problems are quantitatively greater though proportionally no more menacing than those facing this middle-sized New England city. The relevant lesson which can be drawn from this story and applied to the needs of other cities is that we should no longer be repelled by the enormity of our urban problems. New Haven's message to other cities is written in optimism, and it says that progress is possible and success is feasible provided funds are available and a sustained effort is made. It has demonstrated that the work of restoring our cities can be challenging, fruitful, and even fun. I particularly hope that this will have meaning to younger readers, those who are casting about for a career, and especially those who may have been influenced by the counsels of caution and skepticism. New Haven shows that there can be nobility in action, that it is far better to participate than to watch.

A word now on how this book was written. I worked in New Haven from mid-1960 until 1965, and thus was close to most of the events which are described. I began preparation of the book in 1961 by keeping a personal record, and have supplemented it by interviews—many of them taped—which form the basis of the dialogue. In a few cases I reconstructed the dialogue from the recollections of the participants. In those interviews where the speaker is not identified, I afforded him anonymity in deference to his wishes. For background information I enjoyed full access to the Mayor's files, plus those of the Redevelopment Agency, Community Progress, Inc., and Roger L. Stevens. I avoided relying on Mayor Lee's recollections, but discovered that his version of events was fully corroborated. The Mayor's candor was admirable, all the more so because he is still in office.

Of course, as one who has given five years to New Haven I am hardly likely to suggest that its experience has been one of failure. I have tried to see this experience clearly and objectively, yet I feel it only proper to forewarn the reader of my involvement.

The book is organized into four parts. The first deals with Mayor Lee and with the basic program which became an essential part of his political and personal identity. The second part describes how he organized his program and introduces some of his major allies and opponents. This is followed by an account of the application of the program to the physical problems of the city; that is, the reshaping of the face of New Haven. The fourth section tells of the efforts to better the human resources of the city, especially through finding solutions to the problems of racial injustice and poverty. Because so much did happen, and because so many projects were undertaken simultaneously, it may be difficult for the reader to keep the order of events clear. I have therefore included a chronology of events, both national and local, which affected New Haven from 1941 through 1965. Neither the chronology nor the book purports to be a full historical account of the Lee administration or of New Haven; it is intended mainly as a narrative of those events which relate to the city's effort to overcome physical blight and human poverty.

Besides those people prominently mentioned in the book who gave freely of their time for interviews, I am indebted to a number of persons who played important roles in the preparation of it. I owe special thanks to Paul Ylvisaker, Director of the Public Affairs Division of the Ford Foundation, who helped launch the project. For guidance and constant encouragement I am also indebted to Dean Louis H. Pollak, of the Yale University Law School. To Mrs. A. Whitney Griswold, Mrs. Carl A. Lohmann, and Mr. Reuben A. Holden, Secretary of Yale University, I am most grateful for the special help they provided and for the time they gave to fill in areas where the record was unwritten. I also thank Mr. Richard Jackson, co-publisher of the New Haven *Register* for his friendly advice, information, and frankness.

Four people were especially generous and helpful in gathering information and materials. My thanks go to Jan Puckett, Mayor Lee's executive aide since his days at the Yale News Bureau; Jane Mulligan, of the City Hall Staff; Marion Morra and Bette Noble, of the Redevelopment Agency staff.

Several persons helped significantly in the preparation of key parts of the manuscript, and to these friends I express my personal appreciation: David Altschuler, Director of Administration, Community Progress, Inc.; Joseph F. Canny, Project Director, Washington, D.C., Redevelopment Land Agency; Robert Hazen, Director of Downtown Renewal, Boston Redevelopment Authority; Lee E. Stern, of the Mobil Oil Company; Eric Sandahl, Director of Public Information, Community Progress, Inc., and Albert Landino, New Haven's City Engineer.

I want also to acknowledge the use of two books which were particularly informative in gaining some understanding of the history of New Haven. *Three Centuries of New Haven, 1638–1938,* by Rollin G. Osterweis, and *Who Governs?,* by Robert A. Dahl, were useful in providing sources for areas of New Haven history that were especially important to this book.

My final but most important expression of gratitude is to my wife, Elizabeth Speakman Talbot, who gave the book skillful editing, careful rearranging, and knowledgeable suggestions based on her experience in elective office. Not only is she my wife, but for two years she was my representative to the New Haven Board of Aldermen.

ALLAN R. TALBOT

New Haven, Connecticut

I

The Setting

The Setting

1

The Mayor

"The hardest, most frustrating part of this job was getting it in the first place, and the worst single event in my career *has* to be that damned 1951 election," Richard Charles Lee, Mayor of New Haven, Connecticut, said emphatically.

"I had already beaten Celentano when I first ran in 1949," Lee continued. "Sure, the record shows I lost by around seven hundred votes, but what the record never shows is that one of our party workers got drunk with a thousand absentee ballots in his pocket."

"It was closer to two thousand, Dick," Ellen, Lee's wife, added.

"Yeah, Ellen's right. It was almost two thousand and we found the damned things in a desk drawer after the election and all of them were for me. I could have died. Well, we tried for mayor again in 1951. It was a helluva campaign. I took on the local press, I found some hanky-panky in City Hall, and I adopted a hard-hitting, chase-the-rascals-out approach. I had Celentano on the defensive from start to finish.

"I debated him, you know. At the Hotel Taft there was this huge debate and I was so nervous that I got sick to my stomach right before I had to go on. But I had arranged to have a lot of friends in the audience, and any time I said anything, they'd cheer like hell. By the time the debate drew to a close, I was having a fine time. Right up to Election Day I kept on the pressure. I was young, brash, and I kicked the tar out of the Mayor. I also kicked the tar out of my own health. I lost about ten pounds, my nerve ends were raw, and I was just exhausted. On the night they counted the votes, we were at my neighborhood headquarters. The only thing that kept me on my feet was the full anticipation that I'd be the next mayor of New Haven."

Lee now rose from his chair. His small size comes as a mild surprise. One expects there will be much more of him, for his deep voice and big head make him seem a large man. When he talks, a listener's attention is focused on that deep, sometimes booming voice and Lee's wonderfully expressive face: lines that show wear, worry, and experience; youthful eyes that are penetrating and mischievous; and a mouth that can be either firm or drawn in a warm, reassuring smile. But when he stands he is top-heavy. All that equipment is lodged on a delicate frame. "A Cadillac motor on a Ford chassis," he once described it.

He walked over to a cabinet in his bookstacks which is right next to his Kennedy collection, all the books ever written by or about the late President, who is one of Lee's few heroes. He opened the cabinet door and pulled out an album.

"What happened that night is all on these records. I never play them. I don't want to and I don't have to, because I'll remember everything that happened that night until I die. Around six I arrived at this small store on Shelton Avenue, just a block from where Ellen and I lived, where the party has its neighborhood headquarters. The first report we got is that some Republican moderator turned away six hundred Lee votes just before the polls closed. Then the city-wide returns came in. There was confusion from the start. In several wards there were as many as four different sets of returns. The Democrats had one, the Republicans had theirs, the press had another, and the official tally showed a still different story. All of them agreed only that it was unbelievably close."

Lee put down the record album and began pacing up and down the room. He was reliving events that had been repressed for fifteen years. He was no longer talking to anyone in the room nor was he talking to himself. He was addressing a painful grievance to "them" who crop up in moments of emotion when a man feels an injustice and exclaims, "Why did they let it happen?" At the other end of the room, Ellen Lee looked as though she regretted that the unhappy business had been dredged up.

"The Democrats downtown added up their sheets and told me I'd won by a hundred and forty-one votes, but a radio reporter said the Republicans were claiming victory for Celentano by a hundred and fourteen votes. The newspaper reporter in the store with us said the Republicans had won, but by sixteen votes. The official moderator didn't know what the hell was going on and was saying nothing.

"Everyone was in an uproar that night, so the moderator locked up all the returns in the police station and told everyone to go to bed. He would do an official recount the next day and declare a winner. So who could sleep? The next day they did a recount and Celentano was the winner by seventeen votes. By seventeen votes I missed being mayor for the second time, knowing all the while that some Republican moderator turned away six hundred of my votes just before the polls closed. We took it to court, and several weeks later the court made a verdict. Lee lost by two votes, two votes out of more than seventy thousand cast. Can you imagine that?"

The 1951 election was one of the most bizarre municipal elections ever held in New Haven, and it was the turning point in the life of a man and a city. Right after the court ruled Mayor Celentano the victor over Lee by two votes, Lee vowed he was finished with politics. The Irish blood that runs through Lee makes him a man attuned to omens. His two narrow defeats in 1949 and 1951 were signs (at least temporary ones, for an Irishman with some Scotch and English blood has the right to change his mind) that he was not fated for politics. Yet what other field was there for a man who had already made his ego a professional calling, and who stood as a curious hybrid in the only city he ever really knew?

Lee was the product of a number of New Haven institutions, yet he belonged to none. He had hustled himself out of a grimy, factory-class neighborhood where, like roughly 60 per cent of the townsfolk, he had been born and raised as a devout Catholic. He was an early worrier, plotting every move of his escape, sweating out the outcome, and approaching the work involved determined to do the job better than anyone else.

During high school and right after his graduation he had grabbed any job he could get—errand boy, pin boy, newspaper boy, even professional pallbearer. In 1935 he went to work for the New Haven *Journal Courier,* brazenly claiming to be a good typist and being eventually assigned to the City Hall beat, where he got a number of scoops as a *quid pro quo* for typing police reports. He came into close contact with the big names in New Haven's Democratic Party, including Mayor "Honest John" Murphy and Murphy's Director of Public Works, John Golden. By 1939, already restless with traveling the ancient, filthy, high-ceilinged corridors of City Hall as a reporter, Lee decided he would like to work there instead as a politician. In the fall of that year at the age of twenty-three, he ran on the Democratic ticket for alderman in his own neighborhood, the 17th ward, and won.

Shortly after he was sworn in as alderman, he quit his job on the paper and took the more prestigious post of associate secretary of the local Chamber of Commerce. Although he proved to be an ambitious worker for the Chamber—among other things, he organized a Junior Chamber of Commerce and became its president—he made more of a mark as alderman. This was a considerable feat in view of his youth and the peculiar workings and inherent weaknesses of New Haven's legislative body. The thirty-three men and women who serve as city legislators have two ways of using their part-time positions for political advancement. They can either remain quiet and hew close to the wishes of the mayor and party leaders in return for patronage and favors, or they can speak their minds in aldermanic debate in return for notoriety. Not surprisingly, Lee chose to speak his mind. His sponsorship of liberal legislation made him unique among his more conservative, more reticent, and older colleagues. The reward for these performances was neither the passage of his bills nor the approbation of the party hierarchy, who were less struck by the audacity of his proposals than by the warmth of his personality. What he got was recognition. He became a distinguishable figure among the hordes of usually anonymous local politicians.

Lee's health played a major role in the next phase of his career. In 1942 he was inducted into the Army, and after suffering from measles, pneumonia, and recurring peptic-ulcer attacks—as well as losing thirty-four pounds—he was honorably discharged. Upon his return to the city in the spring of 1943, he resumed his aldermanic duties and looked for a new job, one that might offer more satisfaction, excitement, and challenge than grinding out copy for the newspapers or enhancing the image of local business. What he found was not so much a job as an institution and a new way of life.

Yale University was looking for a man to write and edit a wartime periodical called the *Yale News Digest*. Lee got the job, which put him under the direct supervision of the University Secretary, Carl A. Lohmann, who, after admiring the enthusiasm, interest, and devotion his new employee gave to the *Digest*, took him under his wing.

"Caesar" Lohmann was a remarkable man, a connoisseur of music and art, a proficient editor, a master of heraldry, a talented gardener, the keeper of tradition at Yale, and a man of immense good taste and sophistication. He became Lee's mentor, and Lee was so attentive a student that his friends noticed subtle changes in the young man's appearance and manner. Familiar French idioms such as *entre nous* and *en famille* popped up in his conversation; he became compulsively aware of carelessly phrased letters and talk; his dress was distinctively Ivy League. He also had the greenest lawn on Shelton Avenue, and was doubtless the only alderman at the time who knew that a minister should be addressed as "the Reverend Mr." Contrary to what some journalists and writers have stated about the Lohmann influence on Lee, Lohmann never shaped Lee's basic beliefs, such as his liberalism and his genuine concern for the feelings of others, especially the underdog. Rather he showed Lee how to give his beliefs tasteful expression.

In 1944 Lee became Director of the Yale News Bureau, and

built it up from a one-man operation in the basement of Wood-
bridge Hall to a staff of five reporters and photographers, with a
dozen undergraduate assistants, based in a building of its own on
York Street. One of the staff, a tall, slender, attractive girl named
Ellen Griffin, became his wife in 1948. Ellen Griffin Lee's quiet
New England personality has been just the right contrast to her
husband's more volatile temperament. She puts into perspective
the setbacks over which Lee broods and the triumphs which elate
him. But despite the contentment of a happy marriage and the
security of an important job, Lee remained restless. By 1949 he
was, in the words of an associate, "climbing the walls of the
News Bureau" in search of more authority and recognition. But
to a towny with no formal education beyond high school Yale
could provide neither. Although Lee was to become a close
personal friend of the President of Yale, he could not enjoy the
symbols of authority and the recognition he craved.

At the time it seemed as though his parallel political career
might provide that fulfillment. He was now a major force in the
local Democratic Party, serving as majority leader in the Board
of Aldermen. His rise within the party was produced by a
combination of his natural attributes, luck, and the unsettled,
dissension-ridden state of Democratic politics—a condition that
could enable a hard-working young man to rise to the top if he
should happen to support a winning faction among the feuding
party chieftains. In 1945, Lee had supported John Golden in a
major party dispute and from that point on enjoyed the friendship of a man whose influence in the local party was expanding.
Golden is presently Democratic National Committeeman from
Connecticut. With Golden's support Lee waged a successful
primary campaign and became his party's mayoral candidate in
1949. Available records indicate that at thirty-three he was the
youngest man to run for mayor in the city's history. But in 1951,
after his second defeat against Celentano, Lee felt like anything
but a boy wonder of local politics. He looked back on the two
campaigns with puzzlement, anger, and frustration. He had
given to the two elections hard work and personal commitment

and he had attracted attention and seemed headed for success. Yet both efforts had ended in failure—and this was disturbingly uncommon for him.

His natural tendency was to find fault in others, particularly the local party organization, for the operation of the party during the two campaigns had been inefficient. Yet even if the party had functioned more smoothly, the fact remained that both elections were unusually close and no politician should ever have to bank so heavily on a well-tuned party machine for victory. There must be independent sources of support. Lee had to begin the more painful examination of himself as a cause for his two narrow losses.

Up to this point Lee had devoted his energy and talent to the cause of self-elevation. His various jobs, while performed admirably, served more as means for personal advancement than as ends in themselves. So, too, did his political career; nowhere is that clearer than in the tone and substance of his mayoral campaigns.

In 1949 his campaign was a series of promises to do better the things that Mayor Celentano was already doing. While the cry during the campaign was for efficiency in government, the basic premise was that Lee was intrinsically a better man. In 1951 Lee rode one issue, the notion that City Hall was the scene of conflict of interest and even outright corruption, but again the attraction which he hoped would get votes was not a positive issue or a clear-cut alternative to Celentano but the magnetism of his own personality. However, such magnetism was not enough to attract the support he needed. At the age of thirty-five Lee had developed what successful politicians must have—poise, shrewdness, apparent self-confidence, and a sufficient ego to withstand personal abuse. Still he lacked the quality of purpose which makes a successful politician outstanding. He needed to attach his personal dynamism to a public cause.

It is virtually impossible to reconstruct the process or events which ultimately convinced Lee that the monumental job of reconstructing New Haven would be his cause. The decision

itself seems to have been made in 1953, but the elements of it
stretched as far back as Lee's boyhood in Newhallville, an area
which typified the decrepit state of many of the city's neighborhoods and hinted at the rock-bottom slum condition of still
others. In the early nineteen-fifties ugliness and obsolescence
were spreading over New Haven like weeds in an unkempt
garden, and not just in the poor neighborhoods but in the
downtown retail section and in industrial areas. The symptoms
of the city's over-all decline were observable within a three-block
radius of the ancient City Hall. Just two blocks behind this
symbol of the city's government were the marks of industrial
progress which had been rampant in the nineteenth century but
which had diminished in the twentieth. There was, first, the
railroad that had slashed through the town, spewing soot and
grime along its path. Then came the smokestacks and bulky
frames of city industry, which blackened the air and spoiled the
rivers and the salt-water harbor. By 1950 many of the factories
were gaunt and deserted, for the industries had moved to the
suburbs where it was possible to build the flat, horizontal plants
preferred for contemporary assembly techniques.

To the south of City Hall was New Haven's downtown area.
Above the fake-marble and neon glitter of first-floor shops were
story after story of vacancies. The shabbiness of the area proclaimed what building records could document, that there had
been little major capital investment in that declining retail section since before World War I. The streets in and around
downtown were choked with trucks and cars, some looking in
vain for a place to park, others looking for the other end of
Route 1, which would take them elsewhere in New England.

Like his fellow townsmen, Lee was aware of his city's decline.
Yet until 1953 he, like so many others, had accepted New
Haven's unhappy condition. The problems were not new and
they did not scream for action. They were, instead, old problems
that had merely worsened with age, and the townspeople had
adjusted accordingly. The reformer within Lee manifested itself
hardly at all in 1949 and 1951. His promises were routine: to

deal with isolated and superficial symptoms of the city's over-all physical and economic decline, such as the need to provide a better street-paving program, a new playground in one neighborhood or a better school in another. The approach was not different from that used by the man whom Lee had tried to unseat. Mayor Celentano had run for office on a pledge to attack one small area of the city's problems, and this piecemeal attack, combined with accumulated community boredom over the fourteen-year administration of Celentano's Democratic predecessor, "Honest John" Murphy, had vaulted him into the mayor's chair.

The inability or refusal to address themselves to the broad problems of New Haven was a failing not only of the politicians but of all leadership groups within the community. With a 1950 population of 164,443, New Haven was of sufficient size to sustain the anonymity of city life; the notion of community responsibility had become blurred against the background of group interest. Whether the group was business, labor, Yale, or church leaders, there was a notable reluctance for any one of them to depart from their specialized interests and fill what had become a vacuum of community-wide leadership. All had a stake in the problems of New Haven, just as each had contributed directly or indirectly to them, but the common reaction seemed to be "Why bother?"

It is quite likely that if Lee had not lost in 1951 he, too, would have continued to take a limited view of what was wrong and what could be done. But, rejected twice and forced into a painful process of self-definition, he could now look at his city from a new perspective—that of a man who felt alienated, who was a stranger to himself and to his city—and from that fresh vantage point he could see that there was indeed a local position available for one of his hybrid development, the post not of mayor but of community leader. He could also see that there was a fundamental issue for a political campaign in New Haven, and that the issue was as pervasive and as basic as the sorry state of New Haven, which affected everyone who lived there. Thus he had found the vital cause which he needed, the cause he was later to call "the rebirth of New Haven."

Once armed with purpose and a new ideology, Lee displayed a resilience that was to serve him well during all his years in office. At that time his resilience could be defined as his ability to interpret his two close defeats not as an omen that he was not fated for politics but as an arithmetic progression at work. If he had lost in 1949 by 700 votes and in 1951 by 2 votes, he was destined to win in 1953 by at least 696 votes. He would run again.

Of course this decision required a reversal of his previous announcement that he was through with electioneering. A good politician avoids a unilateral change of mind. It must appear that the switch is a response to a greater force known as "the will of the people." A suitable petition urging Lee to reconsider was drafted early in 1953. It was signed by a number of people although nowhere near the ten thousand citizens Lee's friends claimed when he announced in the summer of 1953 that he would bow to their demand and run for the third time.

That fall Lee put together a campaign that was markedly different from the previous two. His ideas on city reform had attracted some new and able talent to the political scene, and they formed a group called Independents for Lee. Many of these people were members of the Yale faculty; most were Adlai Stevenson liberals, and in hammering away at his theme for a new city Lee promised to use "the best brains in the city." The Independents mainly attacked Celentano, characterizing him as "old-fashioned" and "indifferent to the critical problems of city planning and urban redevelopment." In the background a new Democratic Town Chairman, Arthur T. Barbieri, though not particularly interested at the time in Lee's renewal proposals but bent on redeveloping the Democratic Party, had brought many dissident party faithfuls back into line. Still further in the background was a ground swell of popular sympathy for Lee, a feeling that while he was still a brash young man, he had endured the ordeal of two incredibly close defeats and had a victory coming to him. The combination of this sympathy vote, an improved party organization, and an active and articulate citizens' group, along with the new Lee ideology was too much for Celentano. After four years of frustration and heartbreak, Lee was elected Mayor of New Haven at the age of thirty-seven by a margin of 3,582 votes.

2

The Program

Night and day separate the jubilation of election victory from the realization that one has finally arrived at the seat of power. Election Night for a victorious candidate is happily crowded with party well-wishers who quite naturally attribute success not to the appeal of the candidate but to the work of the party. In the minds of most party faithfuls, candidates do not win elections; they just lose them.

The morning after, the loneliness of public responsibility sets in, broken only by congratulatory calls and letters which have to be carefully answered. Now the candidate must face two inter-related questions.

The first is how to grasp the reins of power and exert influence and leadership. Elected executive posts in government offer no power transformers through which executive will may be auto-matically translated into public policy and then into government action. Rather, they offer varying legal powers, an important title, and some ceremonial trappings and the symbols of leader-ship. The impact a mayor makes and the power he exerts result from the blend of his personal convictions, his strength, and his skill with the built-in titular, ceremonial, and legal prerogatives of the job. But the quality of the man is much more important than the authority of the position. A man with strong convictions and effective powers of persuasion can take a so-called weak or even ceremonial mayoralty and make it the center of community action. Conversely, a man who avoids conflict and is interested only in personal security or gain can be given the most potent legal authority and still be remembered only by his family and perhaps the Bureau of Internal Revenue.

The second question a new mayor must ask is what it is he wants to accomplish. Many mayors get excited about maintaining efficient city services, minding the tax rate, and maneuvering loyal party members and friends into available jobs. While all that is commendable or at least understandable, it has little bearing on the obvious problems that plague America's urban centers—the slums, the run-down schools, the choked streets, the filth, the human misery, the declining economic base, and the widespread ugliness.

Lee's answers to these questions had already been formed during his four-year waiting period, and perhaps even before that. "It may sound much too dramatic," he said recently, "but as I look back I think I was preparing for this job all my life. By 1951 I wanted it so bad I was like a rookie dying for the chance to show the manager that I was ready. Finally, when he sent me to the plate, it rained. But in 1953, after I finally made it, I was more ready than ever. I had a general idea of what I wanted to do. I felt I knew how to do it. The bat felt good in my hands."

Lee's background as a City Hall reporter and an alderman had given him a unique insight into the mayor's job and the personalities he would have to deal with. One long-time municipal employee, a maintenance man, offers this picture of an early trip of Lee's to City Hall after his victory:

"He was all fired up and in he comes through the front door. The place was suddenly full of noise, with Dick shaking hands with secretaries, the elevator men, and all. Everyone he greets with a smile, and he knew all our first names and we knew him. Dick was no stranger to City Hall."

Lee's knowledge of the personalities in city government included higher-level officials. One veteran city executive recalls his impression of Lee's victory in these terms:

"All of us knew Dick before he got elected, and I can't think of anyone who really disliked him. He was friendly, always had a smile. Of course everyone knew him from being an alderman and as a reporter. I suppose there was some uneasiness now that he was mayor, the same as there is whenever there's a new boss. But on a personal basis, he still seemed like the same Dick Lee."

Lee's grasp went beyond the first names and official titles of those in the city government. He had accumulated a formidable mental file on their strengths, weaknesses, and even some of their indiscretions. All this proved useful once he became mayor, as was his almost encyclopedic knowledge of the general lay of the city land. For instance, his personal secretary, Mrs. Robert Puckett, remembers that during the early days of the administration a request came in from Samuel Lubell, the voter analyst, for a profile on all New Haven wards, including the social and economic characteristics of the residents, election trends, and subleaders. Lee was interested in the request and took half an hour to dictate a memorandum so detailed it would have taken a Yale graduate student weeks of research to prepare. A staff should have an employee or a consultant with a thorough knowledge of its target area. The New Haven staff had Lee.

What lay under his knowledge, technique, and charm? "A simple, yet intense moral purpose," suggests Eugene Rostow, former Dean of the Yale Law School and now the Undersecretary for Political Affairs in the State Department. Rostow, no aloof observer of the New Haven scene, is a friend of Lee's and served as a co-chairman of the Citizens for Lee Committee in the 1953 campaign. "Very few of us at the University took any great interest in Dick's first two attempts to become mayor. He was a part of Yale, so we followed the campaigns, but they were really ordinary affairs with Dick hitting conventional themes of efficiency and honesty. But when he campaigned to rebuild the city, in 1953, he struck a responsive chord. He was attacking fundamental ills of our time, the moral, economic, and social injustice of the slum.

"Dick is no ordinary politician. He has successfully developed the skills of that trade, but he has used them to help others. I believe the reason he finally won in 1953 is that he abandoned the stock clichés of electioneering and allowed his morality to come through. Voters sense this in a candidate. From 1953 until now, the people have understood that Dick means it when he says that slums are evil and the city must be rebuilt. They sense his commitment and that's more important to them than any mistakes he might have made."

Some New Haveners might quarrel with Rostow's last comment, but it would be a matter of emphasis. One searches vainly in the papers, in the general political rhetoric, in the statements of opponents in New Haven from 1953 to the present for an attack on Lee's sincerity, his commitment, or the integrity of his program goals. Many disagree with him, some stress his mistakes, others patronize him with adjectives like "misguided," but no one attacks on grounds of a difference between what Lee has said he will do and what he tries to do. Lee is what the politicians call a "doer"; he stands for something, and he and his program are inseparable.

Between his election in November, 1953, and his inauguration in January, 1954, Lee spent most of his time developing the general course of his program to rebuild the city. This meant finding out more about the federal redevelopment program and what the city had done in renewal and planning, and then determining how the program was to be run under his administration.

The means for city rebuilding at the time was the Federal Housing Act of 1949, which was on the verge of being amended by the broader Housing Act of 1954. Both acts provided for government loans and grants to buy run-down property, clear it, and sell it to a developer who was willing to put up a new building that conformed with a redevelopment plan. The 1949 Act was aimed at blighted residential areas; it stressed total clearance, and did little to encourage comprehensive planning. The 1954 Act aimed at "predominantly" residential areas— meaning that commercial redevelopment was possible; it insisted on comprehensive city-wide planning, and encouraged spot clearance and rehabilitation as opposed to blanket clearance of run-down areas. The federal grant was for two-thirds of the total cost of a redevelopment project. The local or city share of one-third could be met with cash or capital improvements. In 1954 urban renewal was still in the pioneering stage. Little had been accomplished in any city under its provisions.

Fortunately for the new administration, there had been some local spadework in exploring the possibilities of redevelopment and in city planning. It had been done by a number of individuals, including Mayor Celentano, who, while not adventurous in leading the city toward the potential benefits of redevelopment, was receptive to the planners' ideas and has always supported the goal of rebuilding wide areas of the city. His attitude was typical of the attitudes of a great many mayors today who actively support redevelopment, but with the same intensity that they support a modern fire department, failing thereby to see the difference between providing a new opportunity and improving a traditional service through City Hall.

Under Celentano's administration a redevelopment agency had been created in 1950. In March, 1951, the fledgling agency had received a federal grant to survey potential redevelopment areas, and in August, 1952, another federal grant was received for detailed studies in the Oak Street area of the city. By March, 1953, the agency had staked out project boundaries. The generating force behind the agency was the city's planning department, which seems to have provided the sustained support and push that made the new agency possible. Some members of the City Plan Commission—including its Chairman, Angus Frazier, and Myres McDougal, of the Yale Law faculty—were concerned that a strong redevelopment agency might pervert the planning process by applying expedient solutions to long-range problems. But they also recognized that a new agency was the only way the city's master plan could ever come close to implementation. Their fears were eventually to be realized not because the agency perverted the planning process but because it actually took it over, which in the eyes of some planners may mean the same thing.

In 1954 New Haven was one of the few American cities which had a master plan to guide its physical development. Unlike other cities, it did not have the problem of deciding how to plan for change and future growth; its problem was to find ways to realize an already completed, highly sophisticated planning document. Maurice Rotival, a French planner, had developed it in 1941 when he was on the Yale faculty and refined it in 1951 when he was a full-time private consultant. Rotival's theory was that New Haven was basically a traffic distribution center, and that any effort to eliminate urban blight and protect the city from further disintegration would have to be based on this role. The heart of the Rotival plan was to redesign and rebuild the city around a new system of interstate roadways that were then on the drawing boards of the State Highway Department. Briefly, the plan called for a new harbor-front entranceway to New Haven—then called relocated Route 1 and today known as the Connecticut Turnpike—which would cut along the water's edge in a southwest-northeast direction. Rotival called for an interchange somewhere around the middle of the new highway's journey along the harbor, which would connect the harbor thruway with a new highway cutting through the city to the north and for a bypass artery going west of the city's downtown area to connect eventually with the existing Merritt Parkway.

Within the framework of this proposed highway system, Rotival and City Plan Director Norris Andrews had sketched nine renewal areas. Two were in the downtown area, one was a proposed industrial-wholesale area along the harbor, and the remainder were predominantly residential. In the neighborhoods the redevelopment areas were to have the highways as a screen against nearby commercial or industrial areas, in downtown as a new entranceway, and in industrial-wholesale areas as a means of convenient access to an efficient transportation system. Under the plan, approximately 25 per cent of the city's land area would have to be redeveloped.

This bold blueprint was easy to endorse, as some groups like the Chamber of Commerce did, because it was only a general policy statement which had yet to be distilled into specific proposals about what blocks would be cleared, what families and businesses would be moved, and what new buildings were to be created.

With appropriate boldness, Lee decided that the Rotival plan would provide the basic concept of his rebuilding program. The politician who had found a cause now had a plan. As he studied the plan in the late fall of 1953, the basic elements of his program began to take shape. Federal redevelopment law had made the Rotival blueprint feasible. The city planners had already negotiated the construction of the Connecticut Turnpike along the harbor, while the State Highway Department had indicated a readiness to build some sort of downtown connector.

"The elements of a comprehensive program were there when I became Mayor," Lee later explained. "Someone had to fuse them, and give the program direction and purpose. On a national basis urban renewal in the early nineteen-fifties was waiting for someone to show it could work. In New Haven we had an excellent master plan which could work only through urban renewal. The town seemed ready for change if I could show that concrete progress was possible. In short, the market was ready for the large-scale program I envisioned."

The remarkable aspect of Lee's stewardship in New Haven is that urban renewal became the centerpiece of his administration and his personal and political reason for being. The process of public control of physical change intrigued and delighted him. It also lent itself to the undisciplined exaggerations of the Lee mind. As we shall see, he eventually began calling every improvement of his administration, from fire hydrants to sewers, "a product of our renewal program." A newcomer to New Haven, taken aback by these dramatic flourishes or Lee's personal color, might wonder how much substance, originality, or sincerity there is under his effervescent surface. Those who have spent time with him and have witnessed his interminable project tours, his angry notes to shoddy architects and landlords, and the great thrill he gets out of seeing models of new buildings can more easily discern the truth about him: he believes.

The renewal of any city requires strong, understanding leaders. It requires, as well, a good basic plan. It also needs vigorous day-to-day direction by someone who can make the plan a working blueprint, fight the battles a mayor cannot afford to fight, cement the agreements a mayor suggests, and produce the program results a mayor needs to get re-elected. New Haven had the plan and the leader. Now it needed a good doer. Finding such a man was a major preoccupation for Lee during the post-1953 election period.

A name which keeps popping up in the jammed Lee appointment book in the late fall of 1953 was Edward J. Logue, a man who over the years has been variously described as "a brilliant programmer," "the toughest man in the world," "a perfectly charming man," "an egotistical S.O.B.," "one of the best friends I ever had." He is, as one might deduce from those comments, a man for all occasions, fortified by a sense of drama second only to the man who was to be his boss in New Haven from 1953 until 1961, when he left for Boston, Massachusetts. Today, at the age of forty-five, Logue has risen to become one of the best-known and successful renewal chiefs in the nation by virtue of his work in New Haven and Boston. In December, 1965, *Life* in a special feature on the American city featured Logue as the "Bold Boston Gladiator." In the fall of 1953 his reputation was more modest. He was known mainly to Connecticut politicians as an energetic young lawyer who had worked as a special assistant to Governor Chester Bowles. Logue was a Bowles "bird dog." He carried out the Governor's orders on state reorganization, education, and labor problems. After Bowles lost to John Lodge in 1951, Logue became Bowles' special assistant in India, where he helped direct all phases of the Ambassador's activities and learned what Logue has described as "the great sense of urgency which should accompany public service—the feeling, as Chet once put it, that 'if the problem exists today, it should be dealt with today.' " Logue's drive has been his most salient characteristic in public service. It has given him the image of a tough, able, and often abrasive man of action.

The Eisenhower victory of 1952 meant that both Bowles and his aide were out of work. Logue came to New Haven in 1953, but it had nothing to do with professional plans. His wife, Margaret, was expecting their first child and had a strong preference for a local obstetrician. Neither she nor her husband were strangers in town. Margaret's father was the late William C. DeVane, Dean of Yale College. Logue had gone to undergraduate and law school at Yale.

Logue knew Lee while Lee was Director of the Yale News Bureau. When Lee ran for Mayor in 1953, Logue was weighing his career choices. He took a breather from the demands of choice and worked in the Lee campaign, organizing local lawyers behind Lee and supplying ideas on redevelopment. Right after the election, the new Mayor casually asked him, "How'd you like to work for me?"

"Doing what?"

"Helping me put the redevelopment program together."

"In what job?"

"I don't know for sure," Lee said. He reached into a desk drawer and pulled out a city charter. "Take a look in there and see if anything appeals to you."

"I looked through the charter," Logue recalled, "and there was absolutely nothing of interest. I went back to Dick to tell him so, but before I could refuse he upped the ante and asked me if I'd like to be his deputy mayor." At this point in his recollection, Logue broke into a laugh.

"What an absolutely evil proposal. Dick quickly acknowledged that there was no such position, but said he would give me the authority informally to act as a deputy mayor. For budget reasons, he said, I would be listed as Mayor's Secretary, which paid only $4,000 a year, but Dick said he would get it raised to $6,000.

"Well, I started to explain that was not enough money, that I had some Washington offers, and that I was also considering setting up a private practice in New Haven, but Dick broke in and in typical Dick Lee fashion said that he would even let me practice law on the side, which he knew—and I should have known—would be next to impossible while working for a guy like him. Well, I accepted."

Such was the beginning of the Lee-Logue alliance, the most significant development of the post-electoral period. It brought together two men of unusual talent, ability, and will. The remarkable aspect of their relationship was that it lasted as long as it did. "We fought continually, right up to Ed's departure in 1961," said Lee. "And I'd fire him once a week, sometimes twice." "We had some awful, just plain ferocious fights," said Logue. "It was terrible." Each of these admissions was given with the broadest of smiles. Neither man remembers the precise reason for the fights. It seldom had anything to do with programs, but was mainly a matter of Logue's role in the administration. In those days Lee was an admitted penny pincher on staff salaries and insisted that his aides, including Logue, stay in the background. "Well, money was a problem during one quarrel," Logue has said, "but usually it was a question of role. I was ready to be a behind-the-scenes fella. But there's a difference between being a subordinate and a slave. Once Dick cut the ground under me in public. I forget the issue, but I remember that was the most serious quarrel from my point of view. When he did that, I just got up and quit."

Whenever Logue quit or Lee fired him, it took days of intensive bargaining through intermediaries to patch things up. Mitchell "Mike" Sviridoff, President of the State A.F.L.–C.I.O., a Lee appointee to the Board of Education, and later the director of the city's anti-poverty program, was a regular mediator. He remembers that the problems between the two men were caused by the fuzziness of Lee's original proposal to Logue. "Ed was acting like a deputy mayor from the start, and Dick was treating him like one behind the scenes," says Sviridoff. "But whenever Ed emerged publicly as a strong force in the administration, Dick would try to cut him down. Part of it may have been personal insecurity, but I think it was based mainly on Dick's sensitivity to public reaction. This town was not used to high-powered public executives, especially one like Logue, and I think Dick was mainly trying to keep Ed under wraps."

Keeping a man like Logue under wraps is something like hiding a tiger in the cellar. By the end of the first year of the Lee administration Logue was running the city's Redevelopment Agency. By the beginning of the second year, he became the redevelopment czar through his appointment as Development Administrator, a new city post which put him in charge of all city agencies which had anything to do with redevelopment. His only boss on an organization chart or in reality was the Mayor. Thus the conflict between the two men stemmed from the natural problem of how two such strong-minded people could coexist in a milieu of action and power. Yet the full character of their relationship is best indicated by the fact that twelve years later, and separated by a hundred and twenty miles, both men used exactly the same language in summing up their quarrels: "We fought like brothers."

Lee and Logue approached the problems of New Haven with the fervor of a moral crusade and the pragmatism of practical politics. "Dick was often like a preacher," Logue has observed, "but the two-year term sometimes made it necessary to depart from the sermon and take some expedient action to show results." Each man staked his considerable ego on the outcome. Generally, it was Logue who proposed what should be done and Lee—the accepted boss—who decided what would be done and how, although everyone intimately connected with the program can recall at least one occasion when Lee did all three. Logue has never been happy with how writers have treated Lee in their descriptions of the relationship. "Somehow," he says, "it's implied, even stated, that I was the brains of the outfit, and Dick was the con man who got things done and served as a front. That's an enormous injustice to Dick. He percolates ideas, and he has a marvelous sense and appreciation for good planning. He also knows how to use people, and that's one of his great strengths."

Logue is a general by instinct and a generalist by choice. His specialty by training is the law, and he continually builds records for decisions he reaches based on his interests and intuition in other areas. He is no planner, but he has the planner's sense of unity in dealing with city problems. He is no architect, but he has developed a keen appreciation for building design and spatial relationships. He learned the lessons of administrative control and the benefits of thorough staff work under Bowles and he developed his expertise under Lee. He thrives on conflict, which makes him suited for politics—although his abrasive manner in resolving conflict does not make him a politician. He is tough and smart, and he loves cities. And he has attributed part of his success to being "reasonable, by which I don't mean being agreeable."

When Logue joined Lee in 1953, his knowledge of city rebuilding was restricted to his observations in India, his natural interests, and lectures Maurice Rotival used to give at Yale (after which Logue and his wife would gather Rotival's discarded sketches and paste them on their quonset-hut home). On the eve of Lee's inauguration, the combined Lee-Logue knowledge of the details of their intended program was negligible. Aside from Rotival's plan, some preliminary work by the Redevelopment Agency, and a campaign pledge to rebuild the city, they had nothing to fall back on save the intensity of their convictions, their determination to succeed, and their willingness to experiment. They were on their own. McGeorge Bundy once said that the form and direction of government is the product of ". . . continuous, sustained, and intense effort, generally uncertain at the beginning of what the outcome will be, always responsive to the situation as it is . . . and not of some abstract plan of what it ought to be. . . ." Bundy's observation helps make the almost nonchalant innocence of Lee's pre-inaugural period materialize as respectable and even responsible. The political administrative history of the years that followed makes the observation more understandable. Some years later Logue summarized the administration's feeling at the time:

"We were anxious, willing, and optimistic. We weren't really sure of how far we would go or how we would get there. It was not until 1956 that I realized what we were really trying to do. That year Paul Appleby* came to see us, and with his ability to

* The late Dr. Paul H. Appleby, who had a distinguished career in both education and public service. He served as the Assistant to the Secretary of Agriculture and Undersecretary of Agriculture in the Roosevelt administration; was Assistant Director of the Bureau of the Budget in the Truman Administration; served as Director of the Budget in New York State under the Harriman administration; and was a Professor of Political Science and Dean of the Maxwell School of Citizenship and Public Affairs at Syracuse University. Appleby's son, L. Thomas Appleby, worked in New Haven as Executive Director of the New Haven Redevelopment Agency, Development Administrator, and is now the Executive Director of the Washington, D.C., Redevelopment Land Agency.

drive right to the heart of a matter in a few words asked me, 'What the hell are you guys trying to do?' I stopped for a minute, thought, and then replied, 'We're shooting the moon, that's what we're trying to do.' "

II

Organizing Support

3

Tacky's Job

Lee's first two years in office were devoted largely to reshaping
and controlling the city bureaucracy so that it could support
large-scale municipal reconstruction. A hint of the problems he
encountered is given in an incident, which has now become a
legend, about a friend of his named Tacky Dwyer who worked in
the Public Works Department. One of the laborers Tacky supervised wanted desperately to get promoted, and regularly
hounded Tacky to see what strings he could pull. When Tacky's
friend, Lee, became Mayor, Tacky immediately began putting
pressure on him to see what could be done. Lee finally relented
and told the laborer to come to the Mayor's office. After sharing
gossip for a few minutes, Lee finally asked the man what sort
of promotion he wanted, to which the laborer quickly replied, "I
want Tacky's job." As Lee soon discovered, there were many in
city government who wanted Tacky's job.

The conquest of the bureaucracy broke down into three basic
challenges: establishing the Mayor's authority; reorganizing;
and staffing agencies with competent people. The first challenge was a natural one for Lee. He likes to be on top of things
and he knew enough about the personalities and peculiari-
ties of city government to scramble to the top. The bureaucratic
situation he inherited on January 1, 1954, approached anarchy.
City agencies functioned like a confederation of tribes. There
was no central control exercised by the legislative branch, the
thirty-three-member Board of Aldermen, because it was too
large and because many of the members were not up to the

effort. Those factors, plus the part-time nature of aldermanic duty (they meet in regular session once a month), made the legislature a weak opponent when it came to dealing with the bureaucracy, although some aldermen exerted considerable individual influence in departments to which they were assigned as board members.

In the workings of this bureaucracy the traditional role of mayor was also weak. Citizen boards, which are common to New England local government, sat at the top of most major departments and set policy. A New Haven mayor, therefore, had no direct control over his operating agencies, and although he appointed the board members, a new mayor found that he had to deal with the appointees of his predecessor, since the terms are overlapping. Another reason for the perennial weakness of the mayor's role was that most mayors held other jobs while in office. Lee's predecessor, Mayor Celentano, for instance, was an undertaker, and maintained his business interest while in office. One of Lee's campaign pledges in all three elections had been to become a full-time mayor.

Thus the combination of an ineffectual legislative branch and a weak mayor had enabled city departments to operate according to the wishes of their executive staffs and citizen boards. The only real outside interference came from the city's powerful Board of Finance, which controlled the city's annual budget. The key to unlocking these prevailing bureaucratic practices and establishing his personal authority was clear to Lee: he had to make his presence known to the isolated departments, and he had to assume control of the city budget.

His first departmental encounter was with the Police Board, a seven-member group of which he automatically became a member under the city charter. The Police Commissioners convened on January 4, 1954, to meet their new member and to ratify a private and not entirely apolitical decision, the appointment of a new Assistant Police Chief. During the closed-door caucus before the official meeting, Lee promptly challenged their choice, announced his own candidate, and gave two warnings: if the Commissioners did not go along with his candidate, he would throw the public meeting into an uproar, and he would keep their votes in mind when it came time for reappointments. This surprise maneuver, although infuriating to the Commissioners, had the desired impact. This is how one observer described the public meeting which followed:

"They were very subdued, even solemn. Dick's candidate was nominated, seconded, and approved. Then Dick suddenly started paying a glowing tribute to the guy the Commissioners wanted for Assistant Police Chief. Then he proposed two motions—one establishing a new position of Assistant Police Chief for Plainclothesmen, the other nominating the Commissioners' man to fill it. Well, the heads had been bowed, you know, but suddenly they looked up in surprise, I guess, and quickly seconded and approved Dick's motions."

The Commissioners got the message. Lee had established himself by getting his man appointed, and then offered the other man an important appointment as a reward for good behavior. An interesting footnote to this encounter is that after the Commissioners' candidate left the force, the position of Assistant Police Chief for Plainclothesmen has been left unfilled.

Lee got away with similar tactics of bravado and surprise the next day during his first meeting with the Fire Commissioners. At their last meeting in the twilight hours of the Celentano administration, the Fire Commissioners had raged a bit out of control. They had elevated seven men to the position of lieutenant, retired the Fire Chief at 90 per cent of his salary (proposing at one point to give him the city-owned Cadillac he was driving), appointed a new Fire Chief, and, with this last-minute package, exceeded their annual budget by around $20,000. It was their intention during this first meeting under the Lee administration to look over the new Mayor and then clean up some odds and ends they had no time for in December—including the promotion of the retired Chief's clerk to the position of Battalion Chief. Lee took over the meeting. He announced at the start that the clerk would not become a Battalion Chief, that he, the Mayor, was going to review thoroughly the executive pension policies of the Fire Department, that he intended to put a freeze on all new hiring, and that if anyone did not like it he would keep that in mind when their appointments came up. He then opened the meeting to some startling new business. He proposed that the new Fire Chief be given $1,000 a year raise. This, he explained, would put the new man on the same level as the Police Chief. This surprise proposal had the multiple effect of embarrassing the new Chief, winning his friendship, and shocking the Commissioners—yet flattering them, too, because the new Chief was their appointee. The new Mayor's first signal was loud and clear. He was for the Fire Department. He wanted it to share equal status with the Police Department, but on his terms.

During a third meeting in his hectic first week Lee met with the Board of Finance to begin a slow, careful process of taking it over. The only dramatic move during this session was Lee's insistence that the city's Personnel Director, who was a regular, albeit ex-officio, participant in the Board's meetings and who had influenced some of its decisions, get out and stay out. "I wanted to be alone with my Board of Finance," Lee explains today. The reason he wanted to be alone is explained by Edward Logue:

"Dick is probably the only Mayor in New Haven's history to do what it says he should do in the Charter, be chairman of the Board of Finance. Before Dick, mayors negotiated with the Board of Finance. The way he controlled them was through his superb understanding of the budget process and his readiness to do his homework before the meetings began."

Lee gave full priority to budget matters during his first year in office. He worked at it himself, and he organized his staff to keep him one step ahead of his fellow Board members. As Logue remembers it, the city budget was his prime assignment that first year. In addition to Logue, Lee hired Fred A. Schuckman, Research Director of the Connecticut Public Expenditures Council, as his fiscal aide. He also appropriated the Controller's Office staff. The two top staff men of that department were quick to appreciate the stronger role of the Mayor and willingly helped him by performing such thoughtful services as clearing Board of Finance agenda with him before the other members saw them. No New Haven mayor in recent history was this well armed in dealing with the Board of Finance, and when fiscal expertise and solid staff support were not enough for Lee to get his way with the Board, he was not bashful about pointing out his control over their appointments, too.

By the spring of 1954, Lee was fully in charge of Board of Finance meetings, and his personal staff—mainly Logue—was preparing the Board's budget recommendation for the following year. The control of budget preparation was tantamount to control of the bureaucracy, because the budget recommended by the Board of Finance generally becomes the official city budget. The Board of Aldermen has no practical role in this process; under the New Haven Charter it usually approves the Board of Finance recommendation without authority to increase the total amount. As Logue made his budget rounds in the summer of 1954 ("like some huge bear poking for food" is how one ex-department head described him), it was becoming clear to city department heads that the Mayor's Office was in charge. There were other pointed reminders of the trend, including an executive order which prohibited any staff hiring without the Mayor's approval, the removal of all department phone numbers and the establishment of a central switchboard, the centralization of purchasing, the elimination of fifty-two jobs from the Public Works Department, the closing of neighborhood police precincts, regular cabinet meetings called by the Mayor "to promote the team spirit," and even the transfer of one outspoken critic of Lee's to the Health Department, where he was assigned as an inspector of all the barns in Connecticut which supplied milk to New Haven. Thus Lee had taken the first step in shaping the bureaucracy: he had established his control.

The next step, reorganization of municipal functions around renewal, was more difficult. Lee was not sure of how much reorganization was necessary or possible. Logue recalls that Lee became fully aware of the chaotic relations between departments during a meeting held with the Highway Department in the spring of 1954. On the city side of the table were traffic planners, city planners, representatives from Rotival's office, members of the Redevelopment Agency, and several executives from other city departments to serve as window dressing. The meeting was called on the alignment of the downtown connector, and every participant offered a different version of where the connector should go. Finally the perplexed Highway Commissioner, G. Albert Hill, asked Lee, "Precisely what does New Haven want?" Lee promised a specific answer for a future meeting, and after everyone left he flew into a rage, vowing that such a meeting would never happen again.

Of course the unruly highway meeting was merely a reflection of a deeper organizational disorder, which affected all areas of physical programming. Because of the previous state of bureaucratic anarchy, some city agencies were barely aware of what was happening in others, and all were unused to working together. Part of the problem was a series of personal and professional frictions. For instance, the New Haven Housing Authority was cool toward the newly established Redevelopment Agency. The reason was basically that the Housing Authority had been in the slum-clearance business since the early nineteen-forties and understandably regarded the Agency as an upstart. Relations between the Redevelopment Agency and the City Plan Commission were also poor. The directors of the two agencies did not get along. There was also poor communication among those agencies responsible for enforcing the various building, health, and fire codes. The Building Inspector, for instance, would sometimes clear construction plans without checking to see if the Fire Department had looked them over, too; and there was no coordination to speak of in enforcing code requirements for existing buildings.

In 1954, as Lee and Logue concerned themselves increasingly with purely renewal matters, they also discovered they had major problems at the very heart of the redevelopment bureaucracy. The Redevelopment Agency, which had been set up by Mayor Celentano to receive federal grants, acquire and clear land, and sell it to developers, was bogged down. It was still several months away from receiving federal approval for its first redevelopment project, Oak Street, for which planning money had been received in August, 1953. The Agency Director, Samuel Spielvogel, had a number of serious problems, including an impatient Mayor who kept pounding his desk for action. Spielvogel's job was made difficult by the complicated, often confusing, and untried process of putting a project together. His poor relations with the City Plan Commission Director made things harder. And as if all this were not enough, Lee had usurped Spielvogel's planning consultant, Maurice Rotival, whose staff, incidentally, included Nicholas deB. Katzenbach, whom Logue had asked to take some time from the Yale Law School to oversee Rotival's New Haven office. The end result of these intrigues was that Rotival was serving the Mayor rather than Spielvogel.* A less deliberate and cautious Agency director might have bowed to Lee's pressure and slapped a project together. Instead, Spielvogel kept on pointing out the problems and dangers of a pioneering renewal program, and put himself directly in the path of Lee and Logue, who, spurred by their sense of urgency, were more concerned with action than risks. A collision took place, and in December, 1954, Spielvogel met privately with Lee to hand in his resignation, which took effect on January 21, 1955. Logue became Acting Director of the Agency. Under his direction and Lee's continual demands the madness of twenty-four-hour workdays hit the once-quiet Agency. By March, 1955, the Agency staff had ground out the final Oak Street Project Report, which was funded by the Urban Renewal Administration in the summer of 1955.

Concurrent with his probing of the Redevelopment Agency and eventually appointing Logue its Acting Director, Lee was still plagued with the broader problem of reorganization. His embarrassing encounter with the Highway Department had im-

---

* Lee's use of department consultants to take over departments was a recurring device. The prototype maneuver, of course, was his clever use of the Controller's Office staff in his domination of the Board of Finance. The consultant device was a variation. The procedure was for Lee to negotiate privately with a department consultant so that the consultant would recommend a proposal which Lee wanted. For instance, Rotival's office later recommended that Logue take over the Redevelopment Agency. It also proposed that he assume a new post of Development Coordinator. Certain changes which Lee wanted in the Police Department and his desire to establish a special traffic department were accomplished in the same manner.

pressed upon him the need for a quick solution. Logue was pushing for a charter revision as the most thorough solution: to create a new post of development czar—i.e., Logue—who, working directly under the Mayor, would head a new development department that would be an amalgam of the redevelopment, planning, traffic and parking, and some code enforcement functions which were then separate. Such a charter change would also include a four-year term for the mayor.

"I've always supported charter reform," Lee says today. "Our city government is obsolete. People expect a mayor to deal with twentieth-century problems using nineteenth-century equipment. It's like playing quarterback for the Giants wearing nothing but knickers and a T-shirt." While supporting charter reform today and being intrigued with the idea back in 1954, Lee has been leery of it, too. In three previous unsuccessful charter reform movements, he had learned that for most voters the issues were easier to reject than to understand. Charter reform with its hearings and referendums meant open combat with an uncertain outcome and Lee avoids both whenever possible, preferring to persuade individual adversaries to his way of thinking. But there was a deeper reason for his uneasiness with the issue. A man of revolutionary objectives, but also of moderation, Lee wanted quietly to tear his city apart and put it back together again. There was no room in his plan for such side skirmishes as changing the social order, taking on major power groups, or even raising the tax rate. Charter reform, with its promise of extensive change of the standing bureaucratic order, was a potential noisemaker.

Yet despite these attitudes, in June, 1954, Lee appointed a Charter Revision Commission, demonstrating another of his qualities. "Consistency," he often says, "is the virtue of fools." No one recalls precisely why Lee finally decided to expose the issue. He would suggest that he was prompted by the basic wisdom of the idea, which may be true, but judging by his more recent actions, it is also likely that he was riding to work one day and read in the paper something a department head had said that bothered him, so he exclaimed to his driver, "I've had enough of these bastards! Get me Logue on the phone when we get to the office." Unfortunately, this attempt at charter revision, like the others, eventually ended in crushing defeat and gave Lee his first public failure.

Perhaps in anticipation of the outcome, but more as an interim measure to get things moving, Lee began reorganizing the city before the Charter Commission even finished its hearings. The device he used, the executive order, was in keeping with his personal style. The legal basis for an executive order is contained in some broad powers conferred on Connecticut mayors by state legislation and in references to state laws within the New Haven Charter. These laws suggest that a mayor can issue orders to make city operations more efficient. The only practical limit on a mayor's use of the executive order is the possibility that someone may challenge it. Since no one ever has, executive orders proliferated in New Haven. One created a new post called Director of Administration. Lee ordered that the Director of Administration—Heman Averill, an ex-city manager—would work for him coordinating traditional services such as police, fire, health, and public works. The original purpose of Averill's job was to solidify Lee's early gains in controlling the city bureaucracy, and to relieve him and Logue so that they could begin reorganizing.

A second executive order, the most important issued by Lee, was a singularly autocratic document which, stripped of its pretentious legalese, simply told department heads that Ed Logue was in charge of all city functions affecting the redevelopment program. The idea of a development boss had been borrowed from Philadelphia, where Mayor Joseph Clark had helped set up a Housing Coordinator for that city's housing programs. Such a job was intriguing to Logue, although he did not like the Philadelphia title:

"*Housing* was too restricted as a term. It did not cover all that we wanted to cover in New Haven. *Coordinator* was a flat, wishy-washy term. Everyone's for coordination, but who really does it unless they're made to? So Dick and I settled on Development Administrator. That had some sex in it."

The executive order creating the post of Development Administrator and appointing Logue to fill it was issued in February, 1955, but only after some preliminaries. One was a fight between Lee and Logue. Lee felt that Logue could be just as effective running development functions behind the scenes without the title. Logue wanted the trappings. That fight was successfully mediated, and their attention then focused on how the creation of the post could appear to be the recommendation of others.

One recurring phrase during Lee's administration was "Let's do it right," and in this case doing it right meant building a suitable legal record for the decision, developing a memorandum for inside political use to justify the decision, and, of course, making it appear that it was someone else's decision. On February 1, 1955, a detailed report was sent to Lee by Rotival's office urging the creation of a Development Administrator, along with the name of Logue, as the only sensible answer to the problem of renewal administration. A few weeks later a four-page confidential memorandum was prepared by another consultant who criticized previous redevelopment efforts ("New Haven should write off its redevelopment past and start with a clean slate") and urged the Logue appointment as a way to ". . . revitalize the New Haven Redevelopment Program." At the end of the month a special committee chaired by a member of the Board of Finance followed suit and recommended the Logue appointment. Lee "bowed" to this pressure, and issued his executive order which gave Logue the authority to coordinate the activities of the Housing Authority, the City Plan Department, the Building Inspector, Traffic and Parking, and the Health Department around the renewal program being executed by the Redevelopment Agency.

During the spring of 1955, Logue, wearing his two hats as Development Administrator and Acting Director of the Redevelopment Agency, began giving day-to-day direction to the redevelopment bureaucracy. He called regular Wednesday meetings during which he outlined administration plans to execute the Rotival plan, and then set down the exact roles of each department. The job of traffic engineering was taken out of the Police

Department and traffic planning out of the Parking Authority and placed in a new agency under Logue's supervision. Much later a Code Enforcement Committee was organized with Logue as Chairman, during which procedures were established for coordinated code enforcement. There was some resistance to these efforts, but Logue cut through them because the Mayor was behind him and because he went to these sessions knowing precisely what he wanted. He met the opposition with logic, forcefulness, and, when necessary, anger. Logue also paid a personal price in these battles. His critics—and there are still many in New Haven—and even those who considered themselves allies felt that during these struggles he became increasingly insensitive to those with whom he worked. A close friend at the time explained him this way:

"Sure he was tough; he had to be to get things moving and to overcome lethargy. For Ed, rebuilding the city was an emergency issue, a wartime situation which meant that anyone who delayed programs was aiding the enemy. Privately he is one of the most decent men I have ever known. But when it came to his work, the program came first, not personal considerations."

A critic, who happens to be a department head and who remembers the sessions with Logue, had this to say:

"There's a difference between telling a man he's done something wrong and humiliating him in front of his colleagues for doing it. Humiliation was a standard Logue device, and by using it he unnecessarily offended and hurt people. I think his approach to people actually slowed the program down rather than moved it."

One important factor in, although no explanation for, the Logue conduct at the time was the crushing work load he carried. He was acting director of one agency, and he was supervising most of the others. He was often seen rushing from one meeting to another reading memorandums and urban renewal regulations en route. He was working sixteen-hour days six days a week. Lee was never sympathetic to the Logue job burdens, for he had his own, including a re-election campaign that fall of 1955. In fact, Lee delighted in harassing Logue so as to challenge him to do even more. Witness these taunting memos of the period:

DEAR ED:

Now who's slipping??

The enclosed memo is the same as the one I received from you earlier today. You are getting old, boy—either that, or you have nothing to do.

                                                                    DICK

DEAR ED:

What have you done about getting [their] programs launched? Precisely what are [they] doing? We might as well go all the way. Precisely what are you doing these days?

                                                                    DICK

Despite the tone of these memos, it was clear to both men that the renewal program was going nowhere unless they got more staff. The immediate need was for a man to run the Redevelopment Agency full time. The program needed a professional thoroughly versed in federal regulations and able to put projects together. In June, 1955, they found H. Ralph Taylor, currently an Assistant Secretary in the Department of Housing and Urban Development, and at that time director of the Somerville, Massachusetts, redevelopment program. In explaining why he chose to come to New Haven, Taylor today also offers insight into the early years of the Lee administration:

"Ed took me around the city on a Saturday afternoon and showed me the wide areas in downtown and in the neighborhoods that were slated for clearance on the maps he had locked up in his office. As he talked, he wasn't talking about something that might happen some day, but as though he could actually see the shapes of new uses that would spring up tomorrow. I was impressed, but I still felt uneasy about how a mayor would feel about this kind of program. I soon found out that Ed wasn't pushing Dick into accepting these plans. If anything, Dick was actually pushing Ed into doing more. There wasn't anything quite like it in the country. In fact, I don't really think there is today."

Taylor assumed full charge of preparing renewal projects and clearing them with the "Feds," and worked with Logue in negotiating with private developers. Much of the credit for the aggressive way New Haven has pursued federal urban renewal money goes to him. At the time of this writing New Haven had received more grant money per capita population than any other city in the United States.

As grant money came pouring into the Agency's accounts to start projects and plan new ones (the money did not go to the city's General Fund, where it would have been controlled by the Board of Finance), it became possible to hire other staff members. There was no shortage of applicants. Apart from the political job seekers, whom Lee regularly referred to Logue for hiring and whom Logue regularly referred back to Lee for other disposal, the spirit of the program as well as the national publicity it was beginning to receive attracted a number of young college graduates or recent graduates anxious to spend all or part of their lives in public service. New Haven presented an interesting opportunity. Those were the Eisenhower years, and federal service seemed stodgy and unexciting. Certainly there were no state governments offering the innovative spirit that such states as New Jersey and North Carolina have seen in recent years. Yet in New Haven, the most unlikely of places, there were two men—a strong, liberal Mayor and a tough, intelligent administrator—who were pioneering a new domestic program called urban renewal. The applications came pouring in.

The screening process was long and personal, much more like being looked over for a fraternity than being interviewed for a job. The criteria for selection were simple and straightforward: intelligence, readiness to work seven days a week, ability to withstand pressure and abuse, willingness to learn, and a high metabolic rate.

The result of the process was an unusual group of high-strung, brilliant, humorous, often naïve, arrogant but friendly, ambitious hard workers. The old-line city executives called them the "young Turks"; the New Haven *Register* labeled them "the whiz kids"; Logue referred to them in fatherly tones as "my boys"; and Lee smilingly called the building that housed them "the Kremlin."

Lee and Logue developed their recruits into a good staff in two basic ways. The first was their stampede approach to administration. Problems were often thrown out to a number of persons at the same time. The man coming up with the best answer got the prize of following through under the direct supervision of the boss. In that manner problems were not merely solved; they were crushed to death. A second method was the use of raw humiliation. If a young staff member carried out a task sloppily or proposed an action that appeared foolish, he would not be chastised privately but would receive a severe tongue-lashing in front of the others. This treatment made the newcomers a highly competitive group. Lee has admitted that he purposely kept the redevelopment staff competing among themselves, as well as with other city agencies. "It kept them on their toes; men often do their best work under pressure." Lee also knew that by encouraging intra-staff competition he could keep the group under control. Someone else might have viewed "the Kremlin" as a personal threat, but Lee knew he had the respect of its members, and his use of devisive techniques was designed mainly to keep them from getting him into trouble, which, because of their youth and inexperience they were quite capable of doing. For example, one staffer began pushing a proposal to build a nuclear reactor in the center of the city. Another casually dropped off an abbreviated draft bill at the state legislature which, according to its preliminary language, gave the Mayor full authority to do anything he wished with the structure of city government. Another wrote a speech for Lee which urged Negroes to block city traffic as part of a protest demonstration.

Everyone intimately connected with the program can also remember with fondness and some lingering trepidation Logue's staff meetings. At the large ones Logue was a no-nonsense boss, for he knew, as did Lee, that the challenge with this staff was not

to arouse enthusiasm but to control it. "You do this, why didn't
you do that, stop doing this," were the orders he barked to individuals around a conference table. Whenever he left the conference to receive a phone call, the petrified silence he had
established would erupt into wild shouting, then subside again
into silence as soon as he returned. Then there were the smaller
"inner club" staff meetings, which were more informal and
during which Logue would get back some of his abuse. Some of
the select of the staff would have the privilege of joining Logue
in his meetings with Lee, and were at first surprised as Logue
would offer a serious proposal with the broadest of smiles; Lee
would receive it with an equally broad smile, and when Logue
concluded, Lee would break into a booming "To hell with you,
Eddie, boy," at which point both men would break into laughter.

It was only through these private meetings that one could fully
appreciate how close the two men were in their thinking and how
their discussion of city business often took on the air of two
brothers talking of family affairs, even of family pranks, with Lee
usually taking the position of the older boy who would be held
responsible for whatever trouble they might get into. Once a staff
member got used to their style and lived up to their demands,
working for Logue and Lee could be stimulating and fun.
Organizational lines and titles meant nothing to those two, and
they delegated important responsibilities and provided wide program experience to the young staff.

The establishment of a small band of energetic, loyal, and
unusually bright staff members provided the manpower needed
to grind out project reports, to negotiate and move the program.
They also became the shock troops to make all city departments
participate. Functions or programs such as capital budgeting,
airport development, zoning, city code revision, school rebuilding, the planning of new streets and sewers, and eventually the
development of the city's anti-poverty program were quietly
performed by the young staff of the Redevelopment Agency,
working under the guidance and supervision of the Mayor and
his Development Administrator. Equally important, "the
Kremlin" offered Lee the chance to get special staff help, and it

eventually proved to be the training ground for new leaders once the old leaders such as Logue and Taylor departed.*

By 1956 the city bureaucracy also reflected Lee's style of operation through his appointments to various citizen boards and his staffing of key positions. Two of his appointees were on the Board of Education, a new Police Chief had been installed, the Democratic Town Chairman was Public Works Director, and Lee had also found a place for Carl Lohmann, his friendly counselor at Yale, on the Park Board. On boards of agencies involved in the renewal program, Lee inclined toward men with professional rather than political credentials, although if the two could be combined in one man, so much the better. Christopher Tunnard, of the Yale Planning School; Louis H. Pollak, now Dean of the Yale Law School; Reuben A. Holden, Secretary of Yale; Herbert Kaufman, of Yale's Political Science Department; Gibson Danes, former Dean of Art and Architecture at Yale; and Maynard Mack were some of his choices from the University, not to mention some outstanding local appointees who had never been directly involved in New Haven city government before Lee. By 1960 Lee's position as an accepted leader was strong enough to allow a reversal of the process he started in 1954. He began loosening his control of the departments and promoting more departmental autonomy, but never the anarchy he inherited when he became mayor.

* L. Thomas Appleby, who, as already mentioned, now directs the Washington, D.C., redevelopment program, took over Taylor's job in 1959. When Logue left for Boston, Massachusetts, in 1961, Appleby became his successor as Development Administrator. Harold Grabino, now a counsel for R. H. Macy & Co., Inc., became Executive Director of the Redevelopment Agency in 1961. Melvin J. Adams succeeded Appleby as Development Administrator when Appleby went to Washington in 1965. Charles I. Shannon and Joel Cogen jointly run the Redevelopment Agency today. All rose from the ranks of "the Kremlin."

Some others who moved up and out of New Haven include Robert Hazen, Logue's Executive Assistant and now director of downtown renewal in the Boston redevelopment program; Clyde Fisher, once Zoning Director in New Haven, now holds that job in San Francisco; Peter Svirsky, who succeeded Fisher, also works in the San Francisco planning agency. Barry Passett, who had worked as Lee's administrative aide, is now Director of the New Jersey Community Action Institute. Howard I. Hallman, who served as Director of the Department of Neighborhood Improvement, moved on to become Deputy Director of the city's anti-poverty program and is now a private consultant.

Lee's struggle with, and eventual conquest of, the bureaucracy went largely unrecorded in the local press, which is fortunate. The slaying of the paper monster was a matter of indifference to the general public, except of course when the blows were broadcast during a formal effort at charter reform. However, there was one group that took a keen interest in the decline of the old bureaucratic empire and the rise of a new one. Jobs, contracts, and patronage were involved. The politicians wanted to be dealt in, too.

4

The Politicians

Lee the politician was a product of the New Haven Democratic Party, but he was neither its servant nor its master. His exposure to other forces in the community, including Yale, gave him a broader perspective than most politicians have. He did not share the usual politician's respect for party power, nor did he indulge in customary subservience to party line. His ego would not permit it nor would his common sense, for he had learned during his two unsuccessful campaigns that the party machine could not deliver victory at the flick of a cigar ash. But if the party was not the efficient, monolithic power it was alleged to be, it was still a community force Lee could not ignore. He felt a personal debt to the party leader, John Golden, who had helped see that the party gave him the mayoral nomination three times in a row. The party also had influence over Lee's political future through its control of nominations. It also had members who were quoted in the press, who had money, and who could help Lee if only by not hurting him. So Lee needed an accommodation with the party.

During his administration Lee has been the third partner in a coalition which controlled appointments, patronage, and day-to-day direction of the Democrats. The other two were Town Chairman Arthur T. Barbieri and Golden, who together had considerably more control over local Democrats than Lee had. An insight into the background of these men is required to understand how the partnership worked, and how Lee prevented the other two from overpowering him.

Of the three, John Golden, at seventy-one, is the oldest, wisest, and most durable political tactician. He has become a landmark along Church Street, which runs in front of City Hall and where he is regularly seen shuffling along, his rotund face topped by an enormous hat with a broad brim more in keeping with Dodge City than New Haven. He looks at no one as he walks, and if he is stopped by a casual acquaintance or someone whom he regards as a fool, he is aloof and will quickly walk away. But with an old friend or someone from whom he needs a favor, Golden will turn on the charm that has helped him in local and state politics for more than forty years. His generosity with favors and his calculating use of patronage have won him many political allies. Although they tend to be older people, and each year their numbers dwindle, they are still a strong force.

Golden is a product of the ethnic take-over of New Haven politics which began in the early nineteen-hundreds. In 1924 he became a ward chairman when the Irish were in firm control of the Democratic Party. He will tell you that he is proud of the fact that he is still chairman of the same ward, despite his other political accomplishments. Golden plunged fully into politics during the nineteen-thirties under the Murphy administration. In 1932 he resigned from a job as superintendent of the Greist Manufacturing Company to become Murphy's Director of Public Works. A few years later he left the job to establish an insurance and bonding business, although he remained a confidant of Murphy's and continued to grow as a political leader. By 1940 most state politicians regarded Golden as the leader of the city's Democrats. During the thirties and early forties, Golden's leadership was challenged several times, but he overpowered his adversaries with cunning, trickery, and, whenever necessary, outlays of personal cash. Right after the war, however, Golden found himself faced with a problem that even money would not solve. The early systematic exclusion of Italians from the Irish-controlled Democratic Party, causing lasting grievances, had boomeranged into a Democratic predicament. During the first twenty years of this century, the Italians had flocked to the Republican Party, whose leader in those days, Colonel Isaac Ullman, offered them the favors, patronage, and influence that the Irish in the Democratic Party reserved for themselves. The growing number of Italians in the Republican Party eventually led to the nomination and election of William Celentano as New Haven's first Italian mayor in 1945.* Celentano's election and reign from 1945 to 1953 meant, of course, that the Democrats suffered all the dissensions usually encountered by the "out" party. But, even worse, the cause of the Democrats' problems, Mayor Celentano and the Italian votes he attracted, provided a license to some Italians in the Democratic Party to push the appealing oversimplification that if they, instead of Golden, headed the outfit, the Democrats could make inroads into Celentano's strength. Such a proposal was clearly unacceptable to Golden. In the face of Italian pressure he decided instead to sprinkle some Italian names on the Democratic ticket.

One of the Italians who appeared on the Democratic tickets from 1947 to 1953 was Arthur T. Barbieri, a big man who looks like a slightly overweight Mandrake the Magician. In fact, Barbieri is a professional magician and hypnotist with a quick mind, a marvelous array of stories, and a sharp sense of humor. But in addition to being a magician, hypnotist, and raconteur, Barbieri is also a bit of an enigma. While on scholarship at Yale in the nineteen-thirties, he dropped out in his senior year to take a job as a $45.00-per-week postal clerk, because, as he remembers it, "that was good money in those days." Barbieri's father was a strong Republican, and despite Barbieri's explanation that "in an Italian family you ask your father how you should vote," he shocked both family and friends by registering as a Democrat. Barbieri recalls that it was a question of philosophy, but he also concedes it might just have been a desire to be different and cause a stir. For if Barbieri has the skill and appearance of Mandrake, he can exhibit the brutish, brawling qualities of Lothar. He likes conflict. Even in the early days of his career, Barbieri often loomed as a political bully. Whatever power he

---

* Ethnic politicians in New Haven also point out that the Republicans appointed the first Italian postmaster in New Haven and elected the first Italian congressman. These "firsts," they suggest, are the main reasons that Italians continue to lean toward the Republican Party in local elections.

could wield, he did so with a coarseness that was to make him suspect later when he performed with equal gusto in the community spotlight. While some see this as a flaw in Barbieri, others suggest that it is a secondary characteristic, and that the man's most important trait is that he keeps his word. Certainly everyone in New Haven does agree that whether he is out to get you a job or just out to get you, Barbieri is a man who does everything he can to honor his commitments.

The Barbieri system of unbreakable pledges was what attracted Golden's attention, for during the clamorous postwar years in the Democratic Party, Barbieri was pledged to Golden and worked hard for him in the teeming Fair Haven section of the city to prove it. In 1951 Golden picked Barbieri to run as Town Clerk on the Democratic ticket. Lee lost that election by two votes, but Barbieri won his race by more than ninety tallies. Lee's loss of two elections made some of the party's Italian members unmanageable. One of them, A. Mark Barbarito, had also been on the ticket in 1951 and had won. Suggesting that Lee had been given enough chances, he claimed that he, an Italian, deserved a clear shot at Celentano in 1953. To quiet Barbarito and some others who were ready to dump Lee, Golden asked Barbieri to take on a special assignment: become the party's first Italian Town Chairman. Barbieri gave up the Town Clerk job he had just won to accept the post, and joined with Lee and Golden in reuniting the warring Democrats. According to Barbieri, his first effort was a mammoth cocktail party to which all hostile party members were invited. On his orders the Martinis and the Manhattans were mixed at double strength. After three rounds, Barbieri, accompanied by a photographer from the Bridgeport *Herald,* maneuvered through the standing crowd, placing enemy next to enemy for photographs. A following issue of the *Herald* contained shots of feuding Democrats with glassy eyes and silly smiles in a grotesque display of party harmony.

During the 1953 election, Golden, Barbieri, and Lee, three colorful and highly individualistic politicians, worked well together. After victory, however, they behaved like any coalition which achieves its specific objective. They began to look at each other and ask themselves who really was responsible for success. Barbieri could clearly perceive that he was the magic ingredient missing in the earlier Lee campaigns. It was he who had united the party, and it was he who formed the link between Lee, Golden, and the alienated Italians. Lee saw things differently, of course. He had waged a personal campaign and had developed his own issues. The victory was his, not the party's. Golden, the party veteran, took a historical view of the matter. He had brought Lee and Barbieri up through the ranks of the party, and while they had fought hard and worked effectively, the fact was that popular opinion shifts from party to party over the long haul, and an "out" party will eventually become an "in" party if its members are patient and disciplined. It was he who had led the Democrats in Mayor Murphy's day; it was he who had held it together during Mayor Celentano's reign; and it was he who would continue to head the party now that the Democrats had joyously returned to New Haven's ancient City Hall. These different perspectives were to affect relations among the men in the years that ensued.

After the election, the three men developed an informal arrangement about who would control what. It was an understanding which was constantly misunderstood. Lee indicated the following: that he would clear his appointments with Golden; that Golden would handle political arrangements with the state machine; that steps would be taken to assure that Golden's insurance business would be given favorable consideration whenever the city required such services; that Golden's candidates would be given serious consideration for available city jobs and patronage; and that Golden would be the senior partner as far as the party was concerned. Lee wanted full control over redevelopment decisions and jobs, although he would clear major decisions affecting the party with the other two. Barbieri the Town Chairman was made Barbieri the Public Works Director. This gift was perfectly consistent with previous practices during most of this century, for Public Works had always been turned over to the politicians. When compared with the full-time politicians who held the job before him, Barbieri was a good

Public Works Director, probably because managing the trucks, bulldozers, and other heavy equipment of the department suited his personal style. It also gave him the chance to run something. He cut fifty-two "unnecessary jobs" from the department ("all of 'em held by Republicans," he later boasted), worked out a new accounting system, bought eight new refuse trucks, commissioned drawings for a new supply house, doubled the rate of street paving, and, when he got tired of administrative matters, issued public statements about the grand job he was doing compared with his Republican predecessor.

This division of the spoils, with the strong implication that Golden was still party boss, could hold up only as long as the two younger men minded their party manners. They did not. As soon as Lee became mayor, he appreciated what he had always understood, that he had immediate control over the city jobs which the party needed. Sometimes by having patronage meetings held in his office, other times by making personal calls to notify those who were to get city jobs, Lee showed the party that he was the supplier and not the delivery boy. During dealings with party leaders he also reflected his broader responsibilities as mayor. He had a city to run, a program to sell. He made it clear that he would not put jobs up for party grabs in the Redevelopment Agency and in other city agencies directly involved in the renewal program. He needed a skilled staff. Barbieri and Golden understood this, but they could never adjust to Logue and the young redevelopment staff, most of whom were imports with no obligation to the local Democrats for their jobs. Their loyalty was to Lee and the program.

"Logue would infuriate us," Barbieri has said. "I'd send a guy over to Redevelopment for a job, and sometimes the guy might be less than able, but the least I expected was that Logue would talk to him. Instead, the guy would come back to me complaining, 'What the hell is this city coming to? That damned Logue just about threw me out of his office.' Logue created unnecessary problems for the party and for Dick in his treatment." Barbieri and Golden eventually began using Logue's gruffness to their own advantage. Sometimes, when a disappointed job seeker returned to them to complain of mistreatment at the Development Administrator's office, Barbieri and Golden would blame it on Lee, who had hired Logue. This convenient way to discharge their responsibilities put pressure on the third partner. Lee also used Logue to take care of job seekers, but in a different way. He would call Logue on the private "hot line" between their offices, and when Logue picked up the phone, he would hear a presumably furious Lee in a dialogue that usually went like this:

"God damn you, Logue, I told you I wanted Smith interviewed for a job. I'm sick and tired of the way you're managing your office and the way you've avoided him. I want him interviewed right away. If he isn't, then you've had it."

"Is he there with you, Dick?"

"You're damned right. I'm fed up with this."

"Send him over right away, Dick. I'll get rid of him for you."

"It's about time you understood. People like Smith are important to me. I'm going to send him to your office right away, and you see him."

"I read you, Dick."

Lee also tried the patience of his two political partners in awarding contracts for goods and services needed for redevelopment. Once the program got moving, there was a substantial increase in city expenditures for construction projects, architects, engineering firms, demolition, and legal services. Normally this would be a political blessing, because the private firms which offer these services are often politically charged operations whose leaders, with the possible exception of demolition contractors, represent the big contributors to political parties. But Lee and Logue imposed a somewhat foreign standard to the process of who got what. They began insisting on quality. This was not always compatible with the customary insistence that contractors be politically acceptable. Nowhere was this more apparent than in the award of architectural contracts. After several nondescript buildings rose in response to Lee's frantic demand for redevelopment action and the staff's frenzied efforts "to give Dick a few buildings," Lee and Logue wondered whether the product was worth the effort. They became extremely design-conscious, even to the point of importing well-known national architects to work on site planning and building design. The words of one builder reflected Lee's interest in architecture when he recalled "I went to Dick to ask what it would take to get in on one of the projects and he said, 'Nothing. Just let me pick your designer.' " Some of the local architectural firms complained. Their point was simply that building design was a matter of taste, but the money they were losing to outside firms was not. Golden and Barbieri put pressure on Lee to be less rigid. Lee is not always a rigid man, so he worked out an interesting solution. National architects, the ones he preferred, were thereafter teamed with local firms. The preferred architect served as the designer; the local firm did the working drawings. Once a few of the national firms started contributing to the party, Golden and Barbieri became less concerned, although their attitude toward all the changes which occurred in the Redevelopment Agency, from personnel to methods of dealing with contractors, remained unenthusiastic, suspicious, but accepting. After all, this was the area Lee had staked out for himself when he first took office.

They began to object when Lee started to make satellite agencies of the redevelopment program as untouchable as the Redevelopment Agency. In the early nineteen-sixties arguments broke out about who would fill vacancies caused by the retirement of the City Engineer, the Purchasing Agent, and the Building Inspector. Particularly for City Engineer and Building Inspector, Barbieri and Golden felt the nod should go to men acceptable to the contractors, while Lee put greater stress on candidates' technical proficiency and readiness to work closely with the redevelopers and planners. Barbieri had lined up his choices and Lee had already made his selections. Both men went to Golden for support. Lee appealed to Golden on the ground that Barbieri was trying to grab control of the party. Barbieri complained that Lee was undermining party strength. Golden complicated the situation further by making his support conditional on placing a job seeker of his. "That old fox," Lee would say in grudging admiration after a telephoned appeal. "He's still the sage of the party." Lee rammed through his candidates, and Barbieri did not speak to him for over a year. There were some other contributing factors to Barbieri's silence which will be covered shortly.

If Golden could play partner against partner during disputes, so could Lee and Barbieri, for they had learned their lessons from "the old fox." Lee was particularly good at it, and his long-range strategy in dealing with his partners in politics was to limit their ability to act independently of him. He would use every opportunity to confirm Barbieri's fears about Golden's plots and vice versa, sometimes with appalling disregard of the facts. He also made no effort to overcome the distrust of the party leaders toward Logue and the redevelopment staff. "If you keep a bunch of tigers fighting each other," Lee once observed, "then they won't attack you." And so he continually tried to be the middle-man whose counsel was sought and whose mediation was required to settle problems which he had deliberately created.

Because party confusion and friction helped Lee in his game of divide and conquer, he would sometimes go around Barbieri and Golden on party patronage. On these occasions he would unilaterally dip deep into the pool of party regulars to make a job appointment which seemed dreadful to his staff. But his choice usually ended up in an unimportant job, or one that could be made unimportant. Selection by the Mayor effectively reminded some of the unwashed of the party that the man in City Hall still cared regardless of Barbieri and Golden. Lee did the same for a number of small contractors. Whenever a general contractor asked Lee to make a suggestion for a subcontract, he had a complete mental file from which to draw a personally suitable name. He would then call the firm to say, "I just put in a good word for you."

For all this feigning, jockeying, and maneuvering for position, there were two inviolate and unnegotiable items in the unwritten contract among the three party partners. From the party's side, it was a standing rule that Golden and Barbieri would oppose and even fight Lee on any proposal which threatened them personally or weakened their idea of party strength. From Lee's side, his actions showed that he would brook no party nonsense which threatened his chances of being re-elected. These rules were operative and definable only at specific times.

One issue on which Barbieri and Golden took firm positions was charter reform. They had dragged their feet on Lee's first effort at charter revision in 1954. In 1958, when Logue and Lee mounted still another charter amendment, the two party leaders opposed the revision. On their orders, party workers "faded" when the referendum was held. Because there was no adequate organization to take the party workers' place, the 1958 charter revision, like the 1954 version and four others before it, was defeated. Golden and Barbieri had opposed the amendment for a four-year term for mayor because it posed a clear and present danger to them: Lee would need help from them every four years instead of two; and, more important, a mayoral election means money for the party coffers, some of which is left over after campaign expenses are paid. If Barbieri and Golden had supported charter reform, they would have collected revenues (about $100,000 for each campaign) only once in four years. There was no philosophy or program consideration involved; it was essentially a question of control and cash.

Lee exercised his rights in the unwritten contract in 1959, the only year the cloud of major scandal, involving careless work by the city's five-man Board of Assessors, hung heavily over his administration. The Board had remained untouched by Lee as part of his accommodation with the party. In fact, four of the five assessors were holdovers from previous administrations and two of them were appointed as far back as Mayor Murphy's day. The Republicans had charged, and their charge was valid, that the Board had illegally reduced assessments on some hundred and twenty-five residential properties, several of which were owned by friends or relatives of Barbieri's. The issue was not centered on whether the reductions were an accurate reflection of value. It was more on the manner in which they were made. Under the system used by the Board, two of the assessors handled residential properties while the others took care of commercial and other properties. The reductions had been made, therefore,

without the involvement of the full Board. Moreover, they had
been made after the legal closing date for assessment changes.
Lee sensed that the issue was political dynamite, so he took steps
to eliminate the Board and replace it with a single assessor, a
professional civil-service career man. He took another bold step.
He dumped Barbieri from his Public Works job. During the
1959 campaign, Barbieri had been charged with running the
department like a private club. These charges, plus the disclosure
that Barbieri's relatives had received "illegal" assessment reductions, made him a liability in Lee's judgment, so he privately
asked Barbieri to resign. Barbieri did not like giving up his job
(he still harbors a lingering grudge over it), but he knew the
rules of the game. This, of course, was another major contributing factor to the year's silence between Barbieri and Lee.

Lee survived his feuds with Barbieri and maneuvered the
party behind—and sometimes out of the way of—his program
for another reason, which is the most obvious and important. He
proved to be a winner, and a big one. Before Lee, the biggest
plurality ever garnered by a politician in New Haven had been
Franklin Delano Roosevelt's 1936 presidential victory, when he
won the city by 21,116 votes. The next biggest was the Roosevelt
victory in 1944. It was by 16,527 votes. The highest victory
margin for a recent mayor in New Haven had been that of John
Murphy, who won by 14,724 in 1937. In 1955 Lee smashed this
record, winning by 20,808, and in 1957 by 23,331. In 1959 he
won by 13,984, in 1961 by 4,000, and in 1963 by 11,345. These
votes clearly reflected the ups and downs of his renewal program.
Once early doubters, Barbieri and Golden are now firm be-
lievers. "Dick's program is the greatest thing that ever happened
to this town," says Barbieri. "This young man [Lee is now
fifty]," says Golden, "is the greatest mayor in America today."
All of which serves to make an important point about politics
and politicians, at least about able pros like Barbieri and Golden.
When newsmen write of city "machine" politics, they use an apt
term, for the party is like a huge gadget and its leaders are like
mechanics who keep it well tuned and smoothly-running. The
gadget cannot run by itself, and the mechanics aren't interested

in driving it; they just want to make sure the wheels and gears are well oiled. The entire apparatus is just waiting for someone to drive it. The professional politician normally has little time for philosophy or programs. But give him a man with a philosophy or a program that can produce votes—gas in the tank—and he'll let him drive. The able pros like Barbieri and Golden quickly appreciated the voter appeal of Lee and his program, and since he kept the party in office, they accepted his departures from normal political practices, and perhaps even allowed themselves to appear gullible in the face of Lee's trickery.

If New Haven has had examples of politicians successfully adjusting to a new program and of citizens raising their expectations of the quality of local public service, it has also had its share of politicians without understanding. During the 1953 mayoral campaign, the Republican Town Chairman, sensing defeat in the air, called on the City Plan Director and asked, "What is this redevelopment that Dick's talking about, anyway?" Unfortunately for the local Republicans, their leaders never did catch on. In each campaign, the G.O.P. would criticize the philosophy, financing, and managing of the program while Lee scurried about the city cutting ribbons or breaking ground for new schools, playgrounds, libraries, housing, and other forms of voter patronage. It should be added, however, that many of these improvements at the time of their announcement or their groundbreaking were little more than a twinkle in Lee's eye or a freshly drawn picture on a piece of paper. The Republicans had other problems besides a lack of understandable philosophy. They simply were not as good at the nuts and bolts of politicking as were Golden, Barbieri, and Lee. When that trio worked together on a campaign, they were particularly clever at raiding the Republicans and winning over or at least silencing some of their promising younger members, or buying out Republican poll workers so they would sleep at the switch on Election Day. So effective have these and other practices been that at the time of this writing the Republicans had no one on the city's Board of Aldermen. Upon the recent retirement of the man who had served as Republican Town Chairman during most of the Lee years, Lee observed sardonically, "There goes one of the best friends I ever had."

A major part of the Republican problem in New Haven during the Lee years was its lack of support from the business community, which in many cities usually represents a strong prop for the Republicans. Their weakness was no accident, but a product of a deliberate Lee strategy of annexation. How the strategy worked politically but failed in other respects forms a significant part of this story.

5

Dealing with Business

Lee wanted New Haven business leaders behind his program because their support would lend it respectability. The effort to bring local entrepreneurs into the renewal coalition was ironic, for here was a young mayor of immigrant stock inviting city business leaders with their Yankee underpinnings to share political power that they had relinquished to Lee's political forebears, the ethnic politicians, fifty years earlier.

New Haven is an old city by American standards. It was settled in 1637 by a businessman and a Puritan clergyman. Theophilus Eaton, the businessman, and John Davenport, the cleric, were dedicated, hard-working men who personified the merger of capitalism and religion which impelled the early development of this nation and which set the tone of New Haven leadership for the first hundred and sixty years. The Eaton-Davenport venture started as a town but soon mushroomed into a colony; it was ambitious, its participants energetic and inventive. But the colony was also unlucky and perhaps at times mismanaged. An effort to establish a direct shipping link with England failed when the colony's ship, packed with wares of considerable value, disappeared. An expensive effort to colonize the southern coast of New Jersey under the New Haven banner also failed during a violent confrontation with like-minded Swedish and Dutch settlers. These two disasters seriously undermined the New Haven economy. Furthermore, the other New England colonies were not only unsympathetic to New Haven's problems but were hostile to its very existence. In 1662 New Haven discovered that the opulent Hartford enterprise had dispatched an emissary to England to discuss long-range plans for Connecticut. The emissary returned to announce that Hartford had renegotiated its charter and that the New Haven Colony was no more; it was to be part of the Hartford Colony. One can trace from that event the emergence of Hartford as the political center of Connecticut, and today, of course, Hartford is the capital of Connecticut, a designation it received in 1873 after outnegotiating New Haven a second time.

Although it was now merely part of a new colony, New Haven retained some autonomy, and until the American Revolution the town leadership followed the Eaton-Davenport precedent. A group of about a hundred Congregational ministers, lawyers, and leading businessmen controlled all aspects of New Haven life, from religion to education, including Yale College, which had moved to New Haven from Saybrook in 1716. This oligarchy survived because its leaders were uniform in their conservative ideology, because the town was small (around 3,000 at the outbreak of the Revolution), and because the political process was rigged in their favor; i.e., there were property qualifications for voting, and those people who attended town meetings, the rules said, had to stand up to oppose prevailing policies, not vote privately.

The New Haven leaders opposed the insurgences and Lexington and Concord, but they eventually were drawn into the full-scale Revolution that followed, and New Haveners made a good account of themselves. Perhaps the leaders should have followed their initial instincts, however, for one result of the Revolution was the wave of democracy which swept over the new nation, bringing with it changes in social status, in ownership of the land, and in the mores of the day. The old order in New Haven and elsewhere found their ideology too rigid and their numbers too small to withstand the pressure. Religion, political processes, education—business itself—were democratized, never again to be extensions of the will of the élite, but decentralized institutions reflecting the will of wide, diffuse groups. In New Haven the liberation of business from its close association with the old order seems to have been a boon. In the nineteenth century new men with fresh talents moved in to use their shops to make machines that created industries. Eli Whitney, inventor of the cotton gin, introduced the manufacture of firearms to the city and developed a system of interchangeable parts that led to mass production. Charles Goodyear developed the vulcanization process for rubber and gave New Haven another new industry. John Cook, Jonathan Mix, and James Brewster made the city a carriage-making center for the nation. Chauncey Jerome, James E. English, and Hiram Camp gave it clockmaking.

The early nineteenth century was an exciting period of growth for New Haven, but it was not accompanied by a total overthrow of the ideas and spirit of the past. A number of the older leaders were still around, and streets bore the names of those leaders who had died. Yale, which played a major role in the city, conveyed some of the flavor of those who had brought it to the town, and its graduates began to assume leadership in local affairs. The new wave of businessmen also inherited the legacy of entrepreneurial failures which plagued their predecessors. In fact, the new businessmen engaged in similar ones. In an uncanny re-enactment of history the new businessmen did well in town, but not when they ventured outside. In New Haven their family businesses thrived and provided ample employment to a local populace, who showed their gratitude and approval by making their business leaders political leaders. From 1842 until 1897, twenty-one of twenty-two New Haven mayors were drawn from local business and industry. But outside the city, where the local leadership tried to make their money work for them in complex deals, they experienced some terrible defeats. An effort in 1815 to start a steamship line to New York put local entrepreneurs in competition with Cornelius Vanderbilt, who started a price war, rammed a New Haven ship, and bought the New Haven hopefuls out. In 1824, $200,000 in local cash went into a canal company which soon found itself competing with a new gadget called a railroad. While racing their barges against locomotives, the local businessmen stubbornly ignored an opportunity to get into the railroad business, which would have furthered the local economic boom. An outside company was proposing to build a line to New Haven from Connecticut's Naugatuck Valley, an area of heavy industrial development. When the plan faltered, New Haven interests refused to step in to make it work. Businessmen from Bridgeport, the third major Connecticut city, moved in and built the railroad to their city, making Bridgeport the Long Island Sound shipping point for the Naugatuck Valley industries. New Haven eventually did get into the railroad business. Local money was invested in the New York, New Haven & Hartford Railroad, and the less said about that the better, except for the observation that when the line was in bankruptcy, it was known only as the New Haven Railroad.

In the early part of the twentieth century the Yankee business leaders who had guided the town through the nineteenth century began a gradual withdrawal from community life. The town was now a city of 108,000 people, and the old-line families did not always like the changes that accompanied the growth. Politically they had been outnumbered by the waves of immigrants who had come to man their plants. Approximately a third of the city's population was foreign-born. Another third had at least one immigrant parent. Life was hard for many of the newcomers: the wages were low, the housing in areas like Oak Street was dreadful, and the city atmosphere could be cold and indifferent. The political parties, however, were receptive to their numbers and needs, and the control of the party organizations and public offices shifted to the ethnic politicians. The nineteenth-century leaders also became less active in local business. Their family-run businesses could not survive twentieth-century competition or the lack of interest of their heirs, and dissolution or merger with national firms was often their fate.

By the time Lee became mayor, New Haven no longer had a strong, unified business community. What it did have was certainly not running the town as in earlier years. The business leadership was a heterogeneous mixture of new ethnics, imports who ran the family businesses which had been acquired by national firms, a handful of firms still run by old-line families, and other established Yankees who quietly served on bank boards, as partners in law firms, or stayed at home clipping coupons. Nor was there any major industry in town, such as insurance in Hartford. About the only thing the businesses did have in common was their awareness of what had preceded them, which was conveyed in such symbols as the central Green, the old factories, Yale, and the buildings and traditions of such venerable institutions as the Graduate Club and the New Haven Lawn Club. Gone were the hard-working, strong-minded Yankee leaders who as a unified group had built the town and given it a university and economic growth. Only the weakest of their legacy was apparent: the rigid conservatism of their ideology and the caution born of their failures. The only true voice of New Haven business was the city's Chamber of Commerce: it neither led nor dragged. It was just there.

Lee's goals, therefore, were not to overcome strong business opposition; they were centered on mobilization—to give the business community the appearance of unity and power, a group whose members from top to bottom were solidly for Lee. The vehicle for this effort was the Citizens Action Commission (CAC). The idea for such a group had been suggested during his 1953 campaign, when he included in his pledges the creation of a nonpartisan group of "the best brains in the city" to help him with his rebuilding program. The idea was refined during a meeting with a Pittsburgh lawyer after the election. On the basis of Pittsburgh's experience with downtown rebuilding, the lawyer urged Lee to become the focal point of any business involvements with the program planned for New Haven. He warned that if the local Chamber of Commerce was left to represent business, it would merely reflect competing interests and different perspectives rather than pull them into a unified force behind the program.

Lee was intrigued with the notion of having his own chamber of commerce, and he began developing plans for it. He decided it would be composed of various committees on metropolitan planning, parking, redevelopment, and education. He would give the committees assignments, they would report to him on their findings, and together they would implement proposals mutually agreed on; i.e., those ideas that Lee wanted. The Ford Foundation and the Carnegie Foundation were asked if they would like to finance such an idea. They would not, nor was there at first much business interest. During his first five months in office Lee was turned down by at least fifteen people whom he approached to become Chairman of the CAC. It was clear to most of them that the CAC was not just another civic organization orbiting quietly around New Haven but a new political organization attached directly to Lee's command post. Some felt that Lee was another awful ethnic politician who wanted to draw on their established respectability. Others were skeptical of his ambitious rebuilding plan. Still others just did not like the idea of working so closely with a Democrat. Lee finally broke down this resistance by getting his friend, A. Whitney Griswold, President of Yale University, to serve as a Vice-Chairman for the group. Then he got a local bank president, Carl G. Freese, to serve as Chairman. With these names as a start, he readily filled out the remainder of the CAC Board with representatives from such firms as the New Haven Railroad, the A. C. Gilbert Company, major local utilities, the Greist Manufacturing Company, and, in a devilish touch, the Democratic Party in the person of John Golden.

With these firms and some recognizable old family names on the CAC Board, Lee began building the image of power about the organization, attributing to it whenever possible the strength and unity that once marked the city's business community. In answering one reporter's query about the role of the CAC, Lee got completely carried away:

"We've got the biggest muscles, the biggest set of muscles in New Haven on the CAC. . . . They're muscular because they control the wealth, they're muscular because they control the industries, represent the banks. . . . They're muscular because they're articulate, because of their financial powers, and because of the accumulation of wealth and prestige which they have built up over the years."

In contrast is the view from a CAC Board member who recently recalled his participation in the meetings:

"The CAC was the Mayor's creation. He initiated it, picked its members, provided the staff support, and sat in on its meetings which were held in his office. He and sometimes Logue would speak; we listened, and then reacted."

The "muscular" view of the CAC, however, prevailed for several years because of a combination of luck and skillful press-agentry by Lee, who continued to characterize it as a strong, unified group that represented business and supported his program. The local press engaged in unusual, though still mild, enthusiasm when the CAC was unveiled by Lee in September, 1954: ". . . The whole metropolitan area," said the editorial writer of the New Haven *Register*, "must wish our young Mayor and the vigorous support he has mobilized every success." Writers from such publications as *Harper's Magazine, Saturday Evening Post,* and *Architectural Forum* were attracted to the CAC as a lead or feature in stories on New Haven in the early days of the urban renewal program. The *Forum* writer, for instance, represented the CAC as a "resurgence" of community and business activity, and went on to suggest that it was ". . . far more than a sounding board. . . . The commission may assume a planning function by making specific recommendations on a proposed project, or it may help set policy by charting the lines the city should follow in attacking its problems." The fact was that the CAC never made a recommendation that had not already been proposed by Lee and never charted a line that Lee and his staff were not already following. There were some exceptions whenever administration plans directly affected the building or livelihood of a firm represented on the CAC Board. Then discussions were usually held only between the Board member and Lee or one of Lee's staff.

The CAC functioned precisely as its creator wanted it to. Its members and the publicity it received gave Lee and his program respectability and, as long as no serious problems developed, an aura of invincibility. It also provided him with individuals who could help sell the program to the community. The *Forum* writer was right when he said the CAC was far more than a sounding board, for Lee did not present his proposals to get CAC ap-

proval; he sold his ideas to the members to arouse their en-
thusiam and, he hoped, that of their community contacts through
a process of social osmosis.

To help him, he assigned Rotival's staff to work with the
Commission, outlining long-range plans and arousing the interest of the members. He also gave the Commission a full-time
director, H. Gordon Sweet, a former businessman who fully
appreciated what Lee was doing. He also took steps to assure
that the organization would never become so aroused that it
might go out of control. One of these steps was an insistence that
Sweet always stay in the background—for instance, by not
sitting at the head table during CAC luncheons. Putting a lid on
Sweet was probably not necessary, but it did indicate Lee's
anxieties over competition, for a man in Sweet's position could
conceivably have led a revolt. He also sprinkled the CAC Board
with such friends as Griswold, labor leader Joseph Rourke, and
Eugene Rostow, just to assure himself that he had a few aces left
if the Board should ever present "sticky problems." Not too
surprisingly, there were no major problems during the first four
years of the CAC's existence. The group sponsored tours to
Philadelphia and Pittsburgh to review renewal programs; it held
exhibits and issued brochures. Its members appeared at public
hearings to support redevelopment proposals, and the chairmen
of its various committees were encouraged to make some of the
announcements of program plans, which must have been a
sacrifice for Lee, but a small one in view of the prevailing pro-
Lee business spirit. The CAC began to falter in 1958 for reasons
that have been described this way by Sweet, who that year moved
on to become director of one of the redevelopment projects:

"The CAC was basically a sales group, and it did a good
selling job. But there comes a time to stop selling and to deliver a
product. Dick and Ed had some problems starting in 1958 with
the downtown program. All the releases and reassuring statements in the world by the CAC just could not change that. . . .
There should be a burial ground for organizations once they
outlive their original purposes, as they all eventually do. The

CAC deserved a dignified, respectful burial. Instead, it was kept breathing."

One problem hit the CAC when Lee, casting about for other uses for the organization, urged its reluctant Board to give public support for his 1958 charter reform proposals. After a carefully worded supporting resolution by the Board was read at the charter hearings, local Republicans uncovered the fact that out of the 355 CAC members, only 12 knew that the Board had held a meeting on the proposals and supported them. This revelation was prominently displayed on the front page of the New Haven *Register,* causing considerable embarrassment and strain among the Board members.

Deeper crises already afflicted the group. The renewal program by 1958 was shaking the conceptual foundation of the CAC; namely, the notion that there was a unified business community in New Haven whose needs and goals could be pulled together and given direction by one organization. Relocation of businesses to make way for new improvements was particularly damaging to the CAC. The initial awkwardness and inconsistencies* of the relocation process bluntly exposed the different situations, needs, and aspirations of those who made up the business community. Some businesses differed in the motivations and sophistication of their owners. These owners ranged

* Much will be said about relocation both of businesses and families later on. It should be noted here that during the New Haven program, federal policy on payments to displaced firms changed considerably. At one time there was no payment to cover moving expenses and equipment losses. Later on, payments of up to $3,000 were provided. At this writing, the maximum payment is $25,000, plus certain loan assistance offered by the Small Business Administration. Another problem was that different federally aided programs have varying policies on business relocation. The Department of Housing and Urban Development and its predecessor, the Housing and Home Finance Agency, were specific in requirements about what payments should be made to firms affected by urban renewal. The Bureau of Public Roads, however, left it to the states to determine if business relocation payments should be paid to firms displaced by federally aided highway programs. Connecticut decided not to reimburse these firms. So in New Haven, where urban renewal and highway displacements were simultaneous, some firms were given payments and others were not. Occasionally, the firm that did qualify and the one that did not were located side by side, separated not by need but by a line between a highway-taking and an urban-renewal acquisition.

from "mamma and papa" grocery-store proprietors who usually packed up and retired in the face of relocation, to ambitious young owners who used renewal to better their locations, and on to those who were knowledgeable enough to use condemnation proceedings to get top dollar for their properties. There were the renters who received no acquisition price for their quarters and the owner-occupants who suddenly found their old buildings were worth something to somebody. Then there were those who viewed relocation in terms of their functions: retailers who wanted new stores as close as possible to their old location, wholesalers who wanted to move closer to transportation arteries, and manufacturers whose major requirement was space. Lee and Logue tried to be responsive to the needs. They set up the nation's first business relocation office and they badgered the federal government about increasing relocation payments. The one thing they never could overcome was the anxiety—even fear—that most businessmen felt. The idea of large-scale displacement was new, and there was no experience to point to.* Facing this unknown, the affected businessmen either remained grimly silent, protested, or sued. The resulting controversy, encouraged by the opposing Republicans, was a severe blow to the euphoria of the CAC.

On top of these problems the downtown rebuilding program —the cause of much of the dislocation and controversy—was bogged down. Lee, *ergo* the CAC, was in serious trouble. The voice of business was no longer channeled through the slick brochures and soothing announcements of the CAC. It was now rumbles of discontent by hundreds of unhappy dislocatees that were being heard on the street, in the newspapers, and in the

* It was not until 1962, five years after the first of the large-scale displacements, that anyone had precise data on the impact of relocation. Indeed, one could not be sure even at this late date of the results, for businessmen are understandably reticent to reveal their financial situations. However, the results then showed that of 124 firms which had been displaced from the city's first two projects, Church Street and Oak Street, 23 went out of business, 16 disappeared, and the remaining 85 survived. Of the 85, 8 had moved out of New Haven, 34 stayed in but away from old locations, and the remaining 43 relocated to blocks they considered close to their former sites. Half the surviving firms said business was up, about a quarter said it was down, and the remaining quarter said it was the same.

courts. CAC Board meetings were no longer a matter of quiet, happy contemplation over plans for tomorrow; they had become the scene of nervous arguments over the problems of the day. This was reflected in the sharp exchanges noted in the minutes and the sudden, unexplained resignation of the CAC Chairman of the period, who was President of the Southern New England Telephone Company and successor to Mr. Freese.

Several of those who were privy to the CAC deliberations of the time have privately observed that the remarkable aspect of the whole affair was that it did not break out into open hostility toward Lee. It could have, and in other cities it might have, yet with the exception of the President of the Chamber of Commerce, no leading businessman in town openly challenged the Mayor. There are at least three possible explanations. One is that while several Board members were obviously annoyed with Lee, they all seemed to respect his goals and were sympathetic to his efforts to overcome the problems. Also, while New Haven did not have a strong, unified business community, it did have some strong individuals who had lent their names and prestige to Lee's program and were prepared to withstand the controversy. The third reason, and perhaps the most important, was one of the legacies of the elite who had run the town in its early years: Yale.

Yale has always been an influential force in New Haven. In the nineteenth century the influence was open and direct. Many of Yale's leaders, for example, were also local community leaders or had personal or family ties with the business leadership. In this century Yale's role is more subtle, but no less important. University buildings occupy much of the center of New Haven, providing a physical link to the city's past. Many local businessmen and professionals are Yale graduates. While Yale is often a target of local criticism about the rowdiness of some of its students or the tax-exempt status of its buildings, it is also a local status symbol, and New Haveners value University acceptance. Acceptance takes on many forms—socializing with the faculty or administrative staff, having a son attend Yale, or avoiding open conflict with Yale officials, which could lead to the dreadful prospect of being subtly rebuked or, even worse, being ignored by Yale.

Of course Yale does not pass judgment on the respectability of local leaders through Corporation resolution. Yale's attitudes are inferred from the words and actions of its faculty, and in this sense there was little doubt about Yale's attitude toward Lee. The jaunty Mayor who barely finished high school had worked at Yale, he was a member of Mory's, and his friends and supporters at Yale could be found everywhere from the maintenance staff to the Yale Corporation. One of his best friends was the University President, the late A. Whitney Griswold.

These ties with an influential university gave Lee a resource which few mayors enjoy. Sometimes Yale served to restrain open reaction against Lee's brand of civic reform. On other occasions, as will soon be described, the University, through its staff and investments, helped Lee realize his program goals.

6

Yale and New Haven: Whit and Dick

Alfred Whitney Griswold, late President of Yale, and Richard Charles Lee, Mayor of New Haven, unlocked a basic secret of good town-gown relations: they thoroughly enjoyed each other's company. They also agreed on most issues. Their friendship spanned two decades, beginning before 1950, when Whit Griswold was the surprise presidential choice by the Yale Corporation. After Lee became mayor, it matured into what one mutual friend has described as a "warm blend of two mercurial personalities who were natural leaders and incorrigible pranksters."

Certainly their humor, and love of a good story well told, was a major reason why these two men of entirely different backgrounds struck it off so well. Griswold's humor was subtle and witty, Lee's more brash and bold. Lee, for instance, was convulsed with laughter as he secretly plastered obscene labels, obtained on the Atlantic City boardwalk, on the suits of Town Chairman Barbieri as he slept during the 1964 Presidential Convention. Griswold, on the other hand, would chuckle as he turned a clever phrase or set down whimsical lyrics to a well-known show tune. Under Griswold's hand the music of "Some Enchanted Evening" became the background to a story of the discovery of an oil well underneath his office; the label on a mayonnaise jar—"Keep Cool But Do Not Freeze"—turned into a private motto for his administration.

Both were sometime mavericks and full-time reformers. In

71

1934, Griswold was one of a two-man welcoming committee from the University for President Franklin Delano Roosevelt's visit to New Haven. He started the Yale Political Union in the early forties, and pushed hard for faculty raises in the postwar years. One device was a rubber stamp with "Raise Faculty Salaries" which he marked on everything from menus at Mory's to family Christmas cards. When he became President of Yale, Griswold did not abandon his reformer's zeal; he harnessed it. While he was known best for his emphasis on the liberal arts, he also made his mark in more mundane areas. He tripled the University's endowment, initiated a $69,500,000 capital funds campaign, doubled faculty salaries, and put $75,000,000 into twenty-six new buildings. Outside Yale, Griswold pushed the rigid code that governs Ivy League football; he fought the disclaimer affidavits in federal loans to students; and he publicly challenged the methods and goals of Senator Joseph McCarthy. "Books won't be burned," he said in 1952. "Ideas won't go to jail. In the long run of history the censor and the inquisitor have always lost."

As for New Haven, Griswold despised the grime, filth, and decay which marked the home of Yale. He was not content to let the University ride with the problems of the city, but just how he could translate his concern into action was not clear during the early years of his presidency. As already noted, the University's strong overt influence in the community had ended at the beginning of the century. But even if the opportunity for direct and open influence in city affairs was possible, it was unlikely that Griswold would have exercised it. He had turned down a rash of invitations to serve on local boards, from banks to the Chamber of Commerce, for such assignments, he felt, would have entailed the sort of gaseous, lengthy meetings that bored him to tears. When his friend became mayor in 1954, however, there was a unique opportunity to forge a personal link between the city and the University for the benefit of both institutions.

In 1949, well before there was any sign that Griswold might become president, he and his family were energetic Lee supporters. In that campaign, Griswold's wife, Mary, called on old

New Haven Yankee families on Lee's behalf. Arriving at the proper 4 P.M. calling hour for ladies, and suitably attired in hat and gloves, she politely canvassed homes in the elegant Ronan-Edgehill section of the city. When confronted with reserved in-difference or close-lipped hostility toward the Irish Democrat, she would ask, "Then might I speak to your kitchen staff?" Between Lee's first defeat in 1949 and his first victory in 1953, the friendship between the two men deepened. They saw much of each other during this period when Lee was Director of the Yale News Bureau, usually in regular, private luncheons at the Gris-wold home. These were informal affairs punctuated by laughter and highlighted by subjects ranging from University problems to local politics. Lee would lecture his boss on the "do's and don'ts" of enhancing the University image while Griswold would try out ideas on Lee.

Lee listened to Griswold as he listened to few other men, for Griswold articulated philosophies that Lee felt. Griswold was not a scholarly skeptic but a learned optimist. Lee brimmed over with optimism. Griswold had no time for those who labeled Western civilization decadent; he felt that it possessed a moral power that would check its faults and reaffirm its strengths. Lee would later characterize the slums of Oak Street as "not a politi-cal or social dilemma, but a moral problem." Griswold believed in the virtually unlimited potential of the human spirit and mind unleashed from orthodoxy and regimentation. Lee would later proclaim that "free men can put their urban house in order." In many ways Griswold placed the footnotes on Lee's convictions. Lee worked hard for his boss during those years of political defeat and frustration. He still feels that one of his great career accomplishments was getting Griswold on the covers of *Time* and *Newsweek* in the same week. A conversation between them during that happy week went like this:

"Getting some obscure history teacher on the cover of two news magazines is quite an accomplishment, Dick."

"You're right, especially when you consider that it's only happened once before."

"You mean someone other than Griswold was on the covers of *Time* and *Newsweek* the same week?"

"Yeah."

"Who?"

"That other great comedian, Milton Berle."

Griswold was one of the people who encouraged Lee not to give up his ambition to become mayor. When Lee finally made it, there was this exchange of correspondence:

DEAR BOSS:

. . . Believe it or not on election night I was actually depressed when I drove downtown and around the University. I had a terrible feeling that I had made a mistake and that I was really at the "point of no return."

I still feel that way, but I'm much more cheerful about it now. I'm not really leaving Yale—except temporarily—I hope.

My warmest regards to you and your wonderful wife. Please don't forget me in your prayers. The Good Lord listens even to Protestants.

Sincerely,
DICK LEE

Griswold then wrote back:

DEAR DICK:

Arrah wisha, me boy. Don't take on like that. Sure it's only across the street you are.

Sincerely,
WHIT.

During the Griswold-Lee years there were several public indications of the new link between the university and the town. One, of course, was Griswold's agreement to serve on Lee's Citizen Action Commission, which in view of Griswold's dislike of committee assignments was a considerable sacrifice of time and patience. Another, toward the end of the period, was an honorary degree which was awarded to Lee in 1961, although it should be mentioned that an alumnus nominated Lee, not Griswold, who was never much involved in the selection of honorary degree candidates. But to appreciate fully the role of the two men in town-gown relations one needs an insight into some of the transactions which took place between Yale and New Haven. A brief description of two events will do: the sale of three high schools to Yale in 1955 and Yale's role as a potential developer in the renewal program in 1956.*

The sale of the high schools was Lee's idea, but Griswold was quick to see how it could benefit both Yale and the city. The three schools—one a trade school and the others academic high schools—were bunched together in an enclave on the Yale Campus. The acquisition of the schools was a good move for Yale, because the University was cramped for space. Griswold also saw in the purchase a unique opportunity to eliminate the problems and frictions of high-school youngsters cutting regularly through the University campus. Lee liked his idea because the three schools were hopelessly outdated, because he had promised to replace them, and because funds from the sale of the old schools would help him make good on his pledge.

The proposal was informally developed with very few in the city government or in the Yale administration aware of what was going on. Of course, even though Griswold and Lee were the heads of their respective establishments, the two friends could not wheel and deal with public property without consulting others, including the Yale Corporation and the city's Board of Aldermen, whose approval was needed on such details as price and the terms of the sale. These details presented problems. On the matter of price, Lee wanted $3,000,000 for the schools, which was all right with Griswold, but later appraisals showed that the properties were not worth quite that much. There was also the problem of when the money should be paid. Lee needed the money—or a large part of it—right away to finance the construction of new high schools to replace the old ones. If that was to be the arrangement, then there was the question of whether or not the city should pay Yale rent for use of the old schools at least to cover the interest on any funds forwarded in advance of University occupancy. Some members of the Yale Corporation and the legal-financial wing of the University took

* A third event, which involved Yale bailing Mayor Lee out of a serious renewal crisis in 1962, is covered in Chapter 9, pp. 127–29.

an appropriately hard line on these matters, although most were in agreement on the basic wisdom of the transaction. Griswold, however, was more interested in the results of the deal than in the mechanics. He was especially sensitive to town-gown considerations and recognized that while the city's payment of rent to Yale for use of the high schools pending new construction made economic sense, the novelty of such an arrangement would present political problems. So he pushed the agreement through the Yale hierarchy. It was announced on July 6, 1955, that Yale would pay the city $3,000,000 for the schools. Moreover, the city could continue using one of the schools until the fall of 1957 and another until the fall of 1958 without paying a rental fee.

Lee also pushed through the sale on the city side. On July 8th, the Board of Education, which previously had only the barest hint of what was going on, voted unanimously in favor of going ahead with the transaction as long as there were no higher bidders. There were none. In August the Board of Aldermen gave its approval, authorizing the issuance of $2,500,000 in city bonds to add to Yale's $3,000,000 for the construction of two new schools, as well as permission to use the same architect on both. The sale became an issue in the 1955 municipal campaign. Lee's Republican opponent, Philip E. Mancini, characterized the transaction as a conspiracy between Yale and the Mayor, and labeled Lee "Little Boy Blue." But the voters would have none of it, and returned Lee to office that fall with a plurality of 20,808 votes, the highest margin ever earned by a New Haven mayor.

Nevertheless, the sale of the high schools ran into other difficulties which put a strain on relations between Yale and the city and which revealed the role Griswold played with the Yale Corporation in times of stress. The chief problem was caused by construction costs of the new schools the city was building. The land for the schools was city-owned parkland, which saved site costs. But the design of the buildings required more money than was available. A number of city officials, including Lee, had made private suggestions to the architects for some exotic items, including an Olympic-size swimming pool. Logue stepped in as a *sub-rosa* design consultant on cost reduction. He cut ornamentation, substituted less expensive materials, and fought with the architects, but he could not convince Lee that an Olympic-sized pool was unnecessary. By the fall of 1956, however, he had cut the schools' cost to around a realistic $6,000,000 and in February, 1957, a construction contract was awarded.

The delay over costs meant that Lee had to go back to Griswold and explain that it would not be possible for the city to vacate the old schools at the agreed-upon dates. The city would need a year extension. On top of that, Lee wanted Yale to forgo its privilege of charging a fee for continued use of the schools under the agreement which had been signed the previous year. Griswold would have been within the rights of the agreement and the bounds of friendship to refuse this request. Some members of the Yale administration and the Corporation were already displeased with the rent-free arrangement and would probably rebel at the idea of continuing it. Characteristically, Griswold granted Lee's request in a private meeting, then went to the Corporation to get its approval of his personal commitment.

This academic brinkmanship of making private decisions and then going to the Corporation for formal ratification seems to have been a standard Griswold device. Sometimes it meant discreet cultivation of key Corporation members at the Griswold dinner table, during which Griswold would charm them into his way of thinking. At other times Griswold would boldly bring a decision to the Corporation and say, in effect, "This is the way it's got to be." Curiously, the Griswold approach to his board was similar to Lee's handling of the city boards, but was much more impressive and daring, for the Corporation Griswold inherited in 1950 consisted of such diverse, strong-minded fellows as Edwin Foster Blair, Dean Acheson, Robert A. Taft,* and others who often made no secret of their exasperation over Griswold's independent decision-making. The actual method used by Griswold to convince the Corporation to go along with a

---

* The Yale Corporation, it should be noted, changed significantly during Griswold's tenure. Only three of the seventeen Fellows who were in the Corporation in 1950 still served at the end of 1962. Those three were Edwin Foster Blair, Wilmarth Sheldon Lewis, and Juan Terry Trippe.

continued rent-free arrangement with the city is not clear, but whether it was private wooing or open charging it worked, and the saga of the schools ended in 1958, when the city finally abandoned the high schools and moved students into the new ones.

Griswold's help in the sale of the high schools was made more significant by a concurrent relationship between the city and Yale which really angered some members of the Yale administration. It centered on Yale's proposed role as a developer in the city's first renewal project, Oak Street. Logue was the one who seems to have taken the lead in interesting Yale in the development of a seven-hundred-unit high-rise apartment complex in Oak Street. Detailed negotiations were then under way with the Southern New England Telephone Company to build its $15,000,000 administrative building in the same area. Lee and Logue felt that the combined announcement of the housing and the telephone building construction would dispel community doubts about the reality of renewal in New Haven. Like the sale of the high schools, this transaction would give the University needed space for new construction.

Roger L. Stevens, the Broadway producer and real estate developer, who became a major character in the New Haven story, began talking to Yale officials about putting together a deal. It was tentatively decided that Yale would purchase a ten-acre slice of the project which it would rent to Stevens, who in turn would construct two apartment buildings of two hundred and fifty units each. Yale would build a third apartment building of two hundred and thirty-nine units, with priority going to students. The only real question was how Yale should acquire the land. By current renewal standards, a negotiated sale based on several independent appraisals would be a perfectly acceptable arrangement. But in 1955, when this apartment development was being planned, private negotiation was not encouraged by the federal Urban Renewal Administration (URA). Urban renewal was a new program and there was sensitivity over the process of land disposal caused by congressional fears of collusion between local officials and private developers. The emphasis at the time was not so much on the quality or purpose of the development, but on the price the developer was willing to pay and the openness of his method of payment. After months of soul-searching, Lee and Logue decided that as a result of URA reluctance to go along with a negotiated sale and of the political criticism which arose over the sale of the high schools to Yale, it would be best if Yale got the land it needed in Oak Street through a bidding process. Yale officials were edgy about getting involved in an auction and were somewhat miffed over the way the land sale, originally the city's idea, was becoming bureaucratized. But they went along with the idea because, as Lee was quick to point out, who would possibly outbid the formidable combine of Yale University and Roger L. Stevens?

Three other groups, however, did express interest in the land once it was announced it would be sold through public auction. One was from New York, the second from West Hartford, and the third from Boston. The auction was called for May 8, 1957, with bids on the land to start at $700,000. The Aldermanic Chambers in City Hall were packed that morning as a workman in overalls went to the microphone, tapped it, and said, "Testing —one million, two million, three million." Everybody, including the University representatives, laughed at this break in the tension, but the atmosphere soon changed as the New York developer and the Boston group began the bidding. The Yale people watched in horror while the bidding between the two jumped from $700,000 to $1,030,000, which was roughly $200,000 more than Yale had expected to pay on a negotiated sale. At $1,030,000, the New York developer dropped out and Yale plunged in, jumping the Boston group in steps of $10,000. But the Bostonians meant business and kept coming back. Finally at $1,120,000 the Yale people were just one step away from their authorized maximum; "$1,130,000" was the reply; "$1,140,-000" gulped Yale; "$1,150,000," said the Boston group. And that was it; the auction was over. The Boston group was happy, Yale was crushed, and Lee and Logue were stunned. Nobody had expected the land would bring in so much money, and although the city officials were concerned about Yale's defeat, they could not disguise their elation over the fact that the project on which they had worked so hard and the land they had cleared were really worth big money. Watching the elation, the attending Yale officials could not help but feel that Lee and his staff were rubbing salt in Yale's wounds, and that the University had been done in. Events proved that the city was the one that was done in. The high land costs incurred by the Boston outfit resulted in serious financing problems for them, a two-year delay in getting construction under way, and, eventually, two apartment buildings which Lee once confided were "the most God-awful-looking things I ever laid eyes on."

On the Yale side the bitterness centered not only on the seeming rudeness of the city officials at the conclusion of the auction but also on the reason for the auction in the first place— the local charges of conspiracy between Yale and the city during the sale of the schools and Lee's decision as a result to avoid a negotiated sale of the Oak Street land. Griswold touched on this during the CAC meeting in June, right after the auction. The minutes of that meeting show this conversation:

GRISWOLD: If Yale is to continue to cooperate [in the redevelopment program], I think you should do something about the undercurrents which occasionally come to the surface. . . . This Commission must smoke out any disposition to show us as a nefarious schemer in this community.

LEE: The climax [to anti-Yale feelings] came with the announcement that Yale and Stevens were going to bid in Oak Street. . . . If Yale had gotten the land, I was ready to shoot a strong statement. . . .

GRISWOLD: I am shedding no tears about the auction. The outcome was convincing proof of the integrity of the operation. The resentment I describe exists everywhere in some degree. . . . We must depend on the Citizens Action Commission, the Mayor, and the community to back us up. This is especially true if Yale is to be considered a potential investor and participant in the future. This is a real problem and we need help.

LEE: Yale's scholarship program is a real factor in breaking down local resentments.

THE CHAIR: In Connecticut we have New Haven, Hartford, and Bridgeport. Yale is New Haven's distinction. If it were not for Yale, New Haven would be another Bridgeport. Nobody wants that.

GRISWOLD: It's also a matter of getting the Yale Corporation to go along with us. I have a real problem here. They are very much slowed down and say, "Why should we put money into a place where we get abused every time we turn around?"

This give-and-take at the CAC was significant in two ways. First it was obvious that Griswold, although addressing the entire group, was giving a lecture to Lee, suggesting in terms that he understood that the Corporation had been quieted this time, but that they were upset by the Oak Street encounter and would not get involved in redevelopment again if that involvement was to be dictated by the Mayor's behind-the-scenes judgment rather than his open declaration that Yale was no "nefarious schemer." Lee's reply—the business about the scholarship program—was an outrageous bit of jockeying with Griswold, who had at this time informally told Lee that Yale was going to drop its practice of offering several special scholarships to New Haven high-school students. Griswold and others at Yale felt the scholarship program had been abused by local principals, who had nominated personal favorites rather than the most-deserving or best-qualified students. Lee had been under pressure from local school officials to stop Griswold from curtailing the scholarships, and with this remark at the CAC meeting Lee was telling Griswold, in effect, "O.K., Whit, I'll behave on redevelopment matters if you'll behave on the scholarship program."* The fact is that had it not been for the friendship between Lee and Griswold, the result of the auction might have meant an end to any productive relationship between the city and Yale from that point on. But Griswold did manage to soothe the hurt and bitterness felt on the Yale side.

* Griswold eventually went ahead and dropped the New Haven scholarships.

The sale of the schools and the Oak Street auction betoken the close relations which developed between the University and the city under Griswold and Lee on specific projects. But the link between the two men had a broader and more subtle impact. One of these was the actual appearance of New Haven; together Lee and Griswold discovered the wonderful world of architecture, and a walk through New Haven today shows clearly the triumphs and failures of this discovery. Despite early setbacks, the men struggled to bring beauty to Yale and New Haven, and it is not by chance that the work of some of the nation's leading architects is represented in both the city and the University. Philip Johnson did Yale's Rockefeller Virus Laboratory and Kline Science Buildings. Paul Rudolph did the Art and Architecture Building at Yale. He also designed a city parking garage and an apartment building for the elderly, and gave advice and help in the design of the Church Street Project. Eero Saarinen was the architect for the Ezra Stiles and Morse Colleges. The Saarinen firm designed the Hill High School. Skidmore, Owings & Merrill were responsible for the Beinecke Rare Book and Manuscript Library and the Conte Elementary School.

Griswold's struggles to break away from conventional building styles could fill a volume by themselves. In May, 1962, he said bluntly:

"I am sick and tired of the use of the disparaging, not to say pejorative, term 'brick and mortar' as if these things were beneath the dignity of universities. Is it not remarkable that man throughout the ages has used brick and mortar to express his highest ideals, his purest and noble aspirations and that these structures are treasured by archaeologists and historians of art as among the most accurate measures of the progress and dignity of the human race?"

An indication of the totality of the architectural battles engaged in by the Yale President was Ingalls Rink, designed by the late Eero Saarinen. No one at Yale was satisfied with the seedy New Haven Arena as a place for the Yale hockey team to perform in or for the Yale faculty and students to relax in. In the early fifties it was generally agreed that Yale should build its own skating facility. Members of the administration and the Corporation felt that for around $200,000 a modern, functional structure could be built somewhere on campus. Griswold, with the private encouragement of Lee and others, was not content with a modern, functional structure. He wanted a modern, elegant structure, so he dispatched a photographer to Cambridge with instructions to take the ugliest possible picture of the Harvard rink to give the Corporation members an idea of what a $200,000 building might look like. The photographer, Charles Albertus, came back with a picture that made the poor Harvard rink look so ugly it might have qualified for urban renewal clearance. The picture produced the desired result, and the Corporation expressed willingness to explore the idea of a rink designed by an architect instead of an engineer. The designer chosen by Griswold was Eero Saarinen, who by some associates was affectionately called "the thick Finn" and who ranks today as one of the foremost architects of this century.

Saarinen earned his nickname because of his rugged independence and strong will in dealing with clients who sought to compromise his designs for the sake of reducing costs. Yale officials were to get a taste of the Saarinen will, not because they wished to cut costs but because they were under a mandate to bring the building in at a cost of around $700,000, which was considerably more than the Corporation was prepared to invest at the beginning of the skating-rink adventure. The increased costs were not so much a result of the materials called for by Saarinen as of the engineering problems posed by the design he insisted on—a design that thoroughly delighted Griswold but one that shocked the architecturally conservative members of the Corporation and the Yale administration. For the rink designed by Saarinen does not look as though it were made for skating—it appears to be ready for flying. Its high curving and inverted roof dominates the building. It seems not to have walls and there is only the barest suggestion that it is affixed to the site. To its detractors, the rink looks like a misplaced dinosaur. To its admirers, the building has the grace of a gull. To its engineers and contractors, the building was one of the biggest headaches they ever encountered. Its eventual cost was not $700,000 but $1,300,000.

As Griswold struggled to allay the fears of the Corporation and smooth the wrinkled brows of University fiscal officials while the building was under construction, a problem developed which threatened to turn difficulty into disaster. One day the Acting Fire Marshal, in a bold gesture of job dedication, arrived unannounced at Griswold's office to tell the President of Yale, man to man, that the inside of his skating rink would have to be gutted and rebuilt because the seating plan violated a local fire law. Griswold protested vigorously, but the Fire Marshal came right back with "Mr. Griswold, would you want your mother to go to a hockey game in an unsafe building?"

Griswold tracked down Lee in New London, Connecticut, where Lee was about to make a speech, and blew up. For five minutes he outlined his position: he had worked hard to bring Saarinen to Yale; he had faced many problems in financing the structures; the architectural future of Yale was in the balance; and no obscure fireman was going to tip the project into chaos. Lee promised to return to the city as soon as possible, and upon his arrival he discovered that the plans for the building had not, in fact, been thoroughly reviewed by the Fire Department, that the Fire Marshal had correctly seen that the rink's seating plan did not meet the requirements for theatres, but that there was a question of whether or not the rink could be classified as a covered stadium, for which the existing seating plan would be permissible. Several weeks later, the city's Corporation Counsel wrote an extensive opinion that the Saarinen rink was a covered stadium.

One thing Lee and Griswold never agreed on was the role of Yale in attracting and supporting New Haven industry. Lee would have liked to see extensive research functions in New Haven, like those along Route 1 near Princeton, New Jersey, or Route 128 near Cambridge, Massachusetts. Lee also thought Yale should offer night courses leading to advanced degrees and applied research linked to business needs. But Griswold would have none of it. To him it smacked of vocational training and detracted from the main purpose of the University—widening the horizons and sharpening the intellects of students and faculty.

But if the University under Griswold was stingy with its academic resources on matters of local business expansion, it was more than generous when it came to helping the Lee administration with ideas, hard work, and free time. Faculty participation in administration affairs has been considerable on everything from speech writing to legal opinions in the past thirteen years. The major reason was that Lee and his small coterie had the audacity to tackle city problems in which faculty members from law and the social sciences were interested. The opportunity for participation, writing, and research was too good to pass up.

But the greatest University contribution was the warmth, help, and humor of the relationship between the President and the Mayor. It didn't just survive the conflicts that arose during their administrations; it thrived on them because both men understood that the changes they sought would inevitably produce friction and conflict.

It was the saddest of days in New Haven on April 19, 1963, when Alfred Whitney Griswold died. His charm, wit, and style were suddenly gone, but the purpose of the man was readily apparent all over the city—in the University classrooms, in the many ties between Yale and New Haven, and in the handsome new campus buildings. Even the Ingalls Rink now seemed less like a dinosaur and much more like a gull.

It was clear that the direction he set for Yale and the tone he established in its relations with the city would be permanent standards to which future generations would refer and by which his successors would be gauged.

Kingman Brewster, Jr., in his Baccalaureate Address of June, 1963, summarized the Griswold contribution:

"Your President spent his life enhancing the abilities and widening the horizons of those who worked and studied here. This passion sustained both his gaiety, and his ferocity. It gave unswerving course to a most volatile temperament. The extraordinary vividness of his word was pale imitation of the moral vividness of the man.

"Bear with pride and gratitude the good fortune that your Yale was his Yale."

Lee's public statement bore none of that literate eloquence. His was mainly the eloquence of unusual quiet, of tears, and of these few words:

"He was my friend and a good one in all the years I knew him."

7

Retailing Redevelopment

Urban renewal, with its large-scale disruptions and technical complexities, is political dynamite and must be handled carefully. The desired results take years to achieve. Meanwhile problems can crop up—problems such as poorly rehoused families or idle vacant land—which call attention to themselves by picket lines or an unwanted crop of ragweed. Lee's answer to these problems, aside from trying to avoid them in the first place, was burning optimism and the "hard sell." Where else in America has a mayor stood before a group of citizens who have seen the center of town flattened for years and quip, "Well, we have no new construction yet, but at least the Russians have taken us off their primary target list."* Of course, not everyone was amused, but enough laughed to indicate that, besides his sense of salesmanship and not really as a result of it, Lee enjoyed widespread community confidence and popularity. His ability to sustain both, even in hard times, was a remarkable testimony to the successful marriage of his naturally warm personality with the cold, complicated program he stood for.

Lee usually stayed out of his office as much as possible, traveling a circuit of bar mitzvahs, church suppers, Communion breakfasts, P.T.A. meetings, and League of Women Voters teas.

---

* This line was used repeatedly before New Haven audiences, but it was first tried out by Lee on a group of Soviet officials who were in New Haven on a State Department tour. It was remarkable to watch the expressions as the translator told them what Lee had said. A few laughed, but most sat in astonishment. It seemed as though their worst fears of American life had been confirmed.

He charmed his hosts with jokes and stories, and by remember-
ing their first names. He was, or soon became, the center of
attraction at any gathering. When it came time for him to speak,
he would hold his audience with extemporaneous statements of
lofty and suitably vague goals, such as, "We're not only going to
lift New Haven into the twentieth century, we'll push it forth into
the twenty-first," or "New Haven will become the first slumless
city, a truly *new* New Haven." These were never the culmination
of long harangues about city problems, but crisp statements of
purpose, designed to inspire or shock and devoid of the details
that might get him into trouble. Lee extended the circuit usually
followed by New Haven mayors to include formerly isolated
sectors such as school classrooms, neighborhood stores, housing
projects, and places of employment, where he would disrupt
routine by mingling with the people, soliciting their problems,
and jotting down notes in his little black book. At the end of the
day the book would provide material for angry memos to department heads and reassuring notes to his constituents. He personified active local government.

Lee soon became known not only as a hard-working mayor
with big ideas but as a regular fellow, too. He made it a point to
be around when people were in trouble, and the best way for this
friend of 152,048 people to be around when they needed him
was to study the obituary notices. By projecting the number of
funerals attended by Lee in a month in 1965, one of Lee's
secretaries has estimated that he had attended more than 7,000
wakes. In a city with a high proportion of Italian and Irish
families, which are usually large and close, Lee's attendance at
funerals has put him in direct contact with much of the city's
population at times when a visit by the Mayor leaves a deep
personal impression. The practice has also required an efficiency
of operation which Lee's chauffeurs—and he has worn out five
of them—call the "wake stop." The wake stop involves dropping
the Mayor off in front of a funeral home, slowly pulling the car
up the driveway to the rear of the home, and idling for approximately two minutes. Meanwhile, the Mayor is wending his way
through the groups of mourners inside, with gentle smiles and

firm handshakes—stopping at the bier for a brief prayer and a quick inspection of the quality of work downstairs—then through the remainder of the crowd to a rear exit and back into the waiting car. To be sure, the practice is somewhat morbid and political, but it is also based on genuine concern. No one around City Hall will forget the time that Lee completely supervised, partly financed, and fully attended every step of a funeral for an obscure employee who died with no close friends or relatives, because "That was the least I could do for the poor devil." It was a memorable scene to watch Lee slip quietly into the church service, attended by only ten others, and pray alone in a rear pew while a priest performed the Mass.

As soon as his renewal program made a physical imprint on the town, Lee began matching his person with his program through carefully created devices designed to make renewal interesting, understandable, and exciting. The interest was aroused through the use of models and drawings which showed what he was trying to achieve. Renewal was made comprehensible by portraying it in homey terms. The opening of a neighborhood playground or a school, or even the installation of a traffic light, would be the subject for a full-blown dedication ceremony, and Lee would dramatically proclaim the improvement "another step in our city-wide renewal program." The excitement was generated by the hoopla that accompanied any achievement of his administration. When a new animal shelter was opened, Lee appeared on television to find homes for dogs and cats. When the first of the slums was to be razed, Lee manned the crane to swing the wrecking ball, and although he almost killed several observers, the excitement of it all led to the practice of inviting visiting dignitaries to join him in crushing a slum. For a few years Lee had his own television show during which he presented models and drawings of redevelopment proposals, and the Sunday Bridgeport *Herald* gave him a column in which he wrote about everything, from his plans for New Haven to comments on international affairs.

Aside from establishing himself and his programs in the minds of the people, Lee also took steps to enhance the post of mayor.

He remodeled the office he inherited, which included a roll-top desk, asphalt-tile floors, a crumbling ceiling, and a huge, abandoned vault used for storing furniture. He modernized the facilities with a rug, draperies, furniture, renovation of the vault into added office space, and the installation of a private hot line to key aides. He held daily press conferences in the office, and conducted as many meetings as possible there. All major news from city departments was issued by his office under his name. Top city staff people even cleared their speeches with Lee. Ralph Taylor remembers, for instance, that for an out-of-town speech he sent his prepared remarks to Lee for clearance. Lee called him to his office, complimented him on the text, and then added, "Just remember, Ralph, it's spelled 'L-E-E.' "

The only regular forum most mayors have for delivering their message to the people is the press, including radio and television. This was an area of Lee's job which he complained about bitterly, but which he secretly enjoyed most. He enjoyed it not only because he was by experience and inclination a newsman but because there were few supporters of Lee's programs among the New Haven fourth estate. Getting the reporters to broadcast his message was therefore a test of his guile and cunning. New Haven has one television station, five radio stations, and two daily newspapers. Only one of the stations was a strong supporter of the Lee administration. The other five were unenthusiastic about administration programs and equated urban renewal with such topics as public safety or National Brotherhood Week. The two newspapers, which were jointly owned, were in basic opposition to the philosophy of urban renewal with its large expenditures of public money and its acquisition of private property. Both papers remain whipping posts for New Haven liberals, and some of Lee's staff have regarded them as biased, vindictive, second rate, and rigidly conservative. The two papers provided the main formal link between the administration and the public, and for that reason their roles will be emphasized here.

The morning paper, the *Journal Courier,* has a circulation of about 30,000, a small staff, and an editorial page which rarely touches on anything more controversial than the beauties of spring or the duty to vote. One suspects that it is subsidized by the publishers mainly to discourage competition for its afternoon paper, the *Register*. The *Register,* with its circulation of over 100,000, has a professional staff at least three times as large as that of the *Courier,* and its editorial page reflects the view of the management. That view is conservative if one considers support of Barry Goldwater to be indicative of conservatism; the *Register* endorsed Goldwater in the 1964 presidential campaign. The two papers are heavy with wire-service material, but on most state and local news they provide on-the-spot coverage, and many of their reporters write under by-lines.

For most of this century the papers were owned and managed by one man, the late John Day Jackson. It is difficult to describe Jackson accurately, for he was a man whose rugged independence seems to have polarized community attitudes on his papers and person. Most politicians in New Haven, regardless of party, characterize him in tyrannical terms. Old-line business leaders talk of him cautiously. There are few alive in New Haven today who knew him well and there are few who speak of him kindly, but this could be because he outlived his generation. It was not until his ninety-second year that he died; he stood virtually alone in a world of changing needs and conditions, and he was not a flexible sort.

It is clear that Jackson regarded both the *Courier* and the *Register,* from their pressrooms to their news columns, as his personal property. It is also clear that he was never blinded by party label in condemning those who violated his idea of what was right. He shocked many in New Haven with his support of President Truman, whom he always regarded as something of a fool, against General MacArthur over the conduct of the Korean War. The reason for his stand was given by one of his sons, Richard Jackson, who is now Co-Publisher of the *Register*:

"Of course, John Day had no time for Truman, but he felt strongly that the boss's word was law, and Truman, not Mac-Arthur, was the boss. The editorial also had some family meaning. He was telling his sons that he, like Truman, was the boss to be listened to." The elder Jackson did not like Lee, his bravado, or his liberalism. Lee disliked Jackson and felt that their relations were permanently poisoned by an incident in the 1951 campaign. Jackson had refused to run a Lee political ad and story that accused Mayor Celentano of having an interest in a trucking firm which was doing business with the city. After a meeting between Lee and the publisher failed to achieve a compromise, Lee took to television to proclaim, "During this campaign, I have been fighting not only an opposing candidate but a biased, slanted, inequitable, and prejudiced press." According to Lee, Jackson saw this performance in his gardener's cottage, and there was born in that humble setting a grudge which he carried to his grave. Richard Jackson has minimized this incident and suggested the problem was more deep-seated.

"Although John Day and Dick differed deeply on issues, the two men were much alike. They were strong-willed, stubborn, and very proud. I have always told Dick that he made one serious mistake with John Day. He never came to him other than to tell him what he wanted or was going to do. He never swallowed his pride to ask for John Day's opinion or advice. Most mayors and even governors had done this, although they would often turn around and do precisely the opposite. Dick could never do it, and John Day never forgot. The two men were just too different politically and much too alike personally to ever get along."

It is ironic that despite his dislike of Lee, John Day Jackson's method of operating inadvertently helped Lee. By refusing to turn over control of the paper to his two sons, Richard and Lionel, and by instituting instead a gradual five-year shift of responsibility, the elder Jackson created a managerial hiatus, so that for the first few years of the Lee administration there was no one person in charge of the papers; as late as 1958 Jackson, at eighty-nine, was still butting into the decisions of his sons and the staff, and this practice naturally created problems, including an indecisive editorial page.

This and other internal problems at the city's two newspapers played a critical role in Lee's efforts to get his message across to the citizens. He was not really dealing with a strong publisher who opposed him and had a monopoly on community news, as Lee, his friends and staff, and at least one observer would suggest.* Rather he was dealing with an organization which was going through a difficult transition from one-man rule to the two-man management by sons who were bent on overcoming the problems of the past and, judging by their subsequent actions, democratizing decision-making for the future. The paper has not undergone any major change in its conservatism, but it has slowly improved in professional and technical quality.

While Lee encouraged the notion that he was being victimized by a monolithic, tyrannical newspaper, he was very much aware of the actual conditions at the papers. He had many sources—including the boys in the shipping department, who still give him a free copy of the *Register* as soon as it comes off the press. While the problems of transition went on at the top, Lee dealt almost exclusively with the men in the middle, the editors and reporters, who were getting the papers out. The two chief editorial men at the *Register* were Charles McQueeney, the Managing Editor, and Robert Leeney, the Executive Editor. Neither man shared Lee's politics, but they liked him personally and seemed to respect him professionally, if not always as a mayor, as an ex-newsman. Both men got daily calls from Lee to share gossip, to find out what was being printed, and to plug stories. Quite often Lee would offer unsolicited but professional advice on how all stories should be handled.

For his own stories, Lee would first call the newsman he had sent it to and suggest the way it should be written and provide any additional information that might be required. As soon as he hung up, he would call McQueeney to make a case for where the story should be placed. The case would never be made in vague layman's language, but would be couched in such terms as "Charlie, this one needs at least a two-column head, preferably above the fold. What do you think, Charlie?" If the story was big enough, Lee would invariably call up Leeney, who wrote most of the major editorials, begin with a polite suggestion, continue with

* Robert A. Dahl, *Who Governs?* (New Haven: Yale University Press, 1961), pp. 256–67.

a stern lecture on editorial responsibility, and often conclude with an angry note, such as one of these:

DEAR BOB [Leeney]:

. . . Do you think the day will ever come when the *Register* can support anything in an unqualified fashion—anything constructive and good, that is, like Church Street?

Regards,
DICK

DEAR BOB:

. . . With all this pioneering in New Haven, these great achievements in New Haven, don't you think there is something to be proud of editorially in our program . . . not lukewarm but enthusiastic?

Regards,
DICK

Sometimes a blast at Leeney was not enough for Lee, so to get things fully off his chest, he would shoot a wrathful note to the top:

DEAR DICK [Jackson]:

I thought you would like to compare this editorial in the New York *Times* last Saturday with your editorial the preceding day on funds for urban renewal. It was quite a contrast! Some day, I am sure, we are going to have an editorial page in New Haven which will properly reflect a progressive and enlightened attitude. . . . When that day will come, of course, I do not know, but I do hope I will live to see it.

Sincerely,
DICK

Jackson's reply infuriated Lee:

DEAR DICK:

In connection with your letter to me . . . "I disapprove of what you say, but I will defend to the death your right to say it."—*Attributed to Voltaire.*

Sincerely,
DICK

However, such volleys fired privately at the editors were the exception. Normally Lee would court them. He would often call

Leeney to seek advice on policy matters in conversations that would go like this: "Hello, Bob. Dick. How are you, Bob? . . . Tell me, Bob, what do you think I should do about this ———— matter? . . . Damn it, Bob, that's an interesting idea. . . . Do you mind if I borrow that phrase, Bob? . . . Thanks, Bob. Tell me, Bob, if I approached it in that way, how do you think the *Register* would treat it? . . . Well, think it over, Bob, and give me a call."

It would be an injustice to suggest the editors were taken in by such antics; they were capable of some cunning of their own. This was indicated whenever Lee organized a letter-writing campaign, called up Leeney to ask innocently if there had been any response, and Leeney, with equal innocence, claimed that he had received nothing at all. One *Register* reporter has described Lee's dealing with the editors in these terms:

"I don't think you can minimize Leeney's and McQueeney's role as a buffer between the publishers and Dick. A key part of that role is that both guys, like Dick, are Irish Catholics, and there is a subtle ethnic thing going. Dick's problem with the two has never been personal as it was with the old man. It's mainly a question of orientation. While I don't agree with everything Dick's done, I understand it, like some other reporters, because I've seen or covered the problems. Leeney and McQueeney really don't. They spend most of their time in the office and they live in the suburbs, and they just really don't appreciate the problems Dick has dealt with, so it's little wonder they don't usually approve or even understand his actions."

This comment not only summarizes the dynamics of Lee's relations with the *Register* editorial staff but also indicates one reason Lee found the reporters were least intractable when it came to ways for him to get the coverage he wanted. They would often sympathize with him because they were eyewitnesses to what he was doing, although the sympathy might be nothing more than the kind an umpire gives when he calls a batter out. Lee made the reporters feel important because he genuinely believed they were. He would walk out of any meeting to talk to a newsman, and he would make sure they got a briefing on a big story immediately before it broke. On major stories he would arrange a news conference which he personally directed with the flamboyance and extravagance of a Cecil B. deMille filming the Bible. Carefully multilithed press kits, enclosed in handsome blue covers and detailing every possible aspect of a story, were hand-delivered to reporters. The principals were herded to New Haven and propped up in the Mayor's Office along with drawings of the proposed improvements. Lee would solemnly enter the room and make his announcement. New Haven had never seen anything quite like these performances.

The reporters did not always respond to these inducements, so Lee employed some other tactics based on his control of what the reporters needed—the release of administration news. It was a relatively easy step to freeze out a hostile reporter by issuing stories on his day off or by giving it as an exclusive to another reporter who was more friendly. He would also play to their egos ("Damn it, why don't you come to work for me? I'll pay you twice as much as the *Register*"), their personal sympathies ("I'm just flesh and blood. I can't be beat around in the press every day and not be hurt by it"), or their insecurities ("McQueeney tells me there may be a shift in the beat soon"). Two things frequently irritated the reporters. One was based on the skepticism that reporters can develop on any beat when they get to know the personalities and problems and learn that the world is not quite as rosy as it appears in a handout. The other was peculiar to New Haven, where Lee and Logue's young staff clashed regularly with the newsmen. The reporters felt that "the whiz kids" were overpaid, which was understandable because the reporters were sometimes underpaid; that they were highhanded, which was a natural conclusion because some of the staff were considerably smarter than a few of the reporters and delighted in proving it; and that they were just plain arrogant, which a number of them were.

One of the redevelopment staff, Harold Grabino, was high on all the reporters' lists. Grabino, who was the Agency's counsel and later Executive Director, was proud of his ability to give one-word replies to any newsman's queries and, for some strange reason, insisted on calling some of them "Daddy-o." He was openly contemptuous of the newspapermen and would go out of his way to taunt them. One of his favorite tricks was to call *Courier* reporters at their homes early in the morning, waking them up to complain about a story written the night before.

The biggest complaint of the newspaper establishment was the secrecy which cloaked the administration plans and programs. On the surface, the complaint looks valid, for a lid was placed on specific project plans, negotiations with private developers, and proposed public improvements. Public announcements were held up until details were completed or were timed for the greatest dramatic impact, with the emphasis often placed on the impact. But the nature of redevelopment negotiations and the hostility of Jackson had a lot to do with it, too. Lee would often say, "Businessmen don't like to negotiate on a card table on the New Haven Green," and Logue, in lecturing his staff on staying away from the local press, would say, "You can't play square with the Jacksons because they are out to get you at every turn."

Lee was one of the first politicians to employ the full use of polling techniques to provide him with some reading on the results of his varied devices for shaping public opinion. In fact, it seems to have been Lee who introduced John F. Kennedy to the work of Louis Harris, who was Kennedy's pollster in the 1960 presidential campaign and was Lee's personal pollster or "witch doctor," as the staff called him, during the fifties.* Harris and, later, Oliver Quayle studied the city several times during an election year, and their assessments of voter attitudes were amazingly accurate, although their predictions of voter conduct could be quite fallible. Their work was helpful mainly in shaping campaign themes and cheering Lee up, for they were likable, intelligent men whose company the Mayor enjoyed. Sometimes

* A letter from Senator John F. Kennedy to Lee on December 9, 1957, said:
DEAR DICK:
I am returning to you your copy of the Lou Harris survey. He certainly does a thorough and constructively helpful job; and I am definitely going to try to talk to him one of these days about what he might be able to do for me.
Sincerely,
JACK

Lee twisted their survey results to square with his impressions of citizen opinion which he claimed he received "through the antenna down here in my gut."

Lee's record of interpreting these impressions was not perfect, but it was accurate enough for one to marvel at his ability to pick up subtle shifts of opinion and to adjust his words and actions accordingly. His ability to speak when it was time to speak, to say what people felt, to act when there was impatience with talk, or to remain silent for fear that official words and action might tip the delicate balance when opposing community forces converged represented an eloquence—the finest of the political arts—of which Lee remains a true master. This Lee mastery was precisely what the Harris, Quayle, and other studies of voter attitudes uncovered, for there was a significant voter identification with the Mayor. A Quayle survey in 1963 summarized this identification in these terms:

> As always has been the case, Lee shows greatest strength as a person. His personal profile remains rich and warm. . . . The voters like him very much. He is a friendly and warm man who is honest and deeply dedicated to a better New Haven. . . .*

Anyone who has worked for Lee has his favorite pollster finding which dramatized Lee's attraction—the political-science poll in 1959 which showed that more schoolchildren in the city knew who the Mayor was than who the President of the United States was; an earlier finding which showed that 50 per cent of the sample not only liked Lee personally but regarded him as a close friend of the family.

But while the voters liked Lee, they often disagreed with him sharply, particularly on sensitive issues like civil rights. One cannot detect in any of the polls any great ground swell of community liberalism. Rather typically, New Haven voters took a somewhat limited view of what their local government should

---

* A skeptic might properly suggest that such a glowing review is to be taken lightly since it was written by someone on the payroll; i.e., a pollster paid by the Mayor. However, I can remember both Harris and Quayle remarking in meetings not attended by Lee that Lee's personal tie with the voters was extraordinary compared to that of most other public officials they had served.

be doing, and their chief concerns were usually on the rapidity of snow removal, the efficiency of garbage collection, the availability of downtown parking, or the level of taxes. Their attitude on urban renewal was either problem-oriented ("Too much business displacement," "Not enough new housing") or very personal ("What's in it for me?").

In the face of urban renewal disruptions and problems, Lee would exude confidence and optimism sometimes to the point of self-delusion. And for the voter who sought a personal spot in renewal, Lee found one. Under his administration urban renewal became as comforting as a new home, as useful as a handsome new school, as liberal as an anti-poverty program, as commercial as a department store, as economic as a new industrial park, as convenient as a new expressway, and as understandable as a neighborhood playground. In the beginning it was a matter of public-relations imagery, but soon it became program policy. Urban renewal in New Haven was no two-step process of tearing down and rebuilding; it became an umbrella for new programs and services dealing with many areas of physical and human need.

It was the popular support that Lee enjoyed which sustained his coalition of other forces in the community—Yale, the businessmen, the politicians, and the bureaucrats. "Group dynamics" is what he would call it, but whatever it was, the careful courting of the voters, the personal link with Yale, the creation of a pro-administration business organization, the accommodation with the politicians, and the control of the bureaucracy had the practical effect of immobilizing his opposition, giving him the support he needed, and creating apparent consensus. From afar the Lee coalition seemed to have the order, body, and unity of a symphony. But in many ways it was a one-man act with Lee assuming the combined role of composer, arranger, conductor, and performer.

No event better portrayed the character of the coalition than Lee's birthday party, which over the years developed into a pilgrimage of those connected with the administration to pay homage to the chief. The parties were usually held in the fading ballroom of the Hotel Taft and attended by about three hundred key persons. Up the small, cramped hotel elevators they would silently ascend, eyeball to neck, then alight and move into the ballroom to find the table where their group was sitting. There was never enough room, so the overflows created unlikely table partners. One could find a fire marshal next to a law professor, a bank president seated next to a ward heeler, a League of Women Voters member next to Arthur Barbieri, or a *Register* reporter next to a young Redevelopment Agency staff man. The three-man string ensemble would play "Marching Along Together," which was suffered in grim silence. Subjects of conversation might be the heavy layer of fried fat on the chicken legs or the appearance of Mayor Lee, beaming, at the head table. After dessert, discomfort would turn to boredom as the master of ceremonies told stale jokes. Finally Lee would be introduced, to accept, with suitable expressions of surprise and gratitude, the gift he had selected two weeks earlier. The ensemble would render "For He's a Jolly Good Fellow" as a conclusion, and the members of the Lee coalition would quickly leave and return to their separate occupations and areas of the city, not to reconvene until Lee was a year older. The remarkable thing about these otherwise routinely dull affairs was that Lee was usually the one most bored by them. The annual convocation of the coalition to honor his birthday was a bit of symbolism to be endured, not an end in itself. He was happy to get his lawnmower or a set of books, but there in the Taft ballroom the coalition was out of place and function. Its members belonged in their natural community setting linked only by Lee, and their purpose was not to bestow gifts on the leader but to play the Mayor's game.

III

Rebuilding the City

8

The Road Not Taken

The massive reconstruction of a city may begin with the fanfare of a crusade, but it proceeds with the pace of a snail and can become as brawling as a street fight. One veteran campaigner, Robert Moses of New York, has put it this way:

"We are told that the walls of Thebes rose to music and that in building Solomon's Temple there was no sound of axe or hammer or tool of iron. Nice trick, if they did it, but in any event, it has not been done since."

The arena of public works is filled with thousands who have different and often conflicting interests. There are bureaucrats with set ways, architects who are temperamental and often political, contractors who are tough, union bosses who can be tougher, businessmen who need profits, landholders with rights, and people who have votes. Lee, Logue, and their staff enjoyed no basic training for the inevitable combat. They merely picked up their lawbooks, memo pads, and maps, stepped into the arena, and began slugging it out with anyone who acted like an opponent. The first adversary was not a group or even a person. It was an idea called the highway-user concept. Very few had ever heard of it, but they soon learned that it had the potential to ruin their urban renewal program.

The concept began with the federal highway program in 1926, and it still prevails today. It suggests that new highways should be built exclusively for the safety, comfort, and convenience of the car, bus, or truck driver who pays for them with his gasoline tax. The driver's spokesman in building roads, according to the user concept, is the industrial complex which serves him—made up of the car manufacturers, road builders, and gas and oil producers. This group's judgment is that roads should be aligned to get maximum mileage for every gasoline tax dollar. Such side considerations as curving a road to avoid a park, tunneling it to preserve a neighborhood, or hiding it with heavy landscaping are discouraged although not always denied. The effect of the road on the driver is paramount; the impact of the road on the land is of minimal concern.

The user concept was a logical *modus operandi,* which presented few problems during the first twenty to thirty years of high-speed road building, when the engineers developed their trade and changed much of the nation's landscape. Their moving of mountains and bridging or tunneling of rivers and harbors represented awesome achievements for which the nation is now famous. But after World War II the user concept became illogical and created serious problems. The proliferation of cars and the national dependence on truck transport made it illusory to separate driver interest from public interest. The growth of the population, the urbanization of the nation, and the subsequent increase in land value made it reckless to align highways as though America were one great potato field. But the concept endured. A practical effect of its survival was indicated by a former engineer with the Bureau of Public Roads:

"One of my first jobs was to review a clover leaf in a Texas city. I took one look at the state drawings and saw the thing was underdesigned. So I widened the ramps, took about 200 more feet of land, sent it back, and never thought of it again; that is, until after I left BPR and got involved on a different level of government. Today I wince every time I think of it. I followed the book, but I had no idea what was on those 200 feet of extra land. It may have been a gas station, a park, a junk yard. It may have hurt someone, it may have helped, but the point is I never knew."

The worst of the problems occurred in the cities, with their population densities and valuable real estate. A motorist traveling through Boston, Providence, Bridgeport, and New York—

just to name a few East Coast cities—will see how his interests have been served in consequence of pushing the user concept, with a strong assist from sluggish city officials. Neighborhoods have been cut in two, industrial areas obliterated, commercial areas sacked, parkland destroyed.

New Haven challenged the user concept with comprehensive local planning, which tucked proposed highways into both the city master plan and specific renewal objectives, so that when the highway engineers moved into New Haven, they encountered a mayor and a staff who knew what they wanted and who skillfully argued their case. Before Lee became mayor, the city had fought and won on the alignment of the Connecticut Turnpike, which had been slated to slice through New Haven on its easterly course from New York. The alignment of the Turnpike provides a rare case of highway planners and city planners reaching quick agreement.

In the Rotival master plan, the Turnpike was to provide a new harbor-front entrance to New Haven. The area Rotival had outlined for the route was vacant tidal marsh, similar to the vast marshland in northern New Jersey near Bayonne and Secaucus, the sort of low-cost, empty, uncomplicated real estate that highway engineers naturally prefer. The potential problem of fill was solved by the Army Engineers who had dredged the harbor and had dropped tons of fill along the shore. The Rotival alignment was followed by the Highway Department, and the turnpike was being built when Lee became mayor. Under the Lee administration the remainder of the marsh was filled later as part of a state-supported redevelopment project and transformed into an industrial park with direct access to the Turnpike. The final product of the industrial park and Turnpike represents a remarkably smooth blend of public actions involving three levels of government.

Lee's opening gambit with the Highway Department was fraught with drama and audacity. He wanted them to build a $15,000,000 six-lane expressway between the Turnpike and downtown New Haven, where Lee had already begun laying plans for large-scale reconstruction including new parking facilities and widened city streets. The Mayor's downtown plans depended on the connector. The Highway Department had offered the previous administration an exit ramp leading to the edge of downtown, but Lee wanted nothing less than six lanes with a terminal point in the heart of the city. By June of 1954 he had succeeded in mushrooming the exit ramp into an expressway, but he had failed in getting it extended into downtown. Still, as a by-product of his negotiations he had gained something just as important, the friendship of the Highway Commissioner, the late G. Albert Hill, who was privately intrigued by Lee's plans for the city.*

During the summer months Lee's staff prepared reports which showed that the exit-ramp-turned-expressway would produce monumental traffic jams if it was not extended five blocks to permit traffic distribution over a larger area. Commissioner Hill was impressed with this argument and became persuaded by it that fall, when he and Lee found themselves in a peculiar political situation. Hill's boss, Republican Governor John Lodge, was up for re-election and was being strongly challenged by Abraham Ribicoff, who, among other things, was attacking Lodge for permitting alleged bungling by some members of the Highway Department. Ribicoff was naturally anxious to have his allies, including Lee, supply grist for the mill. Lee was in a position to do just that with a number of problems, including his connector needs. Mainly out of friendship for the Commissioner, Lee held back from making public statements and Hill recognized that implicit in Lee's silence was a personal loyalty that was unusual in the hurly-burly of state politics. This, plus his interest in what Lee was attempting to accomplish in New Haven and the strength of Lee's case for a five-block extension, moved him to approve the Lee plan in October, 1954. Ribicoff went on to win that election, and on Hill's last day in office he signed the formal agreement to build the connector to the point where Lee needed it.**

* Commissioner Hill was not a professional highway engineer. Preceding his appointment he taught chemistry at Wesleyan University. After serving as Highway Commissioner, Hill directed a local urban renewal program.

** Personal relationships between public officials are key factors in cooperation among agencies and levels of government. In 1966, Mr. Hill died, and Lee

Before the agreement was signed, Lee had to overcome a final but serious problem. Hill could rationalize the immediate construction of the connector only if it was the beginning of a new state route; however, just beyond the connector terminal point in the path of future alignment the Southern New England Telephone Company was quietly assembling land for a new headquarters building. Lee turned near disaster into a tremendous boon for his renewal program when he convinced the telephone officials to become the first renewal developers by moving to a different site in the downtown Oak Street Project, which bordered the connector.

Lee's first year in office was extraordinarily productive. He had convinced the State Highway Department to build a downtown expressway and as a direct result of that he had his first major developer in the renewal program. Both the downtown connector and the Connecticut Turnpike are unusual examples of successful highway planning. The Turnpike was achieved without interagency frictions because both the city and the state wanted the same alignment. The connector, on the other hand, was a product of peculiar political and personal circumstances, and with its six lanes ending abruptly in the downtown area the road seemed to be a Highway Department contribution to the renewal of central New Haven.*

Much more typical of both the damaging potential of the user concept and the tedious negotiations which are required if a new highway is to serve a city's planning objectives is Interstate 91. I 91 was the third major route scheduled for New Haven. It cut

---

wrote a personal letter to the newspapers to mourn the fact that little coverage had been given of Hill's death or his contributions. He went on to give Hill full credit for the connector, and then said:

". . . The vision of this man is something I shall always remember. His interest in the problems of our cities . . . is something every highway engineer should take as a model and a guide. Most important of all, however, he was at all times a fine and decent and courteous human being who brought to his assignment not only tremendous intellectual capacity but decency, compassion, and warmth."

It is the only letter Mayor Lee ever wrote to the newspapers for publication.

* Only now, ten years after the connector was built, is the Highway Department moving to extend it as Connecticut Route 34.

northward from the interchange of the connector and the Turnpike to Hartford. As originally conceived by the highway engineers in 1952, the road started its journey in the old Wooster
Square neighborhood of New Haven, destroying hundreds of
homes, some of distinguished architecture, and blighting a small
city park. Significantly, the local plea to realign the road, which
was led by Mayor Celentano, was based on economic considerations and not on the desecration of beauty. Using an assessment
map, the city planners showed the engineers that they had picked
the most expensive alignment and that by moving the road
several blocks to the east and out of the residential area they
could save around $300,000. With that compelling argument,
plus pressure from Mayor Celentano, the engineers moved the
road to the allegedly cheaper alignment, which also happened to
provide an effective barrier between a nearby industrial area and
the homes of Wooster Square.

The alignment of Interstate 91 after it passed Wooster Square
was not so neatly resolved. The Highway Department had proposed that the road follow the bed of the New Haven Railroad,
which was fine with the city planners. But as the route reached
the northern boundary of the city, it encountered a large rise
called East Rock. This required a decision to skirt either east or
west. The eastern course involved bridging the Quinnipiac River
and building on marshland. The western route involved cutting
through a park and game preserve and then through the residential area of a suburban town. The inclination of the engineers
seems to have been to build the road on the western route,
because it provided least deviation from the basic north-south
line of the road and followed existing traffic flows. This apparent
preference was reflected in 1956, when the Department unveiled
its proposed interstate system with maps that indicated an Interstate 91 alignment which cut through the park, game preserve,
and suburban homes. The park lovers, bird watchers, and homeowners reacted with a vehemence that shook the Highway Department into proposing several routes falling on both sides of
East Rock and creating further confusion and controversy.

With appropriate statesmanship, Lee stepped into the conflict to suggest that the affected towns join with him in finding an acceptable route. As usual, the Mayor's motives were not sinister, just mixed. He was bothered by the storm the proposed route was causing in suburban towns and he was equally concerned that the controversy would hold up the approval and construction of I 91, which in turn would delay the city's renewal plans for Wooster Square. He suggested a regional corporation to plan the alignment to conform with local plans for residential, commercial, and industrial areas. Seizing on the idea as a way to placate their constituents, who had chosen the closest level of government on which to vent their disapproval of the road, town officials from Hamden, Wallingford, and North Haven accepted Lee's offer and even financed the enterprise, which was named the Quinnipiac Valley Development Corporation (QVDC), after the river which flowed through the affected towns.

Headed by Logue, who was made its secretary, and staffed by "the Kremlin," the QVDC came up with a totally new alignment which ignored existing traffic flows and relegated traffic considerations to an equal status with the road's impact on the land. Much of the QVDC alignment traversed unimproved land and the QVDC report carved out special land areas for recreational, commercial, industrial, and residential development. The report finally produced by the QVDC was more a master plan for the Quinnipiac Valley area than an alignment report. It not only included the proposed highway path, but it showed how exit and access ramps should be tied into present and future roads. It covered proposed zoning laws for the land areas, soil and engineering reports, a survey of industrial interest in the valley, and even preliminary redevelopment plans. The report gave area towns the rallying point they needed. When Interstate 91 finally opened in 1966, it followed the general QVDC alignment, and motorists traveling the road today can already see signs of the development proposed by the QVDC several years ago.

After the release of its reports the QVDC became dormant, much to the distress of many who wanted it to become a full-fledged regional development corporation. Even the city dropped its interest in the QVDC once the general alignment of I 91 and the other roads was settled with the State Highway Department. It turned its attention to making sure that the general agreements were honored and that the detailed highway plans worked. It was clear that these negotiations required a full-time traffic expert on the city staff. As early as 1954, the consulting firm of Wilbur Smith & Associates had made such a recommendation as part of an over-all suggestion that the function of traffic engineering be taken out of the Police Department and incorporated into a new city department of traffic and parking. It was no accident, of course, that this was precisely what Lee and Logue wanted. True to form, such a department was created the following year by executive order.

One of the applicants to head the new department was William R. McGrath, a thirty-one-year-old employee of Wilbur Smith & Associates, who had previously worked for the Bureau of Public Roads and was a research assistant at Yale's Bureau of Highway Traffic. McGrath had a quick wit, a good background, an unproved record of administration, and five children (he now has eleven). He once described his interest in traffic control as developing "from trying to get all those kids in and out of one bathroom in the morning." Lee liked him and hired him. One month after McGrath came to work, he was introduced to Logue over the phone in a conversation he recalls as beginning like this:

"Whom do you think you're working for?"

"I don't know. City of New Haven, I guess?"

"Wrong. Try again."

"The Mayor?"

"Getting closer."

"Well, who, then?"

"Me."

The reason for Logue's assertion of authority was that his friend the Mayor had unilaterally hired McGrath at an annual salary which exceeded Logue's by a thousand dollars—another of Lee's moves to heighten competition among his top staff. McGrath and Logue struck it off well, however, and today

McGrath works for Logue as Transportation Coordinator in the Boston Redevelopment Authority.

McGrath, Logue, and City Plan Director Norris Andrews were chiefly responsible for New Haven's negotiations with the highway engineers once a proposed route reached the stage of preliminary working drawings. It was McGrath who suggested how the ramps should tie in with existing streets, and what local changes were required to handle the increased traffic flow. Andrews' job was to propose how the highway should be aligned to meet precise renewal objectives—should it take this building? run behind that school? isolate a housing project? Logue's job was to blend these two viewpoints, add some others, such as the effect of the highway on existing sewer lines, and develop a unified approach to the highway engineers. Whenever bureaucratic negotiations failed, Lee was ready to go right to the Governor to get New Haven's way. The existence of such a tightly knit professional team headed by a mayor is generally a municipal rarity. In smaller cities there are usually no experts around to deal with the highway engineers, and in the larger cities there are too many.

For the new routes to work in New Haven, there also had to be a comprehensive program of local improvements, which Logue nicknamed "McGrath's toys." These included the widening of major downtown streets to handle traffic from the Oak Street connector, as well as the construction of parking facilities. The city's major downtown renewal project included the provision for more than two thousand parking spaces and a tunnel from the connector for cars and trucks, for off-street parking and unloading. The over-all plan for downtown included the construction of a circumferential artery around the center of the city, enabling traffic to move from one point to another without using cross streets.

McGrath's most interesting toy was his automated signal system, which was designed to facilitate the flow of traffic throughout the city. By means of radio signals beamed to traffic lights, McGrath could time lights to speed the flow on major arteries at peak periods. Outbound city traffic in the morning was sacrificed so that sequential signals on incoming lanes kept the heavier, inbound flow moving quickly. McGrath was a master of the unconventional use of traffic lights to get the maximum service from streets. He figured that drivers did not maneuver their cars along the straightest line between two points, but followed a route, however circuitous, that offered the smoothest movement, because movement is mistaken for speed. Armed with this basic psychology, McGrath used his lights as a means of reward and punishment. On one major artery which was continually over-used, McGrath staggered the lights to make drivers stop at every corner. On a parallel artery which was underused, he synchro-nized the lights for steady movement. Once enough drivers got into the habit of using the new street and the traffic load had been balanced, he synchronized the lighting on both.

He introduced a bizarre downtown one-way system based on punitive traffic lights. Under the McGrath plan, many underused streets on the edge of downtown were made one-way and equipped with lights that blinked red to green as a reward for a driver's use of the new system. Several key streets in the heart of downtown, however, were armed with lights that blinked from green to red as subtle reminders to drivers that they had better search for other routes, which were invariably the new one-way streets that McGrath had incorporated into the downtown sys-tem. Some of his other tactics were less subtle. He started a system of towing away cars parked at curbs on downtown streets during the rush hours. This was the first step toward the elimina-tion of curb parking which will eventually take place in New Haven. Another device was to make key neighborhood streets one-way for about three blocks and then one-way in the other direction, thereby eliminating through traffic from a residential area.

To reduce parking congestion in neighborhoods, McGrath's staff and the Redevelopment Agency began, after a survey of resident interest, to construct small residential off-street parking lots. They were usually large enough for about twenty cars each, with users paying a modest quarterly fee to cover maintenance.

The lots represented the city's effort to make improvements both functional and attractive. The layout was developed by the traffic engineers, but the final design was by architects and landscape planners. As a result, the areas are not blocks of black asphalt placed carelessly in a neighborhood but handsome open spaces framed by fencing or low brick walls, hiding all but the tops of the cars, and set off with hardy perennials. New Haven today abounds with examples of how prevalent traffic fixtures like parking areas, street signs, and sidewalks can be made to enhance the appearance of a town. Along many streets are extensive tree plantings, redesigned lamps, streamlined street signs, and new flower tubs. In renewal areas, a persistent effort has been made to remove poles and place ugly overhead wires beneath the ground or to consolidate them into one thin wire. But the effort is expensive, and most of New Haven still looks like a clothesline for a Bunyanesque washerwoman, for so far no one has found a more efficient way of conveying electricity than the one introduced by Ezra Cornell more than a hundred years ago.

Most of the highway and traffic improvements programmed for New Haven have been completed or are under way. They stand as perhaps the most a city can wring from state highway engineers under the present ground rules—including the user concept—if the city has its own traffic plan and the determination and expertise to implement it. Generally, the new roads, like the Turnpike, the connector, and Interstate 91, have been a boon to the town. They provide efficient access to the city from the region, they link New Haven to other major market areas, and they reaffirm the city's role as a distribution center. They also provide entrances and physical boundaries for areas of the city rebuilt under urban renewal. Their relation to the city street system, fortified by McGrath's one-way streets, synchronized lights, and off-street loading and parking areas, makes New Haven remarkably free of congestion when compared with other cities of comparable size.

While the new roads and highway improvements are efficient, they are far from perfect. No one, except McGrath and the engineers, could judge the new road network as beautiful or even good-looking. Paul Rudolph once argued that the downtown connector should have been a tree-lined boulevard rather than the barren expressway that it is. The view from the connector is good, because some of the new buildings that line it are well designed, but the view of the connector from the buildings is dull, as Rudolph has complained. Interstate 91 is fine for the half mile it travels through the edge of Wooster Square, but through the remainder of the city the view of it and from it is depressing as the artery cuts through the older sections of the city.

There are some in New Haven who argue that the new highways have actually been destructive. Their chief citation is a proposed connecting road to link I 91 with a major north-south artery. It uses as its path the same park and game preserve that were once threatened by I 91. The connecting road was publicized as part of the final alignment of I 91 which grew out of the QVDC studies, but nearby residents apparently were unaware of it until the bulldozers moved into position. Their eleventh-hour protest was sufficient, however, to halt the construction temporarily and to precipitate restudy of the alignment.

A curious sight to behold in the controversy is that of Mayor Lee privately spurring the protesters to attack the Highway Department for a plan he was a party to several years ago. If the controversy follows the established pattern, Lee will probably emerge with some statesmanlike compromise. A useful measure that has already resulted from the controversy is a state law which requires local legislative approval, including a hearing, on any new road which traverses a town or city and cuts through parkland. The law encourages wider citizen participation in highway planning, and some unruly public hearings and bothersome construction delays will probably occur. But this is a small price to pay for wider participation in the compromises which accompany highway alignments and which up to now have been made by only a handful of highway engineers and local officials. The participation will also produce a wider understanding of the heavy price the nation pays in land for constant reliance on private automobile transportation.

But perhaps the most interesting side effect of the local legislative action and public hearings will be the sounding of the death knell for the user concept. The professional defenders of the user concept will have a difficult time rationalizing the theory to a group of angry homeowners, park lovers, and bird watchers who arrive at the hearings in their cars. Then again, when the hearing ends, the homeowners, park lovers, and bird watchers may feel a bit silly as they climb into their cars, the cause of it all, and drive home.

9

Downtown

In time it may become an established principle that to make a city better you must make it over. Richard Lee learned that even in a smaller city such as New Haven, and even when only the downtown core of the city is involved, the effort of urban renewal may shatter not only the buildings but the government of the city as well.

The realization of a new well-planned highway system for New Haven put Mayor Lee in the renewal business. The initial effort took place downtown, and the first project was in the oldest and worst slum, the Oak Street area near the central business district just two blocks from the Yale campus. There was nothing delicate about the planning. The new link to the highway terminated in the heart of the area and bulldozers leveled the remainder. Since 1957, new buildings have gradually and painfully emerged from the rubble. First came the new telephone building, which Lee had by negotiation kept free of the projected right of way of the connecting road; next came a small office building, a modest retail plaza, and then the apartment buildings erected by the Boston outfit which had outbid Yale. During the construction stage, the project was a source of pride to the administration, but when the buildings were finished, their drab design and the generally sterile appearance of the new Oak Street convinced Lee and his staff that total clearance was not always the best answer and that more attention would have to be paid to design. Only recently has the area been saved from complete aesthetic disaster by the construction of three striking

Mayor Richard Charles Lee arrives at his office on the first day of his administration,
January 2, 1954.

Urban Renewal often meant winning support for what Lee called the "sticky challenge" of apparent chaos, such as could be seen in central New Haven in 1958, during demolition for the Oak Street Connector (right). Support was needed from the politicians, headed by Arthur T. Barbieri and John Golden (at center and right, bottom left photo), and from the bureaucracy. At bottom right, Lee is studied admiringly by Edward J. Logue (right) as the Mayor outlines the benefits of team play to an old-line city official.

(Photo by Robert C. Child III)

(Photo by Larry Fried)

(Courtesy Yale News Bureau)

Yale's support was based largely on the deep friendship between Lee and University President A. Whitney Griswold. One of the great moments in Lee's career occurred in 1961 when Griswold, on behalf of the University, awarded Lee an honorary degree

(Photo by Cunningham-Wednigg)

w Haven's redevelopment started at Oak Street, where new construction (above) dually, sometimes painfully, emerged from the worst of the city's slums (below).

(Courtesy NHRA)

Increasingly, New Haven used the scalpel rather than the bulldozer in restoring neighborhoods. This emphasis started in Wooster Square, where for the first time renewal combined clearance of the worst slums with the rehabilitation of serviceable residential structures or those architecturally worth saving.

(Courtesy NHRA)

(Courtesy NHRA)

ccasionally the city undertook pilot rehabilitation projects of its own to spur neighbor-
ood interest in self-renewal. The Court Street Project meant transforming a row of
abby rooming houses (above) into family residences (below).

(Courtesy NHRA)

(Courtesy NHRA)

(Photo by Charles R. Schulze)

Lee strived to make every achievement of his administration a happy community event, as when he stopped to talk with this group of children at a school groundbreaking (left). New Haven was one of the first cities to build low-cost private housing, the "d3" housing of the National Housing Act. In this project (right) families can own their homes without bearing a heavy financial burden.

key part of neighborhood renewal has been the replacement of old "inner city"
hools with new facilities. The Conte School, shown here, is one of seven school-
mmunity centers available to the public day and night with educational, recreation
d service programs for all ages.

The "main drag," Church Street, before Lee became Mayor. Few people in New Ha
were happy with the looks, or the apparent future of the downtown section of the c

(Photo by David Brooks)

e threw his dynamism and reputation into a grandiose plan to rebuild downtown. To p promote the program he appeared on television with Roger L. Stevens (above, at i) and Logue. However, the wide-open spaces and project delays were often more quent, as in the 1961 view below. The Oak Street Connector is in the foreground.

(Photo by Photo Associates)

(Photo by Stuart Langer

The project as it now appears. Above are the new parking garage and department store
below is the project as seen from the New Haven Green. The office tower is at left
the new hotel at right, and in the foreground are street level retail shops.

(Photo by Charles R. Schulz

(Photo by Reginald Jackson)

heart, renewal means enriching the city for people, including stimulating citizen
erest and involvement. Above, members of the Hill Recreation Committee, aided by
I neighborhood workers, plan a recreation program. Below, a new neighborhood
·k proves an obvious success.

(Courtesy NHRA)

because of its wide-scale approach. These aerial photos testify to the dramatic changes which have occurred in just one area—the Central Business District.

(Photo by Harvey and Lewis Co.)

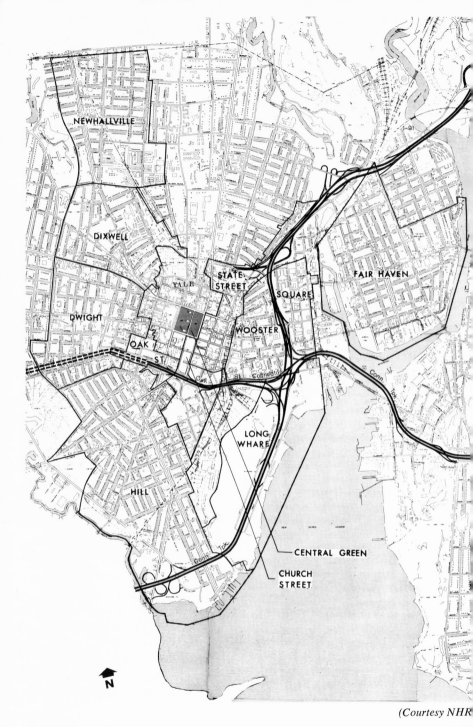

New Haven's Program Areas.

buildings: a research facility by Philip Johnson, a public housing apartment building for the elderly by Paul Rudolph, and a third apartment building by Chlothiel Smith.

Oak Street had its problems, but it was no failure. When it began, Lee and Logue were driven by the notion that removal of families from slum hovels to better housing was sufficient moral justification for the drastic public action of total clearance and relocation. Some six hundred and sixty-five families were removed from the worst housing in the city. Logue still calls it "one of the most sensitive relocation jobs ever performed anywhere." The project also provided economic benefits, for its new housing and new offices eventually brought around three thousand middle-income families and shoppers to the doorstep of the central business district and set the stage for a project to rebuild the heart of downtown New Haven.

Lee and Logue turned their full attention to this district in 1955, after federal approval of the Oak Street Project. The area started at the central Green, included four blocks of valuable retail land between the Green and the new connector, and then fanned out to include the city's food-wholesaling district. This prime real estate included the city's largest department store, many of its movie theatres, one of its largest banks, and its 100-per-cent-retail corner.

Several events made some degree of downtown reconstruction possible. One was the Oak Street connector. Another was Lee's intention to construct a mammoth downtown parking garage. A third was the intention of the First New Haven National Bank to construct a new headquarters building in the area. The last came from an unsuccessful effort by a local businessman to build a five-and-dime store on one of the blocks, which left him holding a ground lease to a key parcel in the area that was cleared and ready for development.

Lee and Logue figured that the scale of downtown reconstruction depended on how much private capital could be attracted. In 1955 they found a man who they believed could bring millions to the project and give it flair, skill, and prominence. He was Roger L. Stevens, real-estate entrepreneur and Broadway

producer, whose financial skill, patronage of the arts, and aid to
the Democratic Party had made of him a private businessman
with a public image. The program was presented to Stevens as a
pioneering effort, a venture which could make money and at the
same time prove that the downtowns of America were not
doomed but could be revived to compete with suburban shopping centers. Nor was Stevens stingy with his thinking. Among
his credentials for grandiose planning was his 1951 purchase and
later sale of the Empire State Building. The momentum from
several such ambitious financial coups swept Stevens into New
Haven's planning, which was, of course, already marked by Lee's
and Logue's penchant for the spectacular. Rather than check
those two with conservative business judgments, Stevens actually
swelled their thinking with his entrepreneurial shownmanship. Lee
himself was shocked when Stevens one day looked over the
project area and told his two new friends:

"You know, the problem with our deal is it doesn't go far
enough. We should expand our thinking to include the full width
of the Green and include four more blocks."

The target area eventually agreed on in 1956 was a four-block
retail area between part of the Green and the connector. It was
smaller than Stevens wanted, but it was still spectacular. Land
assembly and clearance would be through urban renewal. The
city would sell most of the land to Stevens, who would develop
approximately $25,000,000 of new construction, including a
hotel and office tower, a department store, and a huge retail
complex. The bank would also participate with its new building,
and the city would construct a parking garage and a project
tunnel, and also widen adjacent streets. Because the project
jutted into the heart of the city from the connector, it was not to
be an economic oasis but a life line to draw new shoppers and
dollars into the rest of the city. In the fall of 1956 the proposal
was fitted into an urban renewal project application. Project
boundaries were extended to include some residential properties
on the other side of the connector in order to qualify it for
assistance under the 1954 Housing Act, and the city's improvements counted for most of the city's share of costs. After the

Urban Renewal Administration indicated informal approval in the spring of 1957, Lee dramatically announced the newly named Church Street Project in June.

The town's response was one of shock; the local press was dubious; the national reaction, particularly in the real estate field, was incredulous. Nothing on this scale had been tried before. The effort meant bucking the economic trends of the day. Downtown property was on the decline, the victim of age, neglect, and the new craze for suburban shopping sprawls with their acres of free parking. The proposal was thus akin to a heart transplant; New Haven was trying to revive a half-dead patient with massive, experimental surgery.

The atmosphere around Lee's office that June was euphoric. But over the months that followed the spirit turned gradually into semi- and then full depression, for among the kudos, applause, and shock were three lawsuits which ground the project to a standstill.

The administration was prepared for some litigation, but no one was prepared for the two-year effort it took to get the project out of the courts. One suit came from the Central Civic Association, an emergency alliance of downtown shopkeepers whose leaders claimed to represent a hundred and fifty merchants, most of whom would be displaced by the project. For one year the Association sought through its lawyers to have the courts declare the project invalid while the leaders of the Association pressed for specific answers on where they would go, what help they would receive, and whether they could go back into the project. They were unimpressed by an offer by Stevens to give them a 10-per-cent rent reduction in the completed project, largely because it was not clear what Stevens' eventual rents would be. In June the following year, the Association dropped its case partly because of mounting legal fees but also because the Redevelopment Agency posted a specific relocation schedule, offered financial assistance, and promised to help build the merchants temporary quarters, to which many of the Association leaders eventually moved.

The second suit came from the Hotel Taft, which sought to

enjoin the Urban Renewal Administration from financing the project on the grounds of "commercial cannibalism." In other words, the Taft was distressed that federal funds were being used to finance a project which would result in a competitive hotel. This suit was eventually dismissed by the courts in January, 1959.

The most time-consuming suit came from a local jeweler, Robert R. Savitt, who had purchased land and modernized a building in the project area. Savitt claimed his building was too good to be demolished, that the project violated state redevelopment law, and that the city was wrongly using a public power of eminent domain to help Stevens' private interest. Stevens had approached Savitt to buy his property before the project was announced, and Stevens' inability to make a deal with the jeweler had been made part of the city's legal record to show that major private development was not possible in the area without city participation through its powers of eminent domain and a renewal write-down* of the land. The Savitt case lingered through 1957 and was temporarily dropped in June of 1958. In October the Redevelopment Agency, after failing to purchase Savitt's property through negotiation, went to the State Superior Court to acquire it through condemnation. Savitt challenged the Agency, lost his case, and then appealed to the State Supreme Court of Errors. On March 17, 1959 the Court unexpectedly ordered a retrial because of insufficient evidence.

"That day was one of the worst in my career," Lee has observed. "We were confident in our case, and felt that once the court made its decision we'd get the project moving. All the merchants had been moved except Savitt. When the court gave its retrial order, our plans were smashed and we faced another long delay. That night I was scheduled to give a speech, and who

---

* "Write-down" refers to the lower value of land that has been cleared of old buildings and offered for new development. The lower cost of renewal land is partly an incentive to attract builders. But it is also a product of the market. The site which contains the worst slum in a city can be worth considerably less after the slum has been removed. The value of urban land is a product of both the location of the site, and its ability to support maximum development, and the building on it, because the building can generate income either through rent or sale. Take away the building and the land is worth less.

should be sitting in the front row but Savitt. He had a big smile on his face and I felt that he and the others were now laughing at me, so I really let them have it. I vowed that if it killed me, I'd make the project happen."

Community confidence was seriously shaken by the court order. The preceding litigation had already placed a heavy cloud over the project. It had been almost two years since the plan was first announced. Now it appeared that another year would pass without construction. The worst consequence of the retrial order was that it placed the city in default of its contract with Stevens, who was supposed to take title to his land that May. "Some of my partners wanted me to use the opportunity to get out," Stevens recalls. "They were bothered by our high land cost. Potential retail tenants didn't seem interested in New Haven. I'm too proud, I guess. I was in the deal determined to make it work. When Lee called me about the Savitt thing, I told him I would stay in."

In April, 1959, Redevelopment Agency lawyers and Savitt's counsel gathered in separate wings of Lee's office to reach a settlement. The Agency had originally offered $705,000 for Savitt's building, and this had increased by around $200,000 during negotiations before the condemnation proceedings the previous fall. Savitt was holding out for $1,305,000. With Lee serving as mediator, the lawyers finally agreed that Savitt would get $1,105,000 and the Agency would get Savitt's building by June 1st. Community reaction to the news was mixed. Some regarded it as a vindication of the little guy in the struggle against the big bureaucracy. A member of the CAC saw it differently, complaining to Lee that the large settlement was a blow to the small merchants who had quietly moved out of the project after receiving a negotiated price for their properties. Another wrote to Lee complaining that the settlement proved ". . . that if one is wealthy enough and uncooperative enough, and makes a big enough nuisance, he can get what he wants."

The resolution of the Savitt problem generated a spirit of guarded optimism within the administration. A new land contract was drawn up which enabled Stevens to buy his sites in steps. The purpose was to ease the burden of the high land price that had been agreed upon. Under his original agreement with the city, Stevens was obligated to buy all the land (230,274 square feet) at one time for a unit price of $18.69 per square foot, or around $4,300,000. Under the new agreement the unit price stayed the same, but the land was to be purchased at intervals. High land cost was proving to be a principal factor in retail disinterest. Nearby shopping centers were offering sites with comparable access and parking for as little as $2.00 per square foot. Best's, B. Altman, Macy's, and Lord & Taylor were some of the major New York stores which had told Stevens they could not appreciate why New Haven locations were worth so much. This had left Stevens without a major retail tenant, a big department store around which smaller retailers cluster thereby providing rental prospects that are crucial in obtaining construction financing.

To solve this problem, Stevens approached a local department store—then the city's largest—the Edward Malley Company. "I wanted Malley's to be included in the project from the start," Stevens has explained. "They had an old store at one end of the project, but Lee and Logue wouldn't take them for political reasons." Relations were not smooth between Malley officials and the Lee administration during the nineteen-fifties. New Haven's declining retail sales compared with those of the suburban shopping centers had been a principal reason for the project, and every time Lee hit this theme, which was often, he was taking a sideswipe at Malley's by virtue of its leading retail role. Logue had engaged in direct combat with Malley's. In May of 1955 he flatly asserted that downtown New Haven was "dying" and this infuriated the store's executives. One of them openly criticized Logue, then announced a $1,000,000 refurbishing job to prove that Malley's was alive. Lee described the relationship of the store to the project this way:

"Roger kept insisting that we take Malley's. He was still pushing the idea in 1959 before the Savitt settlement. I told him that it was impossible. How could I convince the town that the only way to save a sagging project was through more demolition, this time of the leading department store? The store was old, but it was in good condition and it was worth millions. I finally told Roger that if he wanted Malley's, he would have to work out a deal privately."

Starting in 1959, Stevens did precisely that, and later conceded that it proved to be his biggest problem.

"It was a very complicated deal because it involved dealing with an estate. As seemed to be the case everywhere I turned in New Haven, Wiggin & Dana were representing the estate. They were by far the most important law firm in town and, unfortunately, had become used to doing things their own way. I do not want to criticize their abilities as lawyers, but in my experience over a period of years, I have found that there are lawyers that approach a project with the desire to see how they can do it, and there are others that seem to be so careful they make you feel that they want to see how one can prevent a deal from being closed. They were of the latter type. As I have pointed out to them directly, I felt the greatest problem I faced was the delay caused by the overzealous care in closing the various aspects of the project. It is possible that my remarks, which one might consider tactless, only made matters worse."

Stevens' negotiations and final agreement with Malley's illustrate the incredible complexities of urban real estate. They also reveal Malley's understanding that they held the upper hand. Stevens had to deal with two groups in his store negotiations: the store and the Estate of the store founder, Edward Malley, which owned the site and building that were rented to the store for $180,000 a year. The agreement, reached in September, 1959 (immediately announced by Lee, who was starting an election campaign), was basically a switch of sites between Stevens and the Estate. Stevens would take over the old store and site, and the Estate would take over a site at the other end of the project which Stevens was scheduled to purchase from the city. Stevens would then take a ground lease to the new Estate site on which he would construct a new $5,000,000 department store. Stevens would rent the site from the Estate for $180,000 and he would rent the building to the store for $300,000. "It was a tight deal,"

explained Stevens. "The store cost more to build than we antici-
pated, and since there was no guaranteed income above the local
taxes and the rental payment to the Malley estate, it meant
having $6 million frozen—which, of course, added to our finan-
cial difficulties. Another problem was that because of the long
delay caused by the City being unable to deliver title to their
land, the interest rate structure had changed, and where the
going rate when we started on the project was 4%, now the
rate had gone up to 6%. It doesn't take a great deal of imagi-
nation to see the difference of 2% on a $25 million project,
which capitalized at 10%, means a loss of $5 million unless
the income can be offset by higher rents. Downtown rents were,
if anything, falling at this time."

To consummate this deal with Malley's required a three-party
agreement from Stevens, the store, and the Estate. Estate approval meant tracking down the heirs. The principal of these was
Jane O'Malley-Keyes, but there were thirty-two others scattered
around the globe in such locales as London, Paris, and Malaga.
Illustrative of this complication was the search for Jane O'Malley-
Keyes, a woman in her seventies who regularly embarked on
world-wide trips and who had been taught by her father never to
sign a document unless she read it. The Stevens agreement which
the lawyers wanted her to sign was a lengthy opus filled with
complicated legalese. She was finally located and persuaded to
sign the agreement in New York as she prepared to embark on a
cruise early in 1960. By September, 1960, after these and other
legal complications were resolved, the Malley transaction was
finally consummated.

Until his Malley negotiations, Stevens had no direct interest in
the entire front-block portion of the project which overlooked
the Green. Under the original plan the Malley store was to
remain and the First New Haven National Bank was to build a
new headquarters building next to it. Once Stevens started the
store negotiations that gave him the old Malley building, he
began thinking of a unified front-block development and was
soon talking to the Sheraton Corporation of America about
building a hotel there. This required some accommodation with

the bank, which had already begun excavating its site next to the old Malley building. The bank executives were anxious about the project. Some of the Savitt property was on part of their site, and they were shaken by the court retrial order. When Stevens proposed that he take over the site in exchange for another in a different part of the project, the bank officials made no secret of their concern for what appeared to be mounting chaos, but they went along with it. Stevens offered them a note to cover their initial site expenses as a "gesture of good will."

From the beginning the bank officials had been fidgety and concerned about their new building, and it was generally assumed that they would proceed quickly with construction on the new site. Strangely, the bank did nothing, and in August, 1959, they explained why. Lee describes the event this way:

"Throughout 1959 the community, particularly the business community, was down on the project. My friends at the *Register* seemed to be delighted by the setbacks, for they never believed the project would really happen. My contacts among the conservative business leaders said that many people were now calling the project 'Lee's folly.' I decided to give a full briefing to top business leaders. I borrowed a yacht and invited them to join me on a short cruise during which I would explain where the project stood. Just as the cruise started, the awful news broke—the bank was dropping completely out of the project. It was merging with another local bank. No one at the bank had bothered to inform me. In fact, a couple of the directors were on the cruise. I went to the rear of the ship to be alone, the humiliation was so great. One of the business leaders saw me looking dejected, so he came over, put his hand on my shoulder, and said, 'Dick, don't let these guys get to you. Go back, give your briefing, and show them you have more guts than they do.' I went through with it."

Later in 1959 the U.S. Attorney General ruled that the proposed bank merger violated anti-trust laws. The bank was back in the construction business. This time, however, the bank officials decided to stay out of the project. The site they chose, largely at Lee's urging, was across the street from the project.

The city helped relocate some of the businesses on the site, and the bank's involvement, if not full participation in the project, ended on a cordial note.

During 1960 and 1961 the fortunes of the Church Street Project, as well as those of Lee and Stevens, dropped considerably. The project area was a wasteland of cleared buildings with little construction activity. The steel structure of the new bank was the only new building rising from the rubble. Next to the bank was an excavation for the project tunnel which burrowed beneath Church Street and into the site for the new Malley store. In the fall of 1960 a start was made on the store, but the pace was feeble. Next to the store, the city was building its new parking garage but that project was plagued by a constant series of internal battles involving the contractor, the architect, and the city. A huge lot stretched from the garage and the store to the Green three blocks away, sweeping around the old bank building and the old Malley store, which were all that was left of the retail center of New Haven. At one far corner of the project stood a symbol of Lee's eternal optimism, a temporary cinder-block building called the Progress Pavilion, which contained pictures and models of what the project would look like if it was ever completed—and there were some serious doubts that it would be. There was no prospect of the planned hotel and office tower and there were no firm commitments from prospective retail tenants.

The reactions to the sorry state of the project varied considerably among the major participants. Stevens, who was now losing large sums of money in the project, appeared unruffled and gave the project no new allocation of time, but compartmentalized it, as always, between his other real estate and Broadway interests. Lee and Logue were getting desperate. Their entire program was being judged by this moribund project, as were their personal reputations. Lee faced the gloomy prospect of having to carry an apparent fiasco into the 1961 election; Logue had by this time received his offer to direct the Boston urban renewal program.

Most of all, Lee and Logue were baffled by what they regarded as Stevens' nonchalance in the face of a crisis involving

Stevens' money. Stevens appeared totally unresponsive to the elaborate financial penalties which had been devised to spur him into quick construction activity. In addition to the high land price the city had negotiated, Lee and Logue had avoided giving him tax breaks and tried to push him into buying project land as quickly as possible. The idea was that once Stevens actually invested money in project land and began paying local taxes, he would move quickly in constructing the income-producing improvements. But Stevens' conduct did not change once he became a landowner. In the face of project problems he neither attempted to get out of his commitments nor indicated any alarm or increase in effort. He merely kept moving along at his own pace. "This is where we made a mistake," Logue explained recently. "We misjudged Roger's enormous capacity to absorb financial punishment, just as we overestimated his ability as a developer. Roger was a strong real estate man, and there were few who could match his ability in buying existing buildings, rearranging the financing, and turning a profit. But developing raw land, dealing with builders and architects—this was not Roger's strength, and he demonstrated it in New Haven." What Lee and Logue learned during this chaotic period in the early sixties was that Stevens did not need to be bargained with; he needed help.

Stevens' most pressing problem was the extremely close deal he had with Malley's. It was so tight that no bank would touch the financing. The small amount of construction that had taken place on the new store was generated by Stevens' partnership with the builder—the Gilbane Building Company, of Providence, Rhode Island. Gilbane took a limited view toward the meaning of partnership: he wanted to get paid. When the unpaid vouchers to Stevens' development company reached $600,000, he provided a mere token of construction activity. Stevens described the problems in these terms:

"We shouldn't have purchased the Malley land and started the building until financing was firm. But Lee was always pressuring us, wanted to make announcements all the time. In 1960 I talked to Whit Griswold about Yale getting involved in the project.

Yale invests money all over the nation, why not put some into New Haven? That is what I told Griswold, and he agreed; and suggested I get in touch with Charles Dickey, the Chairman of their Finance Committee. He gave me a very sympathetic hearing, and we worked out a tentative arrangement."

At this juncture, Lee and Logue moved in quickly to help Stevens close his loan with Yale. Specifically it was proposed that Yale provide a $4,500,000 loan commitment to help Stevens finish the Malley store and buy additional project land. Lee went to Griswold for help and Logue paid personal visits to Corporation Fellows—former Secretary of State Dean Acheson among them—to get their support. By September 1961, the transaction was turned over to Yale's lawyers (Wiggin & Dana) and Stevens' lawyers to negotiate the details. "Lee and Logue were a help," Stevens has said, "but the Yale commitment did not help as much as it could have because it was delayed for almost a year. Here again Wiggin & Dana and their conservative lawyers held up the deal while I was holding the Malley land and paying taxes and interest. Everywhere I went in New Haven I ran into Wiggin & Dana."

Under the agreement finally approved by the Yale Corporation, Stevens, and the Board of Aldermen in the spring of 1962, Yale agreed to lend Stevens $4,500,000 upon his completion of the new Malley store and his purchase of additional parcels of land in the project. This paved the way for short-term financing. The agreement also provided that in the event Stevens should not be able to develop the land he acquired under this loan commitment, Yale, or the bank which was to make the short-term loan, would have the option to assume his role as commercial developer under the redevelopment plan for the project. The agreement also provided that if Yale or a bank did not exercise this option, then the city could seize the land, pay the necessary taxes, and sell the land to another developer, paying back to Stevens and his creditors only that amount which was left over. Yale's commitment to the project was an enormous boost, but it by no means assured success. It put Stevens in a position to complete the new Malley store and to buy additional land in the project under his agreement with the Redevelopment Agency. However, he had no office building, hotel, or retail complex, and the entire front end of the project was still in darkness.

The Yale loan commitment came too late to help Lee in his 1961 campaign, during which the project became a central issue and produced Lee's lowest plurality: a depressing 4,000 votes. Logue was now in Boston; Stevens had clearly demonstrated that he was no economic miracle man; and Lee, as a result of his close election, realized that in the interests of survival he would have to assume a stronger role in the project. L. Thomas Appleby had become the Development Administrator and Harold Grabino the new Executive Director of the Redevelopment Agency. Together they attempted a new start, searching for a way to tip the project away from chaos and toward resolution. Lee began dashing off personal notes to New York store executives to see if they might be interested in the project. Rather predictably they were not. He then focused his attention on finding an individual who might be helpful, and, quite accidentally, in early 1962 he found a pressure point.

Among the Yale Fellows who had played roles in the Yale loan commitment was J. Richardson Dilworth, a nephew of the former Mayor of Philadelphia, an executive in the Rockefeller Fund, and a man whose investment skills had placed him in the upper echelons of what Lee, with gleaming eyes, would call "the big New York money." Dilworth and Lee were having lunch at Mory's to discuss Lee's future plans when Dilworth revealed that he was on the board of R. H. Macy & Co., Inc. Lee immediately invited Dilworth to tour the project area where he had "just the right site picked out for a Macy department store." After showing Dilworth the site, which was next to Malley's, Lee drove him around the highway network and showed him the city's new parking garage. Dilworth was sufficiently interested to set up an appointment for Lee with Donald B. Smiley, the Treasurer of Macy's. Lee's meeting with Smiley went smoothly, and the official agreed to dispatch several of his staff to take a closer look at New Haven.

The young Agency staff prepared a full-blown presentation

based on the way Macy officials like their information organized, for coincidentally it happened that the economic consultant to the Redevelopment Agency, Larry Smith, was also an economic consultant to Macy's. The New Haven meeting and subsequent sessions in New York went extremely well. The store officials were particularly impressed by the highway network and the city parking garage, which offered direct access to the site Lee was offering to Macy's. An event that occurred at this time indicates how much the Macy transaction meant to Lee. One day some Macy staff members, city officials, and an over-all project design consultant, one of several consultants who had a part in the project during its stormy history, were gathered in Lee's office discussing the proposed store. Suddenly the consultant suggested that Lee's site was not the one Macy's should choose, that they should locate at a different end of the project. He was just as suddenly interrupted by Lee, who politely asked him to step into a nearby office, where Lee backed him against the wall, grabbed him by the lapels, and through clenched teeth muttered:

"Look, you Viennese S.O.B., one more word from you on a different Macy site and I will hammer you into that site, where you will be a human pile for the store."

By summer's end the Macy staff was sold on New Haven and on Lee's site. In September, 1962, Lee announced that Macy's would build a $5,000,000, four-level department store.

The negotiations with Macy's were unilateral, and although Stevens owned the site Lee was selling to Macy's, he knew nothing of the plans until they were under way. Indeed, while Lee was negotiating with Macy's, Stevens had lined up a Woolworth chain store for the site. Once he learned what Lee was up to, Stevens cooperated fully by holding back on Woolworth's at considerable financial sacrifice, for during 1962 Stevens was, as already noted, paying interest and taxes on the land. He later explained this statesmanship as a sign of how happy he was that Macy's was coming in, because it proved, as he believed, that the project made sense.

The administration's reaction to the Macy store was ecstatic.

"It felt wonderful" was Lee's recollection of his feelings. So buoyed by this coup was Lee that he began assuming a still more active role. He prevailed on Stevens to rent space in a New York hotel to which retailers would be invited to hear Lee extol New Haven's virtues. His staff prepared a model for the occasion. Actually it performed more like a pinball machine; it included a small-scale replica of the entire city, a projection screen, and a billboard, and at the flick of a switch the apparatus, which Stevens termed "a fiasco," came alive with gaudy lights depicting redevelopment areas of the city, with slide pictures, and with an electronic graph showing driving times between New Haven and key points in the retail market. The machine was shown not only to retailers but also to voters in the 1963 campaign. Although no one is sure how many stores or votes it attracted, at least it provided a light interlude in the otherwise heavy proceedings.

By late fall of 1963, Stevens, in a culmination of growing frustration, began laying plans to withdraw as the major developer. The decision was mainly part of his career withdrawal from real estate and his emergence at that time as a leading figure in the federal sponsorship of music, theatre, and the arts.* But the decision was also based on continuing financing problems. Stevens explained recently, "We figured that we sank seventeen million dollars into New Haven. That's more than I spent on the Empire State Building deal. I just got tired of throwing money away." By early 1964, Stevens found two developers to take over construction of the remaining elements of the project—the hotel, the office tower, and the retail complex. One was the Gilbane Building Company, which had built the Malley store, the other was the Fusco-Amatruda Construction Company, a New Haven–based firm which was anxious to expand its activities to include commercial development. Under agreements drawn in the spring of 1964, Gilbane, to whom Stevens' firm still owed money on the Malley building, would

* Stevens is presently Chairman of the John F. Kennedy Center for the Performing Arts, Chairman of the National Endowment for the Arts, Director of the National Council on the Arts, and Special Assistant to the President on the Arts.

develop the hotel, and Fusco-Amatruda would develop the office building and the retail complex. Stevens still retains a major financial interest in the project.

Much of the financial support for Fusco-Amatruda's part of the project came from English investors, although no one was ever sure to whom the contractors were referring when they spoke proudly of "our English money." But the backer of the Gilbane hotel project, John McShain, soon made an appearance. One day in the spring of 1964, he flew to New Haven in his private plane to discuss the hotel with Lee. Among McShain's credentials was his construction of the Pentagon in Washington, which automatically made him an appropriate participant in a project sponsored by the buyer and seller of the Empire State Building. McShain turned out to be a dapper little man with a white mustache, and his eyes sparkled as he talked of his race horses and his trips. He was one of the few visitors to the Mayor's office who could outtalk Lee, and when he finished reciting tales of Dublin and the Irish Sweepstakes, he hurriedly dictated a letter of intent to back and manage the hotel to be built by Gilbane. After delivering a short speech in which he noted that ". . . although my lawyers would disapprove of this procedure, I like the looks of you, Mr. Mayor," he signed his pledge and flew back to Philadelphia.

The transfer of development obligations, including the liquidation of the Yale loan commitment, was approved by the Board of Aldermen in May, 1964, but not until another crisis had passed. While the aldermen sat patiently waiting to approve the agreement, the Redevelopment Agency staff and Fusco-Amatruda were still negotiating the details of a garage to be built underneath the office tower and retail complex. A last-minute disagreement had erupted at about eight o'clock at night, with the discussions getting so heated that the meeting broke down. An hour later they resumed, a settlement was reached, a police car was dispatched to retrieve one of the major participants who had gone home exhausted, and at ten o'clock the agreement, with signatures still wet, was rushed to the waiting aldermen and approved.

At the time of this writing, the McShain-Gilbane hotel building was almost finished, as was the work on the retail complex, the office tower, and the underground garage. There was only one final complication. The city was suing Fusco-Amatruda for $1,000,000.

The problems and frustrations of this project, some of which will probably endure after the buildings are occupied, lend themselves to many interpretations, such as that urban renewal restores downtown, or that developers can get hurt in urban renewal, or that there is a profit to be made in urban renewal, or that urban renewal is simply bad. These are a few of the conclusions to be drawn from the project history and all of them may be true for now, but how many will endure depends on how the project performs. After ten years the project area now has a physical form, but the project economics are not yet clear. The buildings have no adequate rental experience and the stores' sales records are not complete. No one can be sure whether the project has generated downtown economic growth in New Haven, which most agree would justify the disruptions, or whether the project has merely concentrated the limited resources of the city into one tight area. If concentration is the result, then the project is probably a failure.

The preliminary signs are encouraging. Malley officials, never known for chest thumping, openly state that sales during the first two years in the new store are far above expectations. Downtown retail sales are up. Macy's is adjusting to a new market and sales are lower than expected. There seems to be no shortage of tenants for the office building, and hotel officials are optimistic about their prospects as they prepare for the opening.

This much can be said about the project: its basic problems stemmed from its novelty. It was a pioneer project started when downtown real estate was regarded as too risky for investment in an old city like New Haven. To speculators, investors, and retailers New Haven was an interesting experiment, but few firms were anxious to spend money on experiments. When they came to see the city in the nineteen-fifties, it was diverting to have Stevens or Lee pull out maps to show them the highway network or take them to a model of what the city would look like; but when they saw the city as it was—and it was dreary-looking— they left. It was not until the highways were almost finished and the project improvements like the parking garage, tunnel, and access roads were opened that a store like Macy's, for instance, could begin to take the project seriously.

The investor and tenant skepticism was Stevens' biggest problem, although he compounded it with high land costs and his virtual subsidization of Malley's entry. A critic might find Lee and his staff to blame for not helping Stevens, but one must understand that during the fifties there was considerable local suspicion about the project, so they bargained hard. All of them agree today that a city must learn a developer's business at least as well as the developer, and, armed with this knowledge, the city should help him avoid potential problems. Stevens is a sympathetic character in this story because he suffered over problem after problem. But he stuck it out—albeit with a natural reduction in enthusiasm—until others could take over. Stevens, who had made his money and reputation in the big city, got burned in little New Haven. Yet while he lost some money, he kept his honor, and that, to his great credit, always seemed most important to him.

No one will ever know how much this project meant to Lee. It was partly pride that helped him endure the endless frustrations, for in that four-block area of downtown New Haven were not only rubble and buildings but also his career and his self-respect. But Lee was driven by something more than pride. An intense fatalism was at work. It developed in 1958, when Lee passed up an opportunity to run for the U.S. Senate. The party was torn between Thomas Dodd and Chester Bowles. A state-wide movement was under way to get Lee to declare, and even John Bailey, the powerful state chairman, urged Lee to run. But Lee wanted the nomination handed to him before he made up his mind. Bailey refused.

It was a combination of insecurity and morality that held Lee back. He was wary of a possible primary, and at the time the Church Street Project was just entering the tunnel of confusion from which it would not emerge for seven years. After Lee refused and later, when Dodd went on to win in the Democratic landslide of 1958, he became so determined to prove that he had chosen wisely that he mounted fatalistic delusions about the connection between his personal fortunes and those of the project. In its early stages this feeling of personal destiny was self-destructive. Project setbacks and staff turnover such as Logue's departure for Boston were not put in perspective, but loomed as evil portents of a continuing ordeal. The 1961 election, which Lee almost lost, proved to be a most useful gift from the gods, for it reduced his project woes to understandable terms: votes. Lee realized that the project problems were caused by nothing more mysterious than his lack of realistic involvement. From that point on his participation increased, first with the Yale negotiations and eventually with the coup of bringing Macy's to New Haven. In a real sense the Church Street project was a barometer of Lee's career.

Today the city is moving into another downtown area adjacent to the Church Street Project. This urban renewal plan had been on the drawing boards since 1958, but was not unveiled until Church Street passed the danger mark. Perhaps the final judgment on downtown renewal can be made in this present area, which is called State Street. There is no shortage of interest, for two banks are ready to build, and the General Services Administration is ready to participate in a government center which will include a new City Hall. Significantly, there is no great popular or newspaper interest in the project. The novelty of downtown renewal has worn off. Life is less hectic and exciting these days, but a project is easier to put together and finance. This is the strongest indication that the earlier effort, for all its pains and frustrations, was successful.

10

Neighborhoods and Urban Renewal

The top urban renewal professionals who have worked in New Haven—Logue, Appleby, and now Melvin Adams—are generally agreed that the city's greatest success and outstanding contribution has been the restoration of old city neighborhoods. Logue thus summarized his feelings recently:

"There's a lot of lead time in this business. A lot to get discouraged about. They tell me I have self-confidence, but there are days—especially when I talk to John Lindsay about New York* and see the incredible size of those slums. . . . You know, one of the things I thoroughly enjoy is going back to New Haven. There you learn success is possible. New Haven is a village compared to New York, even to Boston, but the problems are really the same, just on a smaller scale. I go to New Haven to get recharged. And I don't go back to see that Church Street Project now that it's finished. No, the place I head for is the neighborhoods we rebuilt. That's where I get my kicks. . . ."

Logue talks slowly and quietly in private, with his thoughts racing far ahead of his words.

"And the place I always visit is the senior citizens' center of the new Conte School in Wooster Square. Around the Square are examples of rehabilitated housing and new housing. And then that marvelous school. When we first planned Wooster Square, the old folks complained about their health and the weather. And now you walk into that new school with that senior center

* At this writing, Logue was Chairman of a special task force on New York City Housing and Neighborhoods.

136

and the smoke is so thick you can barely see the walls. And there are the old-timers, playing cards for money in a public building designed by Skidmore. . . . That is what urban renewal should be all about. People having fun in attractive surroundings. Can you imagine what New York would be like with a hundred Wooster Squares?"

Wooster Square was the first of seven city neighborhoods to be improved through an arsenal of urban renewal techniques: rehabilitation, spot clearance, new schools and other community facilities, new off-street parking areas, the renewal of a neighborhood shopping strip, and a new separate commercial-industrial area. The history of Wooster Square is typical of downtown city neighborhoods. It started as a middle- to upper-middle-class area in the nineteenth century. Its homes and apartments were big and sturdy, the neighborhood itself attractive and pleasant. With industrialization and immigration the neighborhood changed. Tenements sprang up, the air blackened, the original occupants left, and into their place moved the immigrant factory workers. In Wooster Square the newcomers were mostly Italian.

Twentieth-century problems of neglected city services, traffic, and physical obsolescence caused Wooster Square to decline, just as they did the rest of the city. Negro migration to the city accompanied the decline, rather than causing it as some New Haveners believed. (One candid Wooster Square citizen said, "When the colored began moving in, we knew our neighborhood was in trouble.") Wooster Square was ready for urban renewal.

In 1956 and 1957 planning started on the project. It was based on a curious alliance between the city and the neighborhood. The city in the person of Logue and his planners saw in Wooster Square the opportunity to prove "that we could rebuild a neighborhood with a scalpel not a bulldozer" by cutting away the pockets of slums, replacing them with new life, and renewing the old neighborhood rather than building a new one. Many, if not most, of the residents of Wooster Square saw renewal quite differently; namely, as a means of removing Negroes. So while the city staff and the neighborhood residents worked closely on planning (a process which essentially saw the city propose and the residents say yes or no), the motivations were entirely different.

The best way to enter Wooster Square is through Court Street, a narrow artery that starts at the New Haven Green and ends four blocks away at the Wooster Square Green. The first improvement one comes to is a twenty-space neighborhood parking lot, bordered by a growth of ivy and an attractive brick wall. Farther down Olive Street to the left can be seen the top of a modern new fire headquarters building. When Fire Chief Thomas Collins first moved into the building and saw his office with its Danish modern furniture in purple and orange and its bare concrete walls, he complained crustily, "Damn it, Mayor, the men will think I'm a fairy." But Lee insisted on the décor, and Chief Collins' office eventually became his pride and joy, the envy of all the chiefs in Connecticut, who came frequently to see it.

The block of Court Street between Olive and the Wooster Square Green has been closed to through traffic. The street used to be lined with twenty-seven four-story brick row houses, which from 1957 to 1960 had been the scene of seventy arrests—mostly for drunkenness—and a hundred welfare cases, mostly transient men. The Redevelopment Agency convinced the owners of ten of the houses to rehabilitate and purchased the other seventeen from owners who preferred to sell. The city then demonstrated what it meant by rehabilitation. The acquired houses were sandblasted, retrimmed, gutted inside, and converted from rooming houses to town houses with two apartments in each. These were then sold privately with FHA mortgages, the priority going to families displaced by urban renewal. The financing was so good that the monthly carrying charges were almost covered if a family rented one of the two apartments it acquired. Purchasers were required to live in one of the apartments. Today Court Street is attractive, is racially integrated, and houses a mixture of families and single adults, some of whom returned to the city from the suburbs. The little mall that serves the homes abounds with symbols of the good city life—baby carriages and bikes, mothers swapping stories, fathers tending the flower tubs, and small green areas that the city put in where asphalt used to be.

At the end of Court Street is the Wooster Square Green. It is bordered by iron fencing supported by granite posts. Elms give it shade and people give it life. The grass is inviting mainly because it is worn and bare in spots. This is the heart of the neighborhood which the city used as a centerpiece for its renewal planning. Surrounding the Green are the products of the planning lined up like showpieces in a gallery.

To the left along Academy Street are several homes, once battered and neglected and now rehabilitated inside and out. It was here that the city began its rehabilitation program with a small team composed of an architect, a construction specialist, and a mortgage adviser who knew the intricacies of FHA and conventional bank financing. The team operated from a neighborhood office, and, using the Housing Code as a weapon and persuasion as a device, they visited each house, convincing owners not just to improve their buildings to code standards but to enhance them by aesthetic standards.

What operators they were! "My, Mrs. ——, won't your home look lovely if we point the bricks and paint the trim white?" The architect would show the woman a painting of her home as it would look if she followed his suggestions. "Would you like the painting, Mrs. ——?" Indeed she would, and she would fix up her house, too. Such unusual attention was in itself a flattering persuader. With others the architect would sometimes play neighbor against neighbor. "Now, Mr. ——, Mr. Jones down the street is putting up shutters." "What! That cheap Jones is putting up shutters? Well, I'm not only going to put up shutters. Draw me a picture of what a new roof would look like, too." There were some who wanted nothing to do with rehabilitation at first. But once a few of the homes were done, the fear of being the last to improve took over. Neighborhood pride began to replace individual isolation.

Housing rehabilitation has taken place all around the Wooster Square Green and for several blocks beyond. It hasn't been easy. Local banks were a big problem. There was reluctance to lend money in older neighborhoods, especially for improvements on row houses. But the Agency staff pushed FHA financing with the Federal National Mortgage Association (FNMA) as a backup. The Tradesmens National Bank, whose President, Frank O'Brion, was Chairman of the Redevelopment Agency, agreed to be a temporary mortgagee if FNMA would buy the mortgage in the event that other private banks refused. Now local banks are providing conventional mortgage money for rehabilitation. This is one of the clearest signs that residential renewal is working in New Haven.

The far left of Wooster Square Green was once dominated by a nineteenth-century primary school, where, according to old-timers in the neighborhood, Catholic nuns taught some public-school classes. The nuns are no longer there; neither is the school. The first became a casualty because of keener local sensitivities on church-state relations, the second because of the renewal bulldozer. In place of the school are thirty-four units of luxury-priced (by New Haven standards) garden apartments, which represent distinctive yet unobtrusive architecture. These apartments rent for up to a hundred and sixty dollars per month and are fully integrated. They are one of the few new housing developments financed without FHA mortgages.

Along the opposite end of the Green from Court Street is the tower and chapel of St. Michael's Catholic Church, the city's first Italian parish, which never strongly advocated urban renewal, principally because it regards the new city school-community-center next to it as competition for the attention of the neighborhood. The school, which was named for a locally famous pediatrician, Harry A. Conte, is one of Mayor Lee's favorite buildings. He calls it "my jewel." This is the place where Edward J. Logue makes his pilgrimage to gain sustenance and inspiration for his fights with the Boston City Council.

The school site formerly housed a number of factory lofts, one of which burned and killed fifteen people in 1957. One enters the school complex through an arch that bridges two small buildings, one a neighborhood library, the other a senior citizens' center. The arch also bridges the span of life, for the library is usually packed with children and the center with old-timers, who commit two minor and forgivable legal violations—card games for money and the prominent display of a campaign portrait of Mayor Lee, which is guarded carefully by the old folks who know which side their bread is buttered on.

Through the arch is a courtyard which is framed on the right by circular concrete tables with inlaid checkerboards and by two *bocce* courts equipped with lights to accommodate the scores of men who use them. On the left is an auditorium seating approximately two hundred which is regularly used for meetings, small concerts, and plays. Lee has chosen the auditorium for his inauguration in his last two terms.

At the end of the court is the school, a two-story square building with an interior courtyard. The school has classrooms, meeting rooms, a gymnasium, swimming pool, kitchen, and health and dental clinics. It is open until ten-thirty at night for children and adults. On both sides of the school are play areas. One is an athletic field, the other equipped with swings, a green spiral slide, and concrete sculpture for the young to play on. About fifty yards beyond the school is the embankment for Interstate Route 91, and beyond that is a new industrial park, several occupants of which used to be located in the Wooster Square neighborhood.

The school was built by the Department of Education, but the site was chosen by the Redevelopment Agency as was the designer, Skidmore, Owings & Merrill. Design control from the city side was the job of the City Plan Commission, chiefly that of a young planner named Edward L. Friend, who died before the building was finished but whose legacy includes the basic site plan for the school as well as many other buildings and parks in the city.

To the right of the entrance to the Conte School are more rehabilitated homes. The fourth side of the Green was once dominated by a used-car lot complete with waving flags, garish signs, and faded automobiles. The lot is now gone, replaced by a mall which leads to Wooster Street and a new seventy-two-unit housing cooperative, known in the trade as "221 (d) (3) housing." The name comes from a section, paragraph, and line of the

Federal Housing Act under which the development was built. The section provides 100 per cent FHA loans with a forty-year term and a below-market interest rate of 3 per cent to a non-profit sponsor, which in turn hires a contractor to build moderately priced housing.

"D-3 stuff," as it is called by the renewal "in" group, is designed solely for families of moderate income (a family of two, for example, whose annual income does not exceed $6,100). Because of liberal financing, the housing cost to the tenant is considerably lower than that of comparable units built with conventional mortgage money. If the development is rental, tenants pay around 20 per cent less. The seventy-two-unit development in Wooster Square is a cooperative, and tenant-owners pay $325 down and $98 a month for a two-bedroom apartment with heat and hot water. They end up owning the unit. "D-3 stuff" has helped many families buy their way out of public housing into private housing that otherwise would be beyond their income.

"It is a good thing, this D-3 stuff" was the recent observation of Samuel I. Hershman, a grand old man in his seventies who parlayed a scrap-paper business into one of the biggest bankrolls in New Haven and eventually into a family foundation which sponsored the Wooster Square cooperative. One of the great local treats in New Haven is to have Sam Hershman give you a personal tour of "my housing project." During the tour Sam may tell you the story of how he got into it:

"I was in Florida and I get this call from Dick Lee. He says, 'Sam, you're going to sponsor a housing project.' I said, 'My God, Dick, what do I want to do that for?' He says, 'There's no money in it, but it will help a lot of people.' And you know I think the world of Dick, so I says, 'O.K.' After I hang up, I wonder what kind of crazy deal is this, but you know Dick; he won't take no for an answer. Now I'm glad; it's one of the greatest things I ever did."

The actual staff work in the financing and coordination of the project was done not by the Hershman Foundation but by the

Redevelopment staff. Once the project was built and occupied, it was turned over entirely to the tenants who manage it through a cooperative association.

The Wooster Square cooperative is one of several which are now open or under construction in other renewal projects and which are sponsored by such diverse groups as the Junior Chamber of Commerce, the Human Relations Council, the Dixwell Congregational Church, and the New Haven Central Labor Council. The Wooster Square housing is representative of the others, and while all the evidence is not yet in, it seems to make at least two points which are important to the fields of low- to moderate-income housing.

The first of these is that homeownership encourages people to improve their personal habits. Among the most immediately striking aspects of the development are the distinctive shrubs, flowers, and landscaping touches that tenant-owners have given their small plots. An experienced gardener might find fault with the crab grass or the preponderance of radishes in the vegetable patch, but who cares? There's a lot of formerly pent-up pride growing in those gardens, too. The second point is that racial integration can work at the lower ends of the economic ladder, where integration does not usually flourish. The Negroes, Puerto Ricans, Italians, and Irish who live there moved in freely. One could hardly characterize all the relationships as buddy-buddy, but rocks are not being hurled through windows and neighbor is not spitting on neighbor. They are living together, the children play together, and the parents are talking to each other. The chief reason for this surface harmony is undoubtedly the fact that Negroes, Puerto Ricans, Italians, Irish, and every other ethnic or national group share an appreciation for an excellent housing buy when they see one, and they let feelings of brotherhood, pro or con, wait until later. So far, integration at the Wooster Square cooperative has worked.

The racial integration of its housing is perhaps the most significant achievement of Wooster Square. Of course it was no accident, but the result of deliberate choices of housing types, and it was made possible by saturating the neighborhood with such services and facilities as its well-equipped new school.

The original Italian families of Wooster Square have learned a lesson that liberal critics often choose to ignore, that urban renewal does not necessarily mean Negro removal. Some are bitter about being conned into urban renewal, and a few are unhappy with the result. But the Italians of Wooster Square can and do take pride in the peaceful and often generous way they have accepted integration. If they chose, they could certainly look down their noses at posh Anglo-Saxon neighborhoods where prosperous homeowners often sell out in droves as soon as a Negro appears. But not the Italians of Wooster Square, whose feelings were perhaps best expressed by a woman who recently observed, "As long as the Negroes take care of their property and the neighborhood, I don't mind. The fact is the place looks better than it used to."

There are many other interesting sights in Wooster Square, but they require more than a walk around its Green. Along Wooster Street to each side of the cooperative housing, there are more rehabilitated homes as well as some of the city's best Italian restaurants and pizzerias, which have also been spruced up. Next to the co-op is a sixty-unit apartment house for the elderly erected by the Housing Authority. For forty dollars a month, a senior citizen can have a comfortable apartment with a view in an attractive building with a small park in front. Like all the senior citizens' housing in New Haven, this development is small, in the heart of a neighborhood, and within walking distance of shopping and public transportation.

In another part of the project, the city took a decrepit four-block retail strip and got the owners to rebuild, rehabilitate, and provide off-street parking spaces. Across I 91 is the new industrial area where wholesaling and light industrial plants that were once scattered throughout the neighborhood have been concentrated. The design of the new plants is striking. Instead of being bleak and dreary boxes produced by standard engineers' blueprints, the plants are attractive and have been designed by architects. As a result, the area is not just another industrial district the city must put up with for tax purposes, but a distinctive city within a city.

Wooster Square, one of the nation's first neighborhood renewal projects, is also perhaps its most successful. This does not mean one could not find fault with it. No one is completely sure what happened to those who used to live in the Court Street rooming houses. Some owners were too poor to rehabilitate their homes. And I 91, which screens residential from industrial Wooster Square, has made an island out of a public housing project which used to be part of the neighborhood. But the successes of Wooster Square are more numerous. With few exceptions rehabilitation rather than removal of older homes has worked. The unsightly mixture of industrial, commercial, and residential land uses has been unscrambled. Once ugly and declining retail strips have been fixed up and revived. Different kinds of new housing for the elderly and for families of upper, middle, and moderate income have given the neighborhood the variety that city life is supposed to give. New Haven has shown that an old and declining city neighborhood can be restored.

Neighborhood renewal takes a long time. Wooster Square started in 1957 and the project books are still open. But this did not deter Lee from launching several more right away, for he and his staff never liked pecking at problems. All the old residential areas surrounding downtown are now covered by urban renewal. Some of the other projects may outclass Wooster Square; the goals are more ambitious and there are more tools to work with. In 1961, for instance, the Board of Education got bond approval for the replacement of almost half the city's schools. Under a plan developed by Cyril G. Sargent, now a professor at C.C.N.Y., each urban renewal neighborhood gets at least one new school. From the planner's view this gives each neighborhood a facility around which other improvements can be built, just as the Conte School has served as the new heart, along with the Green, of Wooster Square.

The local Housing Authority has an extensive elderly housing program under way in all renewal neighborhoods, with emphasis on small, integrated sites. It has also launched a rent supplement program to house families in private rentals, with the Authority providing the difference between the private rental and the rent the family would pay in a public housing project.

One of the most ambitious renewal projects since Wooster Square is in a predominantly Negro neighborhood called Dixwell which abuts Yale University. The Dixwell planning problems are quite different from those in Wooster Square. In fact, the entire concept of the project is different, for the Negro organizations in the neighborhood want to attract white families to the area while in Wooster Square white residents thought renewal would keep Negroes out. The over-all condition of the Dixwell structures is poorer than that of Wooster Square, so the city, through the Redevelopment Agency, is not in a position to restore an old, declining neighborhood, but is trying, instead, to build a new neighborhood but without tearing down everything in sight.

The Dixwell area has no established center around which a new neighborhood can be built. What it does have is a large, well-equipped elementary school built in 1953 but stuck unceremoniously in the middle of a substandard residential block. Under the project, which was started in 1961, the Redevelopment Agency has broken through to the school by clearing the structures in front of it. In place of these old buildings it will build a park framed at one end by the school and other community facilities and at the other by new shops. The park is to be the new center for the neighborhood. The Dixwell homes are less sturdy and more decrepit than those in Wooster Square. Rehabilitation is working along some streets where the housing is not bad, but much greater emphasis is being placed on new housing, mainly 221 (d)(3) cooperatives. Because one of the larger problems in the Dixwell area was overcrowding, more units have been torn down than are scheduled to be replaced. About seven hundred slum dwellings have been cleared and slightly more than four hundred new ones are scheduled to be built, half of which are already up and occupied.

The first new development, called the Florence Virtue homes after one of the long-time residents of the neighborhood, consists of a hundred and twenty-nine units sponsored by the Dixwell

Congregational Church as a 221 (d)(3) cooperative. In an effort to integrate its project, the church undertook a low-key promotion pitch for tenants with liberal organizations, other churches, and Yale. Since that failed to attract white buyers, the Redevelopment Agency hired an ex-newspaperman named Eric Sandahl to up the key. When Sandahl learned that the church's project was part of four hundred units, that a new school and retail area was part of the renewal plan, and that it all would be close to Yale, he put out a series of promotional pieces which included such phrases as, "Go to where all New Haven is going, the sylvan setting of UNIVERSITY PARK-DIXWELL." That come-on, plus the low housing cost made by 221 (d)(3) financing, produced far more buyers than units, and the project is now filled with a 60–40 Negro-white ratio. The church's project, like the Wooster Square co-op, seems to prove further that people will deal with the problems of brotherhood after they have taken title to a good-looking home at reasonable cost.

The Dixwell Congregational Church and the planners are encouraged by the results of the first housing development. There is a strong hope that the new elementary school in the Dixwell area will be integrated as the other new housing is opened and more white families move in. There are few cities genuinely attempting to use renewal as a means of transforming a Negro ghetto into an integrated neighborhood with integrated schools. The final result in the Dixwell area bears watching.

Credit for much of the success that has been achieved in Wooster Square, Dixwell, and other neighborhood renewal areas goes to the young planners, lawyers, and administrators on Lee's redevelopment staff. Among the many architects and planners who work on the projects there is a romantic affection for the old city neighborhoods, with their distinctive building designs, sound construction, curious alleyways, pleasing vistas, and the genera-tions of wear and tear which have left problems but also warmth, tradition, and mellowness that are rare in a nation of rapidly changing landscapes. The tender loving care that the planning staff has given these old areas is reflected in these comments from one of them, a young and extraordinarily talented planner named Frank Chapman, who in discussing the Dwight renewal area said:

"If only Dwight had been located on water with each house built on a permanent pontoon, then we could float the houses around to achieve the right relationships. There's nothing basically wrong with these old buildings; even some of the commercial buildings have intricate little designs on the façades that no builder has time or money for today. The main problem with an old neighborhood like Dwight is that many of the buildings are in the wrong places."

Soon after he made this comment, Chapman talked the Redevelopment Agency into a plan that calls for picking up a mixture of homes in a two-block area of the Dwight Renewal Project and rearranging them on a new loop road which will be screened from a nearby commercial area. The homes were perfectly sound, but were threatened by the commercial area. Chapman's plan takes care of that, and the homes can be preserved.

To attract and direct sensitive planners like Chapman requires imaginative yet firm executives. This is where New Haven has been fortunate. It had Logue, who was the architect of New Haven–style neighborhood renewal. It had Appleby, who carried out much of the program and gave it his personal imprint of tasteful design and careful, detailed planning. And now it has Adams, who has decentralized neighborhood planning to achieve a sensitive balance between maximum citizen involvement and strong executive control. And, of course, New Haven has had Lee, who has supervised his Development Administrators and the renewal of the city's neighborhoods as a benevolent feudal baron directs his overseer and tends to the needs of the people on his land. He makes countless trips to the neighborhoods, inspecting, advising, and fussing. When he sees something he does not like, he dashes off notes to his staff:

DEAR ED:
One of the new trees we put on Chestnut Street is dying. Get it replaced right away.

DICK

DEAR TOM:

The landscaping at Conte stinks. I told you to put Merion Blue in the specs for the lawn. It looks like plain Rye to me. Take care of this.

DICK

DEAR MEL:

The new Goffe school needs some work before it's opened. I have a list. See me right away.

DICK

Lee's eye for detail and his annoyance with disrepair can move him to send chastising notes to anyone in New Haven. Here is a typical example—a note to Gibson A. Danes, who at the time was Dean of the Art and Architecture School at Yale:

DEAR GIB:

My apologies for bothering you. Please look at the west wall of your building at York and Chapel across from Paul Rudolph's new monument. The drapes are dirty, untidy, and pulled awry—a completely magnificent structure with very poor housekeeping.

Regards,
DICK

His regular visits to the new housing developments find him advising on gardening, discussing interior decorating, and actually barging in on families to see how they are doing, and in the process helping feed the baby, suggesting when asked how furniture might be rearranged, and emptying overfilled ash trays. Perhaps the warmest receptions he receives are at the city's scattered housing projects for the elderly, which he frequently visits "to see how the old folks are doing." After he calls on one of the tenants, a crowd gathers in the corridor outside. Lee moves among them with the warmth of a son returning to a family reunion. He is not unaware of the color of these performances or of the memories they inspire of Frank Skeffington in *The Last Hurrah*. A C.B.S. reporter once accompanied Lee to one of these gatherings and asked how the people were selected to enjoy such comfortable housing. Lee turned to one of the old men in the crowd and said, "You tell him." With a thick Irish brogue the old man replied, "Because we're all lifelong Democrats. That's how, sonny."

11

Beggar with a Bushel Basket

In the federal system, the flow of money historically is upward. The "Feds," as they are affectionately called by the Lee administration, hold the big money because of their huge tax base. The states have a reputation for being comfortably smug, and stingy with their money. The states created both the federal government and the cities, and are jealous of one and often contemptuous of the other. Then, at the lowest level, there are the cities, often run-down seats of civilization, which have the biggest problems and the smallest resources to deal with them. They are the beggars.

Aside from the needs arising from poverty and slums, it is up to the cities to provide schooling, police and fire protection, recreation, and other basic services to the bulk of the population. Each year the problems and needs increase, and the resources to deal with them diminish, for the local property tax is not the most stable of revenues and bond issues are often defeated. One great irony in the federal system is that local government pays the price of the citizens' bitterness for higher taxes imposed on them by state and federal governments. While the federal government can collect billions in income tax with only isolated protest, the local citizens can tear apart a city public hearing on raising the property tax by one mill. As any mayor or local bureaucrat will testify, life can be hard in City Hall.

Lee's financial problems in New Haven were monumental. He wanted to mount a rebuilding program which by early estimates required $100,000,000 in public funds. He inherited an annual operating budget of around $17,000,000, and that was already overburdened with existing services. Another $2,000,000 was raised each year in bonds for physical improvements. To compound the problem, he wanted to avoid any local tax hike to support his program, which he did for the first six years of his administration. Federal and state aid were therefore in order.

While installing taps on the federal and state treasuries, Lee reshaped the local fiscal machinery to make it operate efficiently. He had taken over the budget process during his initial year in office and one of his first innovations had been to put each department under strict financial control.* Annual departmental appropriations were broken into quarterly allotments. If at the end of each quarter a department had not spent its full allotment, the excess was dumped back into the General Fund. Because departments were careless in programming expenditures, considerable portions of their operating budgets found their way back into the General Fund as a surplus, which would sometimes be as high as $400,000 per year. Originally Lee used the surplus to hire staff and consultants to start renewal planning. Some other measures taken by Lee to wring every possible cent from his budget were stepped-up efforts to collect unpaid taxes, the practice of central purchasing, and, thanks to Barbieri, the removal of fifty-two Republicans from jobs in the Public Works Department.

The great temptation for anyone raising money quickly is to borrow it. New Haven gives its Board of Finance, which Lee controlled, enormous freedom in preparing the annual capital budget; i.e., the budget in which the city proposes to sell bonds to finance permanent physical facilities. The Board of Finance recommendation, which is invariably accepted by the Board of Aldermen, becomes the capital budget. In addition to these autocratic procedures, New Haven once had a curious system, inherited by Lee, of using bond money to pay for recurring items one would normally expect to find in the operating budget. Street paving, uniforms, and even some salaries were often financed with bond money, and this was one area of city finance Lee was slow to reform. He placed an expanded street-paving program under the bond program as well as "capital improvements" such

* See Chapter 3, pp. 30–33.

as rolling stock, fire hydrants, and manhole covers. This further loosened the bind on the operating budget and gave Lee a greater surplus to work with in spot financing specific improvements or in getting the rebuilding program started.

Under the Lee administration the capital budget doubled, then tripled, in size. The cause was not the inclusion of "capital improvements" but an accelerated replacement of antiquated schools, firehouses, and other city buildings, most of which formed the basis of the city's financial contribution to the renewal effort. The rest came from the federal and the state government. To understand this requires a brief description of the federal urban renewal program and how New Haven used it.

Lee has always been the beneficiary of a degree of luck, and this was so in his efforts to attract federal urban renewal dollars to New Haven. When he launched his program in 1954 the federal urban renewal program was blessed with money but plagued with problems. Congress had authorized $500,000,000 for the program, but only $74,000,000 had been asked for by the cities. Local officials were either uninterested or afraid of the new program, and federal urban renewal administrators were touring the nation to encourage interest and participation. Lee was something of an oddity at this time, for instead of sitting in his office waiting to be wooed he was in Washington asking for help. He and Logue cut strange figures in those days of urban renewal uncertainties. They would unroll their maps, gesture magnificently, argue persuasively, and feign a professional assurance that created the impression they were direct descendants of Baron Von Haussmann. The federal bureaucrats were intrigued by these performances if not always impressed. So while they expressed great interest in Lee's plans, they made it clear they would supervise New Haven's project planning with the same degree of benevolence they used in overseeing the work of other cities.

The notion of strong federal supervision was distasteful to Lee and Logue, who wanted freedom to develop their plans before negotiating with the Feds. They also understood that a natural by-product of federal influence in project planning would be a

lower federal share of project costs. But to deal effectively with
the New York and Washington bureaucrats they had to know the
rules of the game at least as well as those who had written them.
So Logue memorized the regulations. When Ralph Taylor joined
the Redevelopment Agency, he already knew them. With the
later addition of Appleby and Adams, the city gained two men
who had worked in the federal agency and had helped write
some of the regulations. The assembly of this formidable bargaining unit helped New Haven in the project negotiations, for
its members understood fully the clever financial incentives the
federal government provides for cities to plan comprehensive
urban renewal programs.

The basis for urban renewal bargaining is the preparation of a
project budget, a complicated yet fascinating discipline which
offers those who master it the exhilarating power to make money
multiply or vanish. The elements of it are simple. The federal
government pays two-thirds of a project cost, the city one-third.
The computation of cost is where the complexity and artistry
come into play.

The actual cost of a project includes three factors. The first
comprises the so-called project expenditures. These are the costs
one would normally associate with urban renewal, such as the
planning of a project, the staff and professional services needed
to carry it out, the purchase of land in the project area, the
clearance of buildings on that land, and certain project improvements like sewers or streets. The second factor is something
called an Item 2 cost. Generally Item 2 costs consist of the value
of locally financed improvements which are related to the project. Some examples of Item 2 costs would be the dollar value of
streets, sewers, schools, or other local public improvements. (A
new street or a sewer can clearly be considered a project improvement, or an Item 2 cost, and is therefore transferable
depending on the city's ability to finance it, how it affects the
city's share of costs, and federal approval. This will emerge more
clearly a little later on. Another point is that the local improvement which is counted as an Item 2 cost can be made before the
project starts.) When a city donates land or demolishes a build-

ing in a project, those costs count as well. Item 2 costs do not have to be city-financed. The price of acquiring and clearing land by a hospital or university for institutional use in a project is also considered an Item 2 cost. The gross cost of a project is the combined cost of project expenditures and Item 2 costs.

The third factor in the actual cost of the project is the income derived from the sale of cleared project land to a developer, public or private. This income, when subtracted from the gross cost of the project, produces a net project cost shared by the federal government and the city on a two-thirds, one-third basis. The interesting twist in renewal financing is that the city's one-third share can be met by its local improvements, a federal incentive for cities to participate in a project area with new locally financed facilites. A hypothetical project budget will serve as illustration.

Assume that the project's administration, planning, land purchases, and demolition are estimated at $10,000,000. These are the project expenditures. The Item 2 costs consist of $50,000 in sewers built previously by the city, another $450,000 in sewers and streets proposed to be built by the city, two abandoned schools which are being donated to the project by the city at an estimated value of $1,500,000, and a $1,000,000 city parking garage to serve the project area. Thus Item 2 costs come to $3,000,000. Under plans for the project it is estimated that the sale of acquired land to private developers will generate an income of $1,000,000. Here is how such a project budget would appear:

Project expenditures	$10,000,000	
Item 2 costs	3,000,000	
	$13,000,000	Gross cost of project
	−1,000,000	Land sale
	$12,000,000	Net cost of project
	$ 8,000,000	Federal ⅔ share
	4,000,000	City ⅓ share
	−3,000,000	Item 2 costs
	$ 1,000,000	City cash contribution

In this budget the city's prior expense in the project or its commitment to finance improvements in the project, which totals $3,000,000, is a double entry. It counts in the gross cost of a project and is credited as part of the city's one-third share of the net cost of the project. Clearly, the more local improvements a city can get credit for in a project, the lower will be its cash contribution and the higher will go the federal share. It works like a seesaw. For instance, if the local Board of Education was planning to construct a $4,000,000 high school near this same hypothetical project, and the city could show that 45 per cent of the student enrollment would come from the project area, this would mean that $1,800,000 of the high-school cost could be counted as an Item 2 cost. The sharing would alter dramatically.

Project expenditures	$10,000,000	
Item 2 costs	4,800,000	($3,000,000 + $1,800,000)
	$14,800,000	Gross cost of project
	−1,000,000	Land sale
	$13,800,000	Net cost of project
	$ 9,200,000	Federal ⅔ share
	4,600,000	City ⅓ share
	−4,800,000	Item 2 costs
	+ 200,000	Surplus

Now the city would contribute no cash to the project, and indeed would have generated an excess contribution of $200,000, which it could use as part of its share in another renewal project. The federal policy of allowing local improvements to be counted against a city's share of project costs is a boon to those communities that plan local improvements around their renewal programs. This is precisely what the federal bureaucrats wanted and it is precisely what New Haven did.

Sometimes New Haven may have stretched the meaning of local improvement by combing old city budgets to find as many creditable improvements as possible. As a result some project budgets contain catch basins, tree stump removals, even an abandoned public bathhouse. But in the main New Haven has cleverly programmed the replacement of worn-out schools and other run-down facilities around urban renewal and has received a double return on the investment—the intrinsic worth of the new facility and the federal urban renewal dollars it attracts.

One of the most sweeping uses of the Item 2 device was an $18,000,000 bonding authorization for fifteen new city schools, twelve of which were located in urban renewal projects. Because the twelve schools were built in renewal projects, the Department of Education bought them at a write-down, saving approximately $7,000,000 in land purchase and demolition costs. The roughly $15,000,000 it cost to build the twelve schools was counted as local improvement in the project budgets, and attracted around $30,000,000 of federal urban renewal money; i.e., each city dollar makes two federal dollars under the one-third, two-thirds formula. The magic of it all moved Lee to present some appealing logic to an alderman who recently asked him how it worked:

"It's one of the wisest votes you ever made. We saved $7,000,-000 on the land. We attracted $30,000,000 in federal dough. That makes $37,000,000. If you hadn't voted for the $15,000,000, the city would have lost $22,000,000. Instead we made $22,000,-000, and that's almost as much as we raise in taxes each year. By authorizing the city to spend that $15,000,000 you saved the taxpayers $22,000,000."

The shrewdest of the Item 2 arrangements emerged from a congressional decision in 1960 to permit cities to use the cost of university and later hospital expansion as a local improvement in a project budget. The University of Chicago had urged such a decision, vigorously supported by university towns such as New Haven. The idea was to free city hospitals and universities from the slums that often surround them. Implicit in the new regulation was the recognition that money-hungry cities would quickly gerrymander existing projects or create new ones to include hospitals and universities.

New Haven built the Dixwell Renewal Project around the new Ezra Stiles and Morse Colleges of Yale University, and Yale's acquisition and demolition costs met the city's share of the total

Dixwell Project budget. Some interesting reactions are heard when Yale alumni learn that the handsome new colleges are part of a local redevelopment project and that Lee claims the $7,000,000 construction costs as part of the total private construction generated by his rebuilding program.

In the early years New Haven's success in attracting maximum federal dollars with a minimum outlay of city cash was mainly the result of diligent research and persistent negotiation. Gradually the city gained the reputation as a solid performer, and the federal officials encouraged other cities and even foreign visitors to study New Haven. Lee became a national spokesman on urban renewal. He testified in support of the program before countless congressional committees, served as Chairman of the Urban Renewal Committee of the American Municipal Association, participated in discussions on new legislation, organized a national meeting on urban renewal as part of John F. Kennedy's presidential campaign, and served as President of the U.S. Conference of Mayors. New Haven emerged as a pioneer in urban renewal—not just another city looking for a handout.

In addition to having excellent relations with Washington, New Haven has received substantial Connecticut aid for its urban renewal activities. The development of state urban renewal assistance had its origins in two near disasters: the potential loss of one of New Haven's largest industries and the specter of national depression in 1958.

The industry, Sargent & Co., is a hardware manufacturer with approximately a thousand employees. In 1957 Sargent officials were reported to be considering leaving Connecticut for a cheaper labor market and less expensive land somewhere in the South. Their New Haven plant was housed in century-old structures which were obsolete and costly to operate. Lee had proposed that Sargent participate in urban renewal. He suggested that the city might amend a nearby residential project to include the old plant. The city could then purchase the old buildings under the project and the company officials could use the purchase price to construct a new plant somewhere in New Haven. Sargent officials were interested, but the federal government would have none of it. The federal policy was that renewal projects should stop at natural boundaries, and the huge plant was separated from the project by the Connecticut Turnpike. Also the inclusion of the plant would have cost the federal government around $2,000,000.

With this refusal by the federal government to help keep Sargent, and considering the obvious impossibility of the city's using its funds for such an effort, New Haven had only the state to turn to. The approach for state aid in 1958 came at a time when the nation was experiencing economic recession and there were widespread fears that it might turn into a full depression. In the spring of 1958 Governor Ribicoff convened a special session of the Connecticut General Assembly to consider what his state should do to stimulate the economy. Lee had a proposal. Because Sargent was threatening to leave both New Haven and Connecticut, the state should help keep Sargent. He and local businessmen, including Sargent officials, proposed the creation of a state industrial redevelopment program to include equal sharing by the state and New Haven in a project to buy the old Sargent plant and to provide the site for a new plant in the Long Wharf area—the section of tidal marsh traversed by the Connecticut Turnpike under the highway program. During the special session Lee also joined with other Connecticut cities and towns to suggest that another direct way to stimulate the state economy would be state support of local urban renewal programs. According to this proposal, the state would assume half of a city's one-third share of urban renewal costs.

The response to these proposals and the energetic lobbying which accompanied them was the passage of Public Act 8 and Public Act 24. Under Public Act 8, the state has provided $3,246,127 for New Haven's Long Wharf Redevelopment Project, which today includes a $4,000,000 Sargent plant, a $1,750,000 food terminal, and 120 acres of industrial property ready for development.

Under Public Act 24, Connecticut has authorized $64,000,-000 to help cities meet half of their one-third share of project costs.* New Haven's share of the state program, according to its project budgets of December 31, 1965, was $22,866,365. The result of this state assistance, plus the careful planning of local improvements, is that New Haven will provide no cash outlays for its renewal program. In fact, the Redevelopment Agency is planning to use the state assistance to cover the cost of some city facilities in renewal projects. This can be best understood through a rundown on the current over-all financing plan. As of December, 1965, the net project cost for all federally aided urban renewal projects was $163,447,969, and under the one-third, two-thirds formula the federal share was $108,965,313.** The city share was $54,482,656. To make up its share, New Haven has $41,556,684 in locally financed improvements, including approximately $6,000,000 paid for Yale and hospital expansion with private money. This $41,556,684 plus the state aid of $22,866,365 equals $64,423,049, which is $9,940,393 more than the city is obligated to provide. In fact, the $9,940,-393 is excess state money which the city may legitimately use to finance its improvements in project area.

By careful study and use of federal urban renewal regulations, close planning of capital facilities such as new schools, and help obtained under the state assistance program, New Haven has attracted $108,965,313 in federal urban renewal grants (plus $4,368,581 in relocation grants) with no local outlay of cash. The federal money was attracted for, and the entire renewal program is built upon, the needed replacement of local physical facilities, some of which are now being paid for with state money.

Even more striking is a comparison of New Haven's federal

* Originally, $10,000,000 of this amount was authorized as an outright grant. The remaining $54,000,000 has been provided as a loan which the cities are theoretically supposed to repay once projects are completed. The loans will supposedly be paid from the increased taxes generated from urban renewal projects. Many city and state officials feel that the loan provision is unrealistic and that the law will be amended to make the $54,000,000 an outright grant before any renewal project financed under the program is finished.

** In addition, New Haven has received an outright federal grant of $4,368,-581 to cover relocation costs. This brings the total renewal grant to $113,333,-894.

RANK PER CAPITA OF THE TWELVE CITIES WITH LARGEST FEDERAL RENEWAL GRANT (RESERVATIONS) AS OF DECEMBER 31, 1965

Rank Per Capita	City	Number of Projects	Population	Grants (Reservation)	Reservation Per Capita	Rank By Reservation
1	New Haven	12	152,048	$113,333,894	$745.38	6
2	Newark, New Jersey	18	405,220	112,380,996	277.33	7
3	Boston	23	697,197	152,101,346	218.16	4
4	Pittsburgh	13	604,332	96,869,635	160.29	8
5	Cincinnati	9	502,550	77,803,348	154.81	10
6	San Francisco	8	740,316	91,565,404	123.68	9
7	Philadelphia	51	2,002,512	209,602,569	104.66	2
8	Washington, D.C.	15	763,956	71,884,961	94.09	11
9	Baltimore	21	939,024	71,429,910	76.06	12
10	Detroit	31	1,670,144	114,195,566	68.37	5
11	Chicago	41	3,550,404	168,385,896	47.42	3
12	New York	45	7,781,984	286,182,950	36.77	1

(Capital Grant Reservations by Cities as of December 31, 1965, from UR Directory, 31 December 1965, and U.S. Decennial Census 1960)

grants with those of other cities. Only five other cities have received or are scheduled to receive more federal urban renewal dollars than New Haven: New York, Philadelphia, Chicago, Boston, and Detroit. Each of these cities is considerably larger than New Haven. As a result, New Haven has by far the largest grant per capita record in the nation (see table).

Urban renewal professionals around the nation usually regard the financing of urban renewal in New Haven as the most fascinating and impressive part of the program. During a recent trip to the city, the ex-Mayor of Minneapolis, Hubert H. Humphrey, confided to Lee, "Dick, you son of a gun, what we really ought to do is let the other mayors spend a day with you and your staff. Then they'd understand what we mean by creative federalism."

During an appearance on "Meet the Press" in 1966, one reporter asked Lee how his city had achieved its record, to which Lee gave this candid but hardly modest reply:

". . . I have been able to learn all the nuances of the programs as they arrive. I have an outstanding staff. . . . We study the programs as they evolve in Washington. We help develop this, support the legislation, and in some cases write the legislation, and then when the money is passed out we are there with a bushel basket."

IV

Human Resources

12

The Social Revolution

Urban renewal often uncovers more problems than it can solve. Its critics say that it creates more problems than it is worth. While there are many illustrations of how a massive rebuilding program can turn such long-standing problems as ineffective city planning or small-business decline into immediate crises, no problem is more important than that of human poverty.

The ability of urban renewal to respond to the problems it exposes is largely determined by the inclinations of those who administer it, and the money and bureaucratic control they have. Urban renewal in New Haven began as a program to overcome physical obsolescence, poor housing, and economic decline. It soon became deeply involved in a social revolution caused by increases in the Negro population, Negro impatience, and Negro anticipations.

Negroes have been migrating to New Haven in increasing numbers since the turn of the century, when there were approximately 3,000 non-white* residents. After World War II the Negro migration to New Haven as well as other Northern cities rose dramatically. In 1946 there were about 6,000 non-whites. By 1950 there were 10,000. By 1960 there were 22,000, and today it is estimated that there are at least 27,000. During the nineteen-fifties, Lee and Logue were aware of increases in the city's Negro population, but it was not until the 1960 census that they

---

* "Non-white" is a census designation which includes both Negroes and Puerto Ricans. In 1960, there were 1,169 city residents who were born in Puerto Rico or had parents who were born in Puerto Rico.

understood how great the movement was, not just of Negroes moving into the cities but of whites moving out. From 1950 to 1960, New Haven's net population decreased from 164,443 to 152,048, which meant that while the Negro population had doubled, its percentage of the total population had risen from about 6 per cent to about 14 per cent.

While urban renewal had failed to give local officials a quantitative insight into these population shifts, it had gradually impressed upon them the desperate condition of many slum families, white and black. During the nineteen-fifties, however, no one perceived—or at least identified—any special Negro problem in the slums. Not many public agencies kept racial records, no one was rioting, no one was writing popular books which described Negro "self-hate" or the "invisible" poor, or making a case for the peculiarity of the Negro condition in urban society. This was a period of public innocence, when the civil rights storm was a mere speck on the horizon, when civil rights progress throughout the nation was largely the product of back-door political benevolence.

Lee was—and probably still is—one of the most benevolent mayors in the United States. There is nothing radical or profound in his thoughts on Negroes and civil rights. He is deeply human and emotional in his empathy toward the Negro, whom he regards as society's underdog. Some would characterize him as paternalistic, but Lee has none of the self-serving cynicism that the word has come to convey. During the civil rights turmoil of the sixties, he would raise his hands and exclaim, "Christ, help me do the right thing! I am only a poor Irish boy from Newhall-ville." But during the fifties he was sure of what to do. His view was that the Negro was suffering the same discrimination, unemployment, and poor housing as his Irish forebears had. His initial efforts toward his Negro constituency were characterized by a return to the ways of yesteryear, when many an Irishman was bounced upward from the slums by the impetus of City Hall patronage.

Lee's opening move in civil rights was to appoint the city's first Negro Corporation Counsel, George Crawford. In 1954 that was a bold stroke—an indication of how far the nation and New Haven have traveled since. Heading the city's legal staff has always been a choice job, and during this century it had gone to an ethnic colleague of the mayor. Yet the Crawford appointment, despite its violation of the practice, went over well because of the personal justice involved. Crawford, who was then in his seventies, had established a lucrative law practice and enjoyed widespread respect, but because of discrimination had been denied a prestige appointment or nomination. Lee changed that, and in the process helped some party members relieve their guilty consciences as well as creating pride among the Negro wards of the city. Lee was also repaying a little-known personal debt. After Lee's father died when Lee was still a boy, he turned to Crawford for mature advice. He had delivered groceries to Crawford's home, and during his teens and early adulthood had gone to Crawford on all major decisions about the future. When Lee was discharged from the Army, his first stop after seeing his mother was at Crawford's house.

Building on his initial success with the Crawford appointment, Lee moved to give other Negroes important city jobs for the first time. A Negro woman ran for City Treasurer on his ticket in 1955; he placed a Negro on the Welfare Board in 1956; he appointed the first Negro member of the Board of Education; he appointed another Negro to the Corporation Counsel's office in 1961; and in 1963 a Negro school principal was chosen. None of these moves seems especially impressive today, but this is probably because Lee's administration spans the revolution, and yesterday's achievement is today's cliché.

Lee's upbringing in rough-and-tumble Irish ward politics helped him appreciate that lower-level city jobs were important for Negroes to advance. But getting them these jobs was harder. The competition from the Irish and the Italians, who were still using the jobs as stepping stones for advancement, was often ruthless. Lee's approach to the lower-level jobs was one of quiet negotiation with no fanfare except for throwaways lauding his achievements, which were passed out in the Negro wards during campaigns. Seldom would he talk to the Board of Finance or his two political partners, Barbieri and Golden, about moral commitment. He would rely, instead, on their greater understanding of political debt. Lee enjoyed virtually solid Negro backing at the polls and this was a strength to be cultivated. Of the other two, Barbieri was the more sympathetic. He was young enough and wise enough to appreciate that Negroes were a growing voting bloc. Barbieri soon joined with Lee and sometimes even competed with him in finding city jobs for Negroes. Golden took a calmer view, never rushing to increase job quotas for any ethnic group save the Irish, for whom he had previously established a priority allotment.

Over the history of the administration it has been Lee who has done most in pushing jobs for Negroes. In the face of bigotry he has exhibited violent outrage, implied agreement, displayed bruised sensitivity, hurled charges of disloyalty—anything that would get his way for him. The opposition would disintegrate from the sheer force of his anger, from the warmth of his charm, or merely in tribute to an outstanding performance. From Lee's efforts the number of Negro employees in the city has markedly increased although the totals are modest. According to the city's Commission on Equal Opportunities, some sample increases have been from 1 to 8 in the Fire Department, from 0 to 29 in the Redevelopment Agency, from 3 to 18 in the Police Department, and from 1 to 101 in the teaching staff of the Department of Education.

While this City Hall patronage obviously had little effect on the majority of New Haven Negroes, it did help establish a bond between Lee and the Negroes. Though no one could say precisely what was thought of the Mayor, the election returns and the personal contacts strongly indicated a widespread feeling that this was one white official who really wanted to help.

Respect for Lee was encouraged by the fact that until 1964 he lived in the heart of the city's largest Negro neighborhood, using the location to keep in touch with what his neighbors needed and were thinking. As much as his family life could bear it, the Lee house was often open to anyone with a problem. On many occasions a job need, a housing complaint, or a family difficulty was dealt with in the Lee living room. In the late spring and summer the same kind of business was transacted along the picket fence that surrounded Lee's house. But his personal influence went beyond the block where he lived. At the end of a working day Lee would instruct his driver to maneuver his official limousine down the main artery of the Negro ghetto. "In this way," he now explains, "I could wave at all the people who watched from the curb. I wasn't just the Mayor taking a tour of a Negro ghetto, I was their Mayor coming home for supper." The apparent identification with Lee was strong enough to foster some healthy humor. One neighbor called Lee in 1963 and announced, "Hey, Dick, we finally made it. We're moving into a new house in another neighborhood. The way I figure it if Whitey is taking me, maybe he'll even let you move in."

In 1964, Lee finally did move to a larger house in another neighborhood. The transition made his personal life more comfortable and less hectic, but his political antenna is now in a fringe area, and the signals from the Negro neighborhood are not so sharp as they used to be. Lee confides today that it may be best that he is no longer directly involved. His use of public office helped some Negroes find jobs and solve problems, but it also inhibited and overshadowed indigenous leadership. It was impossible for any of his neighbors to command confidence or leadership while competing with a goodhearted mayor who rode home in a chauffeur-driven Cadillac with a cornucopia of jobs and favors in the trunk.

The lack of mature grass-roots leadership among the Negroes had left the reins in the hands of an established group of ministers, ward heelers, and outright con artists who portrayed themselves as spokesmen for New Haven Negroes. A few were able and sincere, but many spoke only for themselves and a dozen or so who made up their following. Until Lee became mayor, however, they were the ones with whom politicians consulted. Lee went through the motions of continuing to consult them, but he cut them out of major decisions, especially those involving patronage. The idea that they, not he, would take credit for jobs he had fought to open appalled him.

Lee had very little respect for the Negro political leadership because he was sure that none of them could deliver support that he could not get by himself. On two occasions he proved it. One involved a primary fight waged in Lee's ward by some disenchanted Negro leaders who realized they were being manipulated. Lee backed the organization candidate and even canvassed for him, and the race ended with the organization man getting 70 per cent of the vote. In 1963, in another test of strength, a group put up a Negro former Republican as an independent candidate for mayor. He gained barely 1 per cent of the vote, and Lee claims that vote was largely Republican anyway.

It should not be interpreted from these skirmishes that Lee exercised harsh political power only with Negro leaders. He displayed the same cunning with anyone who questioned or threatened his political authority, and in this sense the Negro was getting equal treatment. In other areas, however, Negroes received a subtle yet discernible special treatment. Lee has always enjoyed his visits in the Negro areas of the city. He has always seemed more indignant and emotional in his trips through the Negro slums, and as a result, he has usually given his best fire-and-brimstone speeches before Negro audiences.

During most of Lee's years it was conventional political wisdom not to call attention to the desperate condition of urban Negroes. In a city of many nationalities and ethnic backgrounds it appeared suicidal for a mayor to dramatize the needs of any one group, and the prevalent feeling until only recently was that the Negro was just one more wave in the continuing tide of low-income groups who had used the city as a means to advancement. Lee therefore controlled his emotions, and avoided saying, as he felt, that the Negroes were being suppressed. His restraint was applied not just to public pronouncements but to private conversations with those whom he suspected of harboring anti-Negro feelings.

It was inevitable that Lee would slip, and when he did he slid. In 1960 a young aide gave him a draft speech to be delivered to a Negro audience. It urged Negroes to block late afternoon traffic by sitting in the middle of one of the major arteries leading away from New Haven. The purpose was to force homeward-bound suburbanites to see the slums in which Negroes lived. Lee was struck by the drama of the suggestion but failed to consider the consequences of what the speech really proposed. Here was a public official, sworn to uphold the law, urging Negroes to break the law to dramatize their housing conditions. The speech received national publicity and the copy writers' approach was that in New Haven some nutty mayor was blueprinting and organizing a civil rights demonstration. Editorial reaction was virtually unanimous in criticizing Lee. The *Register* pounced on him with a vengeance, for here was proof of what the owners had always felt, that Lee was a wild, irresponsible, crazy man. They ran four editorials. In the first they called the speech "a flash of mid-summer madness." In another, getting tougher, they accused Lee of "gross ignorance" and "cheap demagoguery." In the last they pulled out all the stops and charged that ". . . this latest blunder of Dick Lee's should remove any doubt . . . as to his usefulness in higher public office than that of Mayor of New Haven—if not that, too."

A week after the speech, Lee went to the Winchester School in the Dixwell neighborhood. Before a group of five hundred Negroes he apologized and then acknowledged that he had been carried away. He urged that they not follow his advice to demonstrate and promised he would support a neighborhood renewal project that would provide Negroes with housing they could afford. The result of that promise is the Dixwell Urban Renewal Project, which is now half completed. But the memory of Lee's slip lingers. Often young civil rights leaders have threatened street sit-outs. When reminded that this would violate the law, they would smile and say they are merely following Lee's advice. At that Lee still winces.

Lee was probably one of the first public officials in the nation to appreciate the real dimensions of poverty. His renewal program displaced more than five thousand families, and among those were large numbers of hard-core, multi-problem families who had endured poverty for generations. Urban renewal could not solve their problems; it merely exposed them on a large scale.

Lee was faced with basic policy decisions which reflect the power of a local official. Between 1958 and 1960, when the relocation problem unfolded dramatically, he could have slackened the pace of renewal and called attention to the plight of the poor and demanded help from the state, the federal government, or private foundations to finance some sort of assistance program. That course of action, however, was fraught with risks not the least of which was the lack of any federal or foundation interest in a problem which had not yet received national attention. Moreover, the city was already committed—legally, economically, and socially—to carry out the program as quickly as possible.

For every slum scheduled to be removed, there were economic or social needs waiting to be met. A business, perhaps already faced with displacement in another part of the city, was waiting to build on the slum site. Or maybe it was a long-overdue school, or new housing. The decision to clear a slum is usually a matter of weighing private sacrifice against the imprecise goal of the public interest, and mayors are paid to watch the scales. If a serious problem like widespread poverty emerges after urban renewal starts, it is difficult at best to stop the process while a solution is devised. It is something akin to asking a juggler to sit down while he has several pins in the air.

Of course, this raises the more basic question of why urban renewal should be started in the first place unless one knows exactly what the family needs are and where the problem families will go. This consideration was not particularly useful to Lee between 1958 and 1960, when his program was already well under way. It also assumes a degree of omniscience on Lee's part. There are probably few alive today who could claim they were fully aware of widespread urban poverty in 1954 when New Haven started urban renewal. Michael Harrington has spoken eloquently of this "invisible land" of poverty, and Lee was one of the first public officials to recognize it. Today, as the techniques for assessing and alleviating poverty have become available, there is no excuse for any city to engage in urban renewal without prior steps to measure human needs and to establish programs to deal with them. Indeed, any city which ignores these needs is acting irresponsibly and immorally. But thirteen years ago New Haven did have an excuse, the excuse of all pioneers— ignorance of the uncharted.

Between 1958 and 1960, Lee had another drastic alternative available in dealing with his poverty problem: to disregard it. This was a great temptation. Very few people were aware of or interested in what Lee's program was uncovering. The social protesters were doing an abysmal job, and the poor themselves were unorganized. Some city officials apparently have exercised this option of inaction, but such a course was as morally repugnant to Lee as the other extreme of halting the program was politically foolish. He chose the middle ground. He approached the Ford Foundation for help in starting a demonstration anti-poverty program, and while these negotiations were under way, he patched together some emergency programs with city cash and urban renewal money.

Under Lee's urging and Logue's dictates the program of family relocation was transformed from the duties of a dull, bureaucratic moving company into a sometimes inspired and always dedicated group which resorted to unpredictable schemes to get former slum dwellers into decent housing. They arranged marriages to get some families into public housing; they conned landlords into accepting Negro renters; they cajoled and threatened real estate agencies into open occupancy; and they offered finders' fees to anyone who could find suitable housing for the displaced families. But in spite of all these efforts they usually failed with indigent older couples, with large-member families, with single older males, and with unwed mothers, who were often placed in condemned buildings fixed up for temporary use, sometimes for two years or more.

Lee helped develop a homemaking program which he innocently figured would solve many of the problems. His stern Irish mother probably provided the inspiration for the program, for according to Lee's description the essential purpose of the homemaking program was to teach slum families "to wash after toilet,

wear clean underwear, and bathe at least once a week on
Saturday." He hired some Negro and Irish matriarchs to run it,
and the program has had an interesting if limited effect.

Still another effort was an after-school program started in
1956 at an elementary school in the city's largest Negro neighborhood. The principal had been trying to find a way to keep
youngsters in the schools and off the streets when the normal
school day ended. He thought the bait of story reading, sports,
arts and crafts, and clubs would be sufficient attraction; all he
needed was some money to try it out. The Community Council
and the Department of Education staff refined the idea, and Lee
gave the school enough money to attract the children after
school and to get their parents to join them after supper. The
program proved so successful that eventually seven schools became full-time after-hours community centers.

Off and on during this period of makeshift programming, Lee
and Logue kept sounding out the Ford Foundation for support
in a large-scale "human renewal" program. Many of the executives at the Foundation were cautious of involvement in the
morass of urban poverty, for it was an area filled with dangers,
including that of failure. Paul Ylvisaker, the Director of Public
Affairs, was the moving force at the Foundation for greater
involvement in city problems. By 1961 he had persuaded his
colleagues to engage in pilot programs in several cities. New
Haven, by virtue of its established pioneering spirit, was tentatively selected as one of the cities, provided it could come up
with a proposal which seemed worthy of support. He transferred
the challenge to Lee, who threw it to Appleby, who turned it
over to a special unit with Howard Hallman as the principal
drafter. Everyone in "the Kremlin" contributed some idea.

Nothing better portrays the capacity of Lee's redevelopment
staff than its effort to develop a pilot "human renewal" program.
They were already heavily involved in the Church Street Project
—then at its lowest point—as well as expanding renewal to the
neighborhoods, and they were working at least six days a week
doing it. None had professional training in social work or education, and there were no established programs to study or emu-

late. Perhaps the lack of professionalism and absence of bench marks were assets. They had no prior commitment to any course of action and relied instead on their spirit of innovation and ingenuity, just as Logue and Lee had done in the urban renewal program seven years earlier. They scoured the available literature and absorbed ideas from a variety of professions. From Mitchell Sviridoff, President of the Connecticut State A.F.L.-C.I.O., they gained ideas on employment programs; from Laurence Paquin, new Superintendent of Schools, they received a thorough rundown on the latest ideas on education programs for disadvantaged children; from Paul Nagle and Frank Harris, of the local Community Council, they learned what was lacking in existing social services; and from Ylvisaker and his staff they got a broad view of what projects were being tried in other parts of the nation and the world.

Out of all this emerged a roster of projects, many of them experimental, that New Haven wanted to try. There were pre-kindergarten, tutoring, after-school, team-teaching, individual curriculum, and job experience programs in the schools. There were projects for teen-age work crews, on-the-job training, and skill training, as well as a proposal for neighborhood job centers. There were proposals for health clinics, neighborhood workers, legal defense projects, and vocational rehabilitation. None of these was earth-shaking by itself, but the over-all program was impressive. The staff proposed that all the projects be launched simultaneously throughout the city in a comprehensive attack on poverty—almost four years before the federal anti-poverty program got under way.

The most notable part of the proposal was its basic philosophy, which was a radical departure from the traditional approach to the problems of the poor. From the days of the settlement house to the welfare programs of the thirties and the growth of massive welfare bureaucracies, the basis for helping slum families was a person-to-person relationship between the social worker and his client, propped up by a weekly handout. The social worker was a lonely crusader in the jungle of the slums. He had nothing to back him but a maze of agencies which did more referring than acting, and behind those an apathetic society which seemed to say, "Here, give the guy some money and keep him out of my hair." The social worker was often a compassionate and convincing salesman for the virtues of hard work, clean living, and self-respect. But when it came time to sign up the customer, the social worker had nothing to sell—no secure job that would allow for a lack of training, no school program tailored to individual needs, no training program that would develop a man's potential. The New Haven plan was designed to provide the opportunity for advancement. It did not retail services and advice; it wholesaled opportunities in education and employment while supplementing services in areas like recreation. In written summaries of program purpose "the Kremlin" staffers would overdo eloquence; however, a most earthy and basic description of the program was once provided by one of the framers, an escapee from the slums, who said:

"If you're really going to help a man beat the slums, you don't do it with speeches, food baskets, riots, bulldozers, public housing, or by being a nice guy. You do it by giving him a handle he can hang on to, and the best handle I know is a job or an education that's going to get him a job. In this country it takes money to get out of the slums, money to climb the ladder, money to be comfortable, and money to give you the time to help your kids forget the past and become a part of the future."

Through the fall of 1961 and into early 1962 the New Haven staff and Ylvisaker's staff refined the plan through the most tedious process. "The Kremlin" was already convinced of its greatness and was anxious to proceed. They had figured their ideas would cost about $3,000,000 to put into effect. Ylvisaker was naturally cautious. His personal reputation was on the line, and he wanted to examine carefully the New Haven proposal, gauge its depth and substance, and evaluate the city's capacity to carry it off. Ylvisaker seemed impressed with Lee, but Lee was not always helpful in the negotiations. He would often show up at the Foundation's Madison Avenue offices with his staff, make a general appeal for quick action and a brief request for support for his homemaking program, and then take off for Roger

Stevens' office several blocks away on Broadway to check on Church Street progress. If Stevens wasn't there, he would drop in on one of his cronies—often Lou Harris at his office in Rockefeller Center—to share political gossip, and then reappear at the Foundation to see how the negotiations were coming. By March, Ylvisaker had indicated his approval of the plan, which at that juncture included the creation of a local nonprofit corporation which would receive a $2,500,000 Ford grant. The corporation called Community Progress, Inc. (CPI), would finance some of the experimental programs, run others, and establish neighborhood offices in the urban renewal neighborhoods of the city. The CPI Board would include a representative each from the United Fund, the Community Council, the New Haven Board of Education, the New Haven Redevelopment Agency, the CAC, Yale University, the New Haven Foundation, and three appointees of Lee's. There remained only the question of who should be the Executive Director. From Boston came the voice of Logue, who to this day is still offering advice. He suggested Mitchell Sviridoff, the labor leader and President of the Board of Education. Lee and Ylvisaker were enthusiastic seconders, and it was time for Lee to plan a press conference. In April the news of the grant, the new local corporation, and the program was announced to a generally surprised public. Lee had carefully screened or selected each CPI Board member, and at their first meeting he politely told them that Sviridoff was to be the Executive Director.

Such were the origins of CPI, one of the first anti-poverty organizations and one of the most successful in the nation. The story of its development and accomplishment will be told in Chapter 15.

13

Civil Rights: Up from the Cellar

John F. Kennedy was the first President since Lincoln to make Americans think about their race problem. With an intensified civil rights movement forming a backdrop, he made frequent and eloquent calls for complete Negro participation in American society. He did not have a full opportunity to transform rhetoric into action, but he did accomplish a great deal by identifying the problem and refusing to allow the nation to ignore it further. One of these accomplishments was to give lower-level officials more maneuvering room in discussing and dealing with the needs. Lee offers one example.

Mr. Kennedy was both a political friend and a personal idol of Lee's. Part of Lee's allegiance was based on Kennedy's Irish-Catholic background. He was no mere son of Massachusetts. To the great band of Irish politicians of New England he was their boy who had risen to the top. For Lee there was special pride when Kennedy became President, just as there was a special edge to his sadness when the President was killed. But quite apart from these personal ties, Kennedy was the national leader who broke the hundred-year silence to call for action, and in so doing he provided a rallying point for Lee and those other public officials who before 1960 had struggled quietly and individually to achieve progress. If the President could speak out, they could now do the same. If the President could call for action, they could now emerge from the shadows, for they were no longer alone. Civil rights had become a respectable issue for a politician.

One result of the new day was an expansion in Lee's efforts to get jobs for Negroes. No longer did he restrict himself to city jobs. He moved into the private sector and selected the local building trades as his primary target. In New Haven, as well as in many other areas of the nation, young men who wish to become plumbers, electricians, masons, painters, or members of any other skilled trade must go through an apprenticeship. In Connecticut the apprenticeship system is based largely on nepotism; the apprentices are usually relatives or close friends of existing tradesmen. The mere fact that there is no one place to go just to get information on how one becomes an apprentice indicates what a closed working society the trades can be. The practice of recruiting from within, while meritorious in some respects, produces ethnic inbreeding, and during the past thirty years it has had the effect of excluding Negroes. In the spring of 1963 national attention was focused on this practice. There were warnings from Washington and demonstrations for change in a number of cities. In New Haven the local chapter of the National Association for the Advancement of Colored People (NAACP), which was being taken over by a new generation of Negroes, joined in.

Lee convened his labor cabinet to see what should be done. This group was an informal coalition of three persons—Mitchell Sviridoff, former President of the State A.F.L.-C.I.O. and then Executive Director of Community Progress, Inc.; Vincent Sirabella, President of the local Labor Council; and Monsignor, now Bishop, Joseph Donnelly, who through his work as an arbitrator and his close ties with labor was considered labor's priest in Connecticut. All three men are close friends of Lee, and the Monsignor was then Lee's priest.

The labor cabinet produced a list of the Negro members— there were two—in each building trade union in the city, as well as a decision for a face-to-face meeting with the union officials to get them to recruit Negroes right away. Lee picked supper at Mory's for the meeting. This was a key decision and a slight digression is needed to explain why.

Mory's and its employees are an informal part of the Lee administration, as well as of the Lee information network. The staff regularly tells him what is going on at Yale, in New Haven, and sometimes, because of the people who eat at Mory's, in the nation and the world. When Lee holds meetings at Mory's, the staff has developed ways of strengthening his hand. On signal from Lee, the waiters can arrange to have anyone in the room called out to receive a fictitious phone call, or, on certain nights, have the Whiffenpoofs come into the meeting, break into song, and thereby change the tone or emotion of the discussions. These diversions have been used many times. When anyone meets Lee in Mory's to discuss business, the Mayor automatically has the upper hand.

In came the unsuspecting union leaders on a Wednesday evening in June. These were tough seasoned veterans of the labor movement. They sensed the general purpose of the meeting, but were highly unsympathetic to the notion of changing procedures for the NAACP, the Mayor, or anyone else.

The evening got off to a pleasant start. Everyone had met everyone else, and Lee told stories and reminisced. To some of the union officials whom he had known for a long time, he threw out barbs based on special needs or favors they had been asking of him. Sirabella, Sviridoff, and the Monsignor mingled informally with the guests, softening them up with small talk and beer. After dessert was served, Lee nodded to Sirabella to get the meeting going. As President of the Labor Council to which all the attending officials belonged, Sirabella had a difficult role. Nonetheless he spoke directly to the point, reminding everyone that the national A.F.L.-C.I.O. was for civil rights progress, that the local Labor Council was morally bound to back civil rights progress, and that the building trades, as members of the council, had to begin opening their ranks to Negroes.

Sviridoff then underlined labor's role in civil rights and reminded the officials that there was the strong possibility of a local clash between labor and Negro leaders over the building trades' job situation. He pointed out that the trades had the choice of either voluntarily opening their ranks to Negroes now or being forced to do so later under the pressure of demonstrations. The Monsignor then discussed the moral aspects of the problem. He admonished the labor leaders, most of whom were Catholic, that the Church would brook no nonsense in the way its members acted on the civil rights question. The vise was tightening.

On came Lee, saying flatly that more Negroes had to be hired on construction jobs in the city. Three of the labor leaders then protested that no discrimination existed within their organizations, that they accepted Negroes, but that the waiting list for membership was already two years old. Lee replied by challenging each union official to say exactly how many Negroes were in his membership. As their faces turned red, Lee reached into his briefcase, pulled out his tally sheet, and then went around the table reeling off statistics on racial composition union by union. The labor officials now began to squirm. Lee pressed on. In an outrageous move he went around the table again, assigning each union a quota he wanted met immediately. The gall of Lee's quota suggestion caught the leaders off guard, so much so that they began to challenge not the necessity of Lee's proposal but its feasibility.

With the issue now centered on feasibility, Lee introduced his *pièce de résistance.* If the unions were not prepared to move quickly, he warned that he would do nothing to help them when the impending demonstrations occurred. In fact, he suggested he would be forced to side with the demonstrators in view of the actual record of Negro membership in the building trades. Then, moving to show that he wasn't totally deserting them, he observed that he and the building trades had a mutual interest in avoiding a construction stoppage. But before the officials could build a defense based on the Mayor's confession that the threatened demonstrations would hurt him, too, Lee dropped a bomb by saying, in the tone of one musing aloud, that the unions would be in a very difficult position if the tally sheet on the actual Negro membership in the building trades should find its way into the hands of the NAACP.

At his point, the Mayor was notified that there was a phone call for him in the next room. Coffee was served. A week later seventeen Negroes joined the ranks of the electricians, the carpenters, and the ironworkers unions.

Lee's encounter with the building trades was a minor incident compared to his next civil rights move—the passage in 1964 of what appears to be the nation's strongest local anti-discriminatory legislation. In June, 1963, the U.S. Conference of Mayors, of which Lee was then President, held its annual meeting in Hawaii. Through his insight into little-known flexibilities of "Robert's Rules of Order," he had managed to get the assembled mayors to support the Conference's first civil rights resolution, a firm endorsement of the proposed Civil Rights Act.

At Lee's request, President Kennedy appeared at the meeting to outline the local government role in civil rights. Kennedy's speech dealt specifically with the need for local commissions to police discrimination and to promote intergroup relations. He made it clear that without support and action by mayors, national legislation and policies would have little impact. The speech was politically flattering to the mayors, but it was also significant because this was one of the few times that a President of the United States acknowledged the crucial role of local government. In effect Kennedy told the mayors that the President can urge, Congress can support, bureaucrats can administer, but little will happen unless local officials are ready to act.

Upon his return to New Haven, Lee drafted a proposal for a Human Rights Committee which would hold hearings, make studies, and report to him on the official steps to be taken to provide full opportunity for Negro advancement in New Haven, including possible anti-discrimination laws.* The formation of this committee was both a response to the President's call and a way of seizing the initiative locally, for 1963 was an election year for Lee and civil rights was bound to be an issue. The idea was that the committee would give extremists from all sides the chance to blow off steam during committee meetings, and Lee

---

* Two years earlier an anti-discrimination bill had been introduced into the Board of Aldermen by a small coalition of liberal aldermen with backing from the NAACP. It was ruled invalid by the Corporation Counsel on the general ground that it conflicted with existing state laws. More crucial to the bill's demise, however, was that Lee was not in full support. He had not initiated it and regarded it both as a civil rights power play and a poor piece of timing; i.e., the community was not ready.

could postpone any sweeping law or new program until after the election for the reason that he was waiting for the committee's recommendations. Most important, the community, after listening to a steady drone of civil rights dialogue, would be dulled to the sensitivity of the issue, making it that much easier for the administration to act.

Lee picked ten men to serve on the committee. There were conservatives like Richard Jackson, Co-Publisher of the *Register,* and the then President of the local Chamber of Commerce, Robert Metcalf. There were three Negroes: a doctor, an alderman, and a young activist. There was also the Chairman of the State Civil Rights Commission, as well as labor leader Sirabella, a member of the Board of Education, and the Republican leader of the Board of Aldermen. Lee's choice for Chairman, Professor (now Dean) Louis H. Pollak, of the Yale Law School, who had argued civil rights cases successfully in the courts, indicated that the committee's studies would be thorough and its recommendations comprehensive. The inclusion of the conservative members, however, meant that the evolvement of the committee's recommendations might be spirited and that if Pollak could get unanimous committee agreement, its recommendations would have a strong chance of implementation. Lee gave Pollak full rein to direct the committee's activities and carefully dissociated himself publicly from it, although he kept in close private contact with its activities. He was not at all disturbed when the group became known as "the Pollak committee."

Pollak's first move was to ask four local attorneys to serve as consultants to the committee by examining existing state antidiscriminatory legislation and drafting any necessary local bills. While the consultants worked on this, Pollak conducted a series of public hearings deliberately designed to publicize complaints of discrimination as well as conditions of poverty, especially as they affected non-whites. These meetings started in the summer of 1963, continued into the fall, passed the election, and ended in late November. A stream of people flowed through the hearings. There were Negro families who complained that they couldn't get housing in certain sections of New Haven and in the suburbs, fathers who revealed the agony of being turned down time after time in their quest for secure employment, state and local public officials defending the integrity of their programs, business representatives who claimed no discrimination in hiring, union officials who echoed them, ministers who called for morality, demagogues who preached militancy, and politicians who condemned inequality. While these individual presentations often sounded like perfunctory readings of lines from a well-known play, the basic drama of Negro inequality and racial suppression in a Northern city still came through.

There were a number of themes—Negro families being forced to live in public housing because it was the only decent housing open to them, the overcrowding of Negro families in high-density slum areas, the inability of Negroes to get bank mortgages, the deceit of some real estate brokers, and the crowning irony of Negroes paying more for slum apartments than whites pay for decent housing.

In employment, the pathos of the story emerged just as clearly as in housing. Because of discrimination and lack of training Negroes were lumped together at the bottom edge of the job market, which was being eaten away by the forces of automation. Non-white workers were plummeting steadily into the abyss of chronic unemployment. By 1963 they formed more than their share of the unemployed, and they would soon account for the majority of the jobless if the trend continued.

While the committee hearings portrayed the vicious cycle of poverty in which most Negro adults are caught, they also showed that their children could hope for little better in future years. Already Negro children formed a disproportionate share of school dropouts and juvenile delinquents, and many were stuck in the academic no man's land of the high-school general course. They were headed for a highly competitive job market in a complex society with no skills and little confidence or hope in their futures.

At the end of the hearings, the committee turned its findings over to the legal consultants with a request that the lawyers make specific recommendations for the committee to act upon. By January of 1964 the lawyers and Pollak had completed their work and proposed that the committee recommend a strong local anti-discrimination law to be enforced by a new local commission. Their proposed statute deliberately duplicated the coverage of the existing Connecticut laws, so that uniformity between the local law and the state law would minimize potential legal problems of pre-emption. The state statute was more than adequate in its coverage, but it was not being enforced vigorously because the State Civil Rights Commission was understaffed. Pollak and his consultants felt that duplicating the state law in a local ordinance administered by a local commission would have the practical effect of intensifying the enforcement of an already acceptable anti-discrimination statute. Their draft, however, did go beyond the state statute in enforcement procedures.

Generally, their proposal called for: prohibiting discrimination in all forms of housing except in two-family houses and boarding homes where the owner was also an occupant; permitting the proposed local commission to seek an injunction to prevent the owner or an agent of housing within the coverage of the law from selling or renting a dwelling unit which was the subject of a discrimination complaint; and allowing the local commission to initiate discrimination complaints itself without waiting for a timid Negro to come forth.

In employment, the proposed law prohibited racial or religious discrimination in businesses with five or more employees and provided for the payment of back salaries for any period that discrimination was proved. In both housing and employment, the draft law provided for financial penalties to landlords or employers who refused to comply with commission cease-and-desist orders in cases of proved discrimination.

While the ordinance spelled out these fairly stiff rules on discrimination, it put considerable weight on preventing discrimination by calling for the proposed commission to educate, to support or develop opportunity programs for Negroes and other minority groups, to promote equal opportunities, and to hold public hearings on general problem areas bearing on equal opportunities. In other words, the punitive powers given to the commission were not an end in themselves but a means for easing the community into a healthier state of race relations.

In February, Pollak and the consultants transmitted their law and a draft report to the whole committee. The committee, after two study sessions, accepted them not particularly at the urging of its Negro and liberal members but, surprisingly, because of outspoken support from the man who was supposed to be such an arch-conservative—Richard Jackson, of the *Register*. It was expected that Jackson would join forces with the Chamber President to block the proposed law. But on the day the vote was taken, Jackson suddenly declared that ". . . the hearings show that we have a real problem and this kind of law is needed. I support it."

This strange turn of events can perhaps be explained by two factors. First, the record of the hearings, which Jackson read assiduously, may have had a strong effect on him, especially because he had been thrust into an active role of responsibility in recommending what the community should do about the problems that leaped from every page of that record. The other possible factor was his respect for the work of the legal consultants. Jackson never agreed with Pollak on philosophy, but he respected his integrity and legal ability. Also, one of the consultants, C. Newton Schenck, was in the local firm of Wiggin & Dana, and Jackson thought highly of him. When both Schenck and Pollak assured him that the law was within the city's legal powers and that it contained adequate safeguards to prevent an overzealous commission from running wild, he felt comfortable in supporting it.

Jackson's support left Mr. Metcalf, of the Chamber of Commerce, temporarily responsible for the conservative cause. Metcalf extricated himself nicely by indicating conditional support for the bill; he then phoned the committee staff a week later to inform them of a sudden change of mind concerning the employment provisions of the bill, and asked that his opposition to any local law prohibiting discrimination by employers be indicated in the final committee report to the Mayor. Apparently he then turned over whatever material he had for opposing the legislation to the Chamber's Counsel, Edward F. Becker, who later was to lead the Chamber's fight against the bill.

When Lee received the committee report and bill, he literally jumped with joy and immediately began to spread the word that Jackson supported it, endorsed it, recommended it, and—in a spurt of Lee excitement—even that he wrote it.

Perhaps Lee's abundant enthusiasm in giving Jackson full credit for the bill was too much for the *Register,* because Jackson, as had Metcalf earlier, suddenly seemed to fall off the civil rights band wagon. In a painfully awkward editorial which used the phrase *"The Register* as an institution" several times, the paper came out against the bill. But this didn't deter the Mayor, who could still joyously point to Jackson's signature on the committee report as he began to line up support for the bill within the Board of Aldermen. In the spirit of capturing an enemy general, Democratic Town Chairman Barbieri buttonholed aldermen on the bill saying, "If it's good enough for Jackson, it's good enough for you."

When the bill was formally presented to the Board of Aldermen in March, it was quite clear where the opposition was—the *Register,* the Chamber of Commerce, the Republican Party, and the New Haven Real Estate Board, which up to this point had twice refused to meet with the Pollak committee on the ground that no one person could speak for the entire Board. They had changed this position for the public hearing on the bill in April and joined with representatives from the Republican Party and the Chamber to attack the constitutionality of the bill. Specifically, they claimed that the State of Connecticut had preempted the civil rights field with its anti-discrimination laws.

The administration was primed for this one. The Corporation Counsel, Fred Mignone, had prepared an extensive brief supporting the legality of the bill, and Pollak had been meeting individually with the aldermen to reassure them. Besides, the audience in the hearing room was in no mood for debating fine points of law. Comprised mainly of civil rights leaders and, as is customary, many City Hall employees, the audience seemed to pose the emotional question: Are you for or against civil rights? As Republicans, Chamber of Commerce, and Real Estate Board representatives indicated that they weren't, they were booed. As friends of the administration proclaimed that they were, they were cheered.

When the May meeting of the Board of Aldermen arrived, the fate of the bill seemed certain. For eleven months members of the community had been exposed to constant talk of local civil rights legislation and they were dulled and prepared. A virtually unanimous committee, including the owner of the *Register,* had recommended that legislation be passed. The Mayor had submitted the committee bill, with his support, to the Board of Aldermen. Questions about the bill had been answered carefully in private meetings with the aldermen. A public hearing had produced a preponderance of support except for a handful of people who were raising some fine legal points.

On the morning the bill was scheduled for a vote, the Mayor made a few last-minute phone calls lining up reluctant aldermen, and Barbieri dispatched individual telegrams to all the aldermen virtually demanding that they support the bill. That night they did. It was anticlimactic but official. The Board passed the legislation by a 26–6 vote.

As one last neat touch before the Commission became operative, Lee convinced an old political foe to become Chairman of the new group in a symbolic but important move toward bipartisan support for a sensitive undertaking. The Commission Chairman was former Mayor William Celentano.

14

Time of Reckoning

Compared with other cities, New Haven was outwardly calm on the civil rights issue during the early nineteen-sixties. But its people were not sheltered from the stormy national events of the period. Whites were confused and shaken by the riots in the North and the demonstrations in the South. Negroes felt the indignities of Birmingham and the pride of the March on Washington. Emotions swelled, stirred by events which tore at the conscience. It was inevitable that some local issue or event would touch off an emotional explosion.

The time of reckoning for New Haven was in June, 1964, shortly after the Pollak committee's recommendations had been accepted. The issue was school integration, and it brought the race problem into the home and placed it on the shoulders of children.

It began innocently enough, or so it seemed, a year earlier. In July, 1963, June Shagaloff, a field representative of the NAACP, together with some local civil rights leaders, met with the Board of Education to see what the Board intended to do about school integration. The Board, which is composed of seven unpaid citizens appointed by the Mayor, was not sure.

A few months earlier, the local CORE and NAACP chapters had complained about school segregation, so the Board, borrowing a page from the Mayor's book, held public hearings to get more information. These hearings revealed that there existed some overcrowding and predominantly non-white student en-

189

rollments in schools in the Negro sections of the city.* This information, plus plans for a comprehensive grade reorganization in 1966 which could include a degree of racial integration, was about all the Board had to offer Miss Shagaloff in the way of progress at the July meeting, which the Board members hoped would be strictly exploratory. Unfortunately, it wasn't.

Miss Shagaloff had come to New Haven to negotiate specific questions. Was the Board going to integrate the schools? Did it have a plan? When would the plan become operative and how many children would be involved? She made it clear that unless the Board was prepared to give immediate and satisfactory answers to these questions, the NAACP would fully support local civil rights groups who were prepared to demonstrate for school integration with sit-downs, picketing, and school construction stoppages.

Miss Shagaloff's list of demands and the urgency of her tone caught the Board by surprise. Individually, the members were sympathetic to the needs of school integration, but they were not

* To guide the reader in this discussion of school integration, here is a brief statistical summary of the general characteristics, including racial composition, of the New Haven public school system. In November, 1963, there were 20,917 students in the schools, of which 12,969 (62 per cent) were white and 7,948 (38 per cent) were non-white. The school system was then composed of 31 elementary schools of which 25 were kindergarten through sixth-grade schools and 6 were kindergarten through eighth-grade schools. There were four three-year junior high schools and two three-year senior high schools.

The problem of *de-facto* school segregation existed in the neighborhood elementary schools and the regional junior high schools. Ten elementary schools had more than 50 per cent non-white enrollments; two junior high schools had more than 50 per cent non-white enrollments. Six schools could be characterized as being heavily segregated if the standard of 75 per cent non-white student enrollment is used. These schools were:

School	(November, 1963) Total Enrollment	Per Cent Negro
Baldwin	290	94.2
Winchester	990	93.0
Lincoln	548	90.4
Ivy	678	88.0
Dwight	265	79.4
Bassett Junior High	614	90.2

Approximately 48 per cent of the Negro students in the elementary schools and 42 per cent of the Negro students in the junior highs attended schools where the enrollment was more than 75 per cent Negro.

prepared to negotiate details. The Board President, John Braslin, seemed to feel it was his responsibility as chief spokesman for the Board to try to extricate himself and his colleagues from the delicate situation, for quite unexpectedly and unilaterally, he declared that the Board would try to develop an integration plan during the coming school year and implement it the following fall, September, 1964.

Would this proposed timetable and indication of good faith preclude demonstrations? Miss Shagaloff indicated they would, and just as suddenly as Braslin's proposal came forth, the meeting with the civil rights leaders came to an end. Two months later, on September 23, 1963, the Board publicly adopted a resolution saying that some plan ". . . to alleviate racial imbalance and to provide a greater intermingling of students of social and economic backgrounds" would be implemented in September, 1964. When the Mayor of New Haven first received word of the Shagaloff meeting and the Board's commitment, he shrugged it off. "A year's a long time," he said, "and a lot can happen between now and then."

When the Board's resolution was passed in September, 1963, Lee was starting an election campaign and was embroiled in a front-page fight with Governor George Wallace of Alabama. Wallace had been invited by the Yale Political Union to speak at the University. Lee regarded the timing of the invitation as thoughtless and unfeeling. Several Alabama Negro children had just been killed in a church bombing, the state was seething with unrest and violence, and the Governor was establishing a national reputation for his greater sensitivity to state's rights than to the rights of state Negroes. Lee publicly criticized the students for their invitation and declared flatly that Wallace would be "officially unwelcome" in New Haven.

Lee was attacked for his remarks by students, conservatives, and civil liberties groups alike. He was also criticized by Wallace, who charged that Lee was invading the Governor's right of free speech. The Governor and the Mayor traded insults for two weeks, much to the consternation of Yale officials, including Provost Kingman Brewster, Jr., who was working quietly behind the scenes urging the students to withdraw the invitation. The *Yale Daily News* learned of Brewster's efforts and portrayed the Provost as a co-conspirator in trampling the Governor's First Amendment privileges. This was hardly helpful to Brewster, who was at that time in line to succeed the late A. Whitney Griswold as President of Yale. (He survived the encounter with the *Daily News*.) It was Wallace who finally put an end to combat. With Southern chivalry he declined the students' invitation and asked Lee to come to Alabama to speak on any subject he wished.

As the Wallace battle was fought and concluded, the integration timetable went unnoticed by the Mayor and by the entire community. The issue rose only once during the election campaign, when a Republican candidate for Tax Collector charged that the Mayor was developing some scheme to bus children all over the city. That, too, failed to make any impression, and ironically the furor over a segregationist governor from a Southern state had served to obscure the significance of a proposed integration plan in a Northern city.

In the late fall of 1963, the Board of Education hired two special assistants to help the Superintendent of Schools gather detailed information on student enrollments and racial composition in the school system. The Superintendent of Schools, Laurence Paquin, who now holds that post in Baltimore, Maryland, offered a general integration plan.

New Haven had four junior high schools which served grades seven through nine. Two of these schools were predominantly white, one was roughly 50-50, the fourth was predominantly Negro:

Junior High School	(November, 1963) Total Enrollment	Per Cent Negro
Bassett	614	90.2
Troup	1,127	52.5
Sheridan	881	16.3
Fair Haven	927	10.2

Paquin proposed to change the elementary-school feeder pattern for these schools by sending more white children to the Bassett and Troup schools, and by sending Negro children who would have gone to the predominantly Negro junior highs (mainly Bassett) to the Fair Haven and Sheridan schools. Paquin also proposed grade reorganization in five predominantly white elementary schools. These schools, which contained 17 per cent of the elementary school enrollment, were on a different grade system from the other elementary schools. They ran from kindergarten through eighth grade, releasing their students for just one year of junior high before they went on to the three-year high schools. The other elementary schools, which contained 83 per cent of the elementary school enrollment, ran only to the sixth grade, after which their students attended three years of junior high before the three-year senior high schools.

Paquin saw three benefits in eliminating this "dual pattern of organization." First, because the five K-8 schools tended to overcrowding, the elimination of two grades would provide them more space. Second, the school system was already scheduled in two years to go on uniform "4-4-4" grade system; i.e., a system of kindergarten through fourth-grade elementary schools, fifth-through eighth-grade intermediate schools, and four-year high schools. He felt that reducing the K-8 schools to K-6 schools would be a step in that direction. Third, because the five K-8 schools were predominantly white, the transfer of their seventh and eighth grades to junior high school would help the cause of junior high integration.

The two researchers worked through the winter plugging the numbers into Paquin's plan and reported to the Board of Education in March, 1964, that it would not only help to integrate the junior highs but would also reduce overcrowding and open up some spaces in white elementary schools for Negro youngsters who wished to be bussed out of their neighborhood schools.

Generally, the Board liked the idea. Four of the seven members were definitely in favor: Louis H. Pollak, of the Yale Law School, who was then also serving as the Chairman of Mayor Lee's Human Rights Committee; Alphonso Tindall, the Board's only Negro member; Phyllis Seton, the Board's only woman member; and Professor Nelson Brooks, of Yale's French Department. The other three—John Braslin, Dr. Frank Cammarano, and Orville Sweeting, who was then a research chemist at Olin Mathieson—had various doubts about the plan, but were limited in proposing another course because of the tight schedule stemming from the commitment to integrate the schools that fall. It was agreed that the Board would take no action on the proposal until they received some reaction from the Mayor, whom they directed Paquin to see about the plan.

Lee was an ex-officio member of the Board, but he rarely participated in meetings. He regarded it as politically unwise to involve himself deeply in educational matters and felt his obligations were discharged by appointing able people to the Board and making himself available on special problems. Aside from the physical aspects of education, such as buildings and equipment, Lee has never shown the interest in public education that he has in a "hard goods" program like urban renewal. Because of Lee's major role in city affairs, the Board often sought his advice, usually respected it, but occasionally ignored it.

At the time of the Board's integration deliberations and its consultations with the Mayor, Lee was preoccupied with his health.* On the day Paquin visited him at his house, Lee believed he was seriously ill and showed little interest in school integration. He gave the plan a cursory reading, indicated vaguely that it might cause some problems, but closed by saying that if the Board thought they had to do it, then they should go ahead, for it was their responsibility.

Paquin relayed the Mayor's reaction to the Board, which was now on its own to decide how to proceed. It was already May, and some plan had to be approved by early July so that the education staff would have a full summer to prepare for the

---

* Lee had a serious inflammation of the intestinal tract, but was convinced he was suffering from some terminal disease. One of his doctors had the good sense to appreciate that Lee could not be dissuaded from his morbid conviction without dramatic proof, so they televised his digestive system. Through an elaborate process involving the use of flashing lights, barium, X-rays, and a television screen, they gave him a "showing" of his intestinal tract with a suitable salesman's narrative proving that there were no flaws in its operation. This medical showmanship had the desired effect; when it was finished, Lee let go a yell of delight and asked if they could do it again. Thus Lee was returned to the road of good health.

opening of school on the new basis in September. The Board decided to go along with Paquin's proposal after getting private reactions to it from two advisory panels, one composed of teachers and principals, the other of prominent local citizens. The two advisory panels were somewhat helpful, although they eventually created more problems than they solved.

Because there were so many members of the advisory panels (thirty-two on each), the plan began leaking to the community. Moreover, one of those selected to serve on the citizens' panel— a furniture salesman named Joseph Einhorn—later used his panel membership as a platform from which he attacked the Board and organized a protest group against the plan. By June 1, 1964, seven days before the Board finally decided it would unveil its integration plan, its "secret bussing plan" was already a major subject of community conversation, and City Hall politicians were conveying hostile feedback from lower- and middle-income white neighborhoods. Some members of the teaching staff were further compounding the problems. There were many who did not like Paquin and were spreading the word that he was the evil culprit who originated the plan. Rather than calm anxious parents who came to their neighborhood schools to find out more about the bussing, some of the Paquin foes went out of their way to spread rumors. Several even duplicated pilfered copies of the report and passed them out.

The Board was in a dreadful position from the start. Community opposition was solidifying and the Board was being attacked for a plan they had yet to present. Consequently, the Board members decided that starting June 8th they would hold a series of six information meetings in different areas of the city to give the plan full and, they hoped, rational exposure to counteract the rumors. At these sessions a sixteen-page booklet outlining the plan would be distributed and questions answered. All this would take place before an official public hearing on the plan and before the Board took final action.

By June 6th it seemed that the only topic in New Haven was the Board's "bussing program," and despite the lack of details on what the Board was proposing, everyone seemed passionately opposed. From what the civil rights leaders could learn, many of them felt the plan did not go far enough. Everyone else seemed to feel that whatever the plan was, it went too far. In two neighborhoods, however, the opposition was very specific, for the parents had managed to get copies of the report and learned that it affected them directly.

One of them was part of the heavily Jewish Westville section of New Haven. It was classified as the Beecher district, after the elementary school which served it. As the Beecher parents read their advance copies of the plan, they discovered that the Beecher School had been chosen by the Board as one of the predominantly white elementary schools which would begin to feed students at the seventh grade to the heavily Negro Bassett Junior High School.

The parents were violently upset on two counts. Up to then, Beecher children had been going at the seventh grade level to Sheridan Junior High School, which served the entire Westville area, and no other school in the Sheridan feeder system was affected by the Board's plan. Why were they alone chosen to go to an all-Negro school? The second cause for upset was that their children were being asked to go to the Negro school, not the other way around. Because Bassett was located in a low-income slum-spotted neighborhood (across the street, incidentally, from Lee's old house), the proposed pupil transfer loomed as a step backward for many who could remember that just one generation before they had hustled themselves from the same kind of neighborhood. Being isolated from the rest of Westville and having their children go to school in the same kind of neighborhood they had struggled successfully to leave were, then, the burning issues among Beecher parents, although related concerns about educational quality and child safety were also expressed.

The other neighborhood where the reaction to the plan was specific and intense was the Worthington Hooker area, named after the elementary school which served the neighborhood. The Worthington Hooker area is composed of ethnic enclaves of Yankees, many of whom are associated with Yale, and of middle-class Irish and Italian families. Up until then the Hooker School had functioned as a kindergarten through eighth-grade school, with children going for one year of ninth grade to a junior high in the eastern section of New Haven before moving on to a three-year high school. Under the Board's plan, starting in the seventh grade Hooker children would be bussed for three years to Bassett Junior High School, the predominantly Negro school to which Beecher children were scheduled to go.

Hooker parents had made it clear for many years that they wanted their children to stay in the neighborhood elementary school for as long as possible, and in fact the retention of Hooker as a K-8 school had been a concession to that wish. They had still complained about sending their children away for the ninth grade before going to high school, and many sent their children to private school for that one year. But now, in the view of the Hooker parents, the Board was making things still more difficult by suggesting that their children leave the neighborhood school at the seventh grade to attend a predominantly Negro junior high school. "If the Negroes really want to integrate," many Hooker parents said, "then let their children come to our school."

The Hooker controversy was complex, for not only were the parents angry with the Board, they were often furious with each other. Some residents of the neighborhood were on the Yale faculty or had Yale connections, and of these quite a few supported school integration in principle and were not shy about saying so during the series of P.-T.A. meetings hurriedly called to discuss and then protest the Board plan. When Yale parents called for school integration on moral and intellectual grounds, they fueled the fires of anti-Yale-eggheadism within other Hooker residents. Debate then shifted from school integration and got caught up in the tangle of city-University relations. During these lapses the combatants would drop all inhibitions, and points were made not on the logic of the argument but on the basis of who could shout the loudest and insult the most.

Word of the growing city-wide opposition and the furor in the Beecher and Hooker neighborhoods soon reached the Board of Education. Superintendent Paquin decided it was his responsibil-

ity to meet immediately with P.-T.A.s from Hooker and Beecher
to explain the plan and allay their fears. He scheduled two
emergency meetings in the auditorium of the Conte School on
Sunday, June 7th, the day before the plan was to be officially
released. Unfortunately, since he was unaware that the parents
had already read the plan, Paquin was proceeding on the as-
sumption that once the facts of the integration plan were clearly
outlined, opposition would be minimized in the spirit of logic,
reason, and good will.

The first meeting that Sunday was with the Beecher parents,
two hundred strong, packed into the school auditorium. Onto the
stage strode Paquin, ready to outline the plan. As he began his
presentation, someone in the audience yelled, "Yeah! We know
all that, and we don't want it!" Everyone applauded.

Paquin begged the indulgence of the group. "Please let me
outline the proposal so you know exactly what it is," he said.

"We already do," said a loud voice. "Why is our school the one
picked for the integration plan? Why should our children go to
an all-Negro school? Let the Negro children come to *our* school
and we'll receive them with good will."

"I hope not the same good will you're showing here today,"
Paquin replied. The audience booed.

"Please," Paquin said, "give me the courtesy of hearing what I
have to say. Then boo me if you wish."

The idea that he would allow the audience to boo him later
seemed to quiet the group, and they let him continue.

For five minutes he outlined what they already knew—that
Beecher children would go to Bassett Junior High in the fall
along with children from the Hooker School. Suddenly an impatient father broke in:

"Look here, Dr. Paquin," he said, "we know all that, but what
about the safety of our children? We understand the girls' bath-
rooms at Bassett have to be locked to keep the boys out and that
fist fights are a common occurrence. Why should our children be
asked to endanger themselves like this?"

"Sir," Paquin said, "Bassett is no more safe or dangerous than
the school your child presently attends. The girls' rooms at

Bassett are not locked. There are no more student fights at Bassett than at any other junior high in New Haven."

As Paquin finished, a woman with a girl of about eleven sitting next to her rose and, in solemn tones, proclaimed, "I am the mother of this young girl." She put her hand on the girl's shoulder. "I have worked for her, saved for her, planned for her, and devoted my whole life to her happiness and well-being. Her father and I sacrificed personal pleasures to buy a house in the Beecher district so that she could go to the neighborhood school —a good school—with her friends and relatives. Now all that we have planned and fought for is threatened by this Board of Education, and you are asking me to send her to a strange school where heaven knows what may happen to her. Well, I won't let you do it. I will defy you! I will go to jail before I—" She broke into tears.

The audience was silent for a moment, then burst into emotional applause followed by boos and catcalls. Paquin's later meeting with the Hooker parents started with a mild boo, was punctuated by a series of louder ones, and ended with a sustained one. He was not prepared for the emotion of the parents, nor was he ready to answer specific and hostile queries about a plan which he thought was not yet public.

The first of the information sessions was held the following night, June 8th, and it picked up in emotion where the Beecher and the Hooker meetings left off except that the audience was larger, the catcalls louder, and the full Board was there to share the abuse with Paquin. The meeting was held in Sheridan Junior High School—the junior high school Beecher children would normally attend—and it seemed as if all of Westville were there to support their neighbors in the Beecher district.

Although most of the audience was hearing the details of the plan for the first time, they had heard enough from their friends in the Beecher area to know that they were against it. They jeered, booed, stamped their feet, and clapped their hands. When, later, Lee heard of the controversy, he groaned and picked up the phone and dialed Paquin's number.

"What the hell's going on, Larry?"

Shaken and angry, Paquin attributed the problem to an outbreak of bigotry, and suggested the town was in the process of purging itself of pent-up fear and racial hatred.

"Well, whatever is going on, I want it stopped right away. Call off the rest of these damned meetings and put the plan on the shelf for another year. You'll never get anywhere this way."

Paquin said it was too late to stop; the Board was committed to going ahead with the meetings, and he was helpless. Lee, confined to his bedroom, was also helpless so he ended the conversation with a vague indication that he would call again later in the day.

Lee spent the rest of the day complaining that in his absence the town was going berserk. He called members of his staff to get their reactions to a "dramatic appearance" he planned at the Fair Haven Junior High meeting that night, during which he would "take on" the bigots and restore order to the community. This proposal was firmly vetoed by his doctor. About a thousand people were on hand at the Fair Haven meeting that night; three-quarters of them seemed against the plan. With the exception of a contingent of about a hundred and fifty Hooker parents, most of the opposition had no specific objections. Judging by their comments, they weren't even familiar with the details and were just expressing general opposition to the notion of bussing children out of neighborhood schools. The approximately two hundred and fifty people in the crowd who seemed in favor of the plan came from all over the city and consisted of Negroes and liberals who, while not particularly enamored of the Board plan because they felt it didn't go far enough, felt obliged to support the principle behind it. Valiantly they tried to make their presence known through sustained applause and cheering whenever one of their members spoke in support of the Board.

The opposition, however, was much more vocal and their spokesmen usually quite effective. The best effort of the evening was provided by Alderman Bartholomew Guida, whose ward included the Lovell School, one of the white schools which would be cut from a K-8 to a K-6 school with most of the seventh- and eighth-graders going to Bassett. Guida reminisced of his student days at Lovell and of his dream for his children to go to the same school and have the same teachers. He talked of how the neighborhood had raised money to buy a Lovell School flag and to finance Lovell School athletic teams. He spoke glowingly of how the teachers at Lovell had grown to know the neighborhood intimately and how the neighborhood had responded with affection and support for the teachers. Then Guida angrily portrayed the Board as a cold, ruthless group who were callously threatening Lovell's peace and stability. By the time he had finished, Guida had his supporters on the edge of their seats ready for action. During his speech, thirty policemen had moved quietly to the front of the auditorium between the Board and the audience. If they hadn't been there, Guida, if he so wished, could merely have said "Charge!" and the Board would have had to run for their lives.

The four remaining information sessions came close to, but never quite reached, the emotional peak of the Sheridan and the Fair Haven meetings, particularly as liberal and civil rights groups rallied more of their followers to get to the meetings early to fill the seats. Indeed, the liberal wing of the community actually managed to hold two rallies attended by about four hundred people—the majority of them white—who expressed support for the Board of Education.

Paquin and Braslin, the Board President, attended a rally on the Green at the invitation of the organizers. They found themselves in a slightly awkward predicament when the master of ceremonies asked everyone on the platform to lead the audience in a suitable song for the occasion. In the next day's papers there was a photo of Paquin and the Board President holding hands and singing "We Shall Overcome," which must have had a very special meaning to them at that point in their lives.

Among Negroes the reaction to the integration meetings was a mixture of shock, disbelief, anger, pity, and, in the incident of the duet, some much-needed laughter. The white man had gone a bit mad. Negroes shook their heads in dismay as they saw white mothers crying and fathers clenching their fists in defiance of school integration. The fury was directed at the school Board, but they knew it was also aimed at them. What seemed to hurt most was that their children were being singled out as something undesirable, not good enough for white schools.

"It's bad enough that I've had to put up with this crap," one Negro man confided, "but when my kids get treated like dirt and it looks like they're going to have to go through the same thing, then I've had it."

"I always knew they didn't like us," said another Negro after leaving one of the Board's information sessions, "but tonight I learned they hate us."

A Negro teen-ager expressed her feelings this way: "If what I saw tonight is an example of what we're supposed to get integrated with, you can have integration. I'd rather be black and poor than be white and sick like that."

Despite anger and provocation, the Negroes showed amazing self-control and moderation. While white families held private protest meetings guarded carefully by self-appointed vigilantes to keep "outsiders" away,* the Negroes restricted their discussions to shops and living rooms, where there were angry discussions and, now and then, calls for militant counteraction. Publicly, however, the Negroes remained silent as the white community fought among themselves.

Over at the *Register* building, the owners and editorial writers were confused and nervous. They carried no brief for school integration, but were appalled by the passion of the fight.

Prior to the week the Board of Education had given itself in early July, 1964, to come to a decision on the integration proposals, the paper offered its editorial opinion on the question. It began by condemning the violence with which much of the community had reacted to integration. It continued with a plea for reasonable consideration of the Board's proposals. It then commended the Negroes for their restraint and concluded by urging the Board to compromise its proposals. Like the rest of

---

* A *Journal Courier* reporter later claimed that he was literally carried out of a private meeting in the Beecher district. Among his bearers were a local physician and a member of the Yale faculty.

the community, including its ailing Mayor, the paper had passed the buck to the Board.

If good judgment, as the ancient Greeks taught, is a product of quiet contemplation, then the members of the New Haven Board of Education could hardly have operated under more adverse conditions during the last days of June. They had to arrive at a decision in early July to give the staff adequate time to prepare for the opening of school that September. The Board members, each of whom held a full-time job, had only the night hours to devote to meetings. They were physically and emotionally exhausted from their month of public meetings. They had been insulted, abused, and threatened publicly. Their homes provided no escape from the turmoil, for they had been subjected to private letters and calls of complaint and vilification.

The fact that they were able to pull themselves together to meet until the early morning hours every day of the last week of June was testimony to their dedication, but the cranky disagreements that often broke out in the sessions reflected the human toll that had been taken. On the first night they agreed that their initial proposals would have to be altered to reflect some of the complaints that had been lodged. To aid them in reshaping the proposals, the Board established an informal network of roughly fifty people who represented various community interests. These included civil rights leaders, teachers, P.T.A. officials from the neighborhoods where the protest had been greatest, some aldermen, as well as Democratic Town Chairman Barbieri. In Lee's absence and in view of the crisis, Barbieri had responded with unusual statesmanship for a party boss. He never initiated contact with the Board and never criticized or urged a course of action despite the fact that the party faithful were in an uproar. When asked to help the Board by gauging community opinion, Barbieri merely said he would pass along whatever information he could and pledged in addition that he would try to keep his boys in line after the Board made its final decision. He did both.

The second meeting of the Board was chaotic. Each member seemed to be proposing a different course of action and each was as strong in the defense of his proposal as he was in the attack of the others. When the Board finally recessed, at 2:30 A.M., it had slipped to its lowest point in morale and physical exhaustion. During its third meeting the Board members rallied to defeat a staff proposal to achieve forced integration in elementary schools with bussing of mainly Negro students to white schools. Most of the members felt this was a compromise of the principle of bussing both Negro and white children, and was therefore a rebuke of the Negroes and their moderation.

On the fourth night, Pollak introduced the concept of pairing the predominantly Negro Bassett Junior High with the predominantly white Sheridan Junior High. Under his plan the children from nine elementary schools entering the seventh grade would go to Sheridan; all the seventh-grade students at Sheridan and Bassett would go to Bassett for the eighth and ninth grades. The white students would be drawn from all the elementary schools in the two fiercely anti-integration areas of the city—Westville and Hooker-State Street. In other words, this idea did not pick just one school in these areas, but took all of them *en masse* and therefore answered the complaints of "Why just my child?" that had been expressed by Beecher and Hooker parents. Pollak's idea also placated the anxious parents of white sixth-grade youngsters who had expressed bitter opposition to sending their children to a predominantly Negro junior high. Under his plan they would go to Sheridan along with large numbers of Negro and white children. This new idea also included the elimination of seventh and eighth grades from all but two elementary schools, thereby opening more elementary school space to alleviate overcrowding and to allow open enrollment; i.e., parents had the option to send their children to any one of several elementary schools within a district. Finally it provided for substantial integration. If carried out, it would make Bassett (formerly 10 per cent white) 46 per cent white, and it would make Sheridan (once 16 per cent Negro) 36 per cent Negro.

The Board was receptive to Pollak's proposal; the members asked Paquin to refine it, and decided to test it on the information network. Over the July 4th weekend Paquin worked day and night on the plan, and the response from the network was that from all points of view this was the least offensive integration plan. The following week Paquin said the plan was workable and the Board decided that they would hold a public meeting on the evening of July 7th to approve it formally. In the meantime the plan was deliberately leaked to the press and word of its contents spread throughout the community. As the Board members headed for their public meeting on the evening of July 7th they did not know what to expect. There was a chance that this might be the end of the first phase of the integration controversy. There was also a chance that the Board might never be able to take a vote during the meeting, for there were understandable fears that opponents might mob the session, demonstrate against the new plan, and shout down the Board.

When the door to the meeting was opened, it revealed the benign calm and small audience which had once characterized most Board meetings and which the members must have felt they would never enjoy again. After the plan was formally introduced and approved, there was a quiet ripple of applause from the audience, which was composed largely of civil rights leaders and Negroes. The issue which had started in June with a bang subsided in July with a whisper. The orderly process of government had overcome enormous odds to subdue the mobs.

Opposition to the Board and its plan did not die; it merely took a different form. Once-screaming mothers and enraged fathers now quietly signed petitions to eliminate an appointed Board of Education and to replace it with an elected group. Neighborhood protest groups merged to hire a lawyer to represent them in a court action to block the integration plan. This injunction eventually failed, as did a related suit to declare the Board's action illegal. The opponents even produced a political candidate to run on the integration issue against Lee in the 1965 campaign—Joseph Einhorn, who ballooned into Republican prominence through his protest group.

In a month New Haven had manifested the most appalling and the strongest characteristics of democratic government. The rights to free assembly and free speech had become license for temporary anarchy. Yet a basic respect and trust in the process of government enabled the town to pull itself together again. It appeared that the great majority of people felt distrust and even disrespect for individual members of the Board of Education. The Board itself, however, was greater than the sum of its individual members. It had the legal authority to act, and despite the fact that its actions ran counter to the will of large segments of the community, its decision was binding. But while government gave the Board the right to take an extremely unpopular action, it also offered opponents the legal options of dissent: petitions, litigation, and political counteraction, all of which were sufficiently exercised to convince the majority of integration opponents that there was no need to create dissenting options of their own. The integration issue reaffirmed the ability of local government to act in an atmosphere of crisis.

Opinions on the effect of integration, pro or con, vary directly with the preconceptions of those who are asked. The Board of Education has reported that the plan has had a favorable impact by reducing class size and teacher-pupil ratios throughout the system. The findings on student achievement, however, are inconclusive. Two junior high schools were integrated, but observation during the 1965–66 school year showed that classrooms were often segregated, largely as a result of placing students of comparable achievement in the same classes. There was no evidence that large numbers of white students had been "chased away" from the schools. The non-white enrollment had reached approximately 43 per cent of total enrollment as compared with 37 per cent two years before, but this seems to be due to population trends that were under way before school integration.

Perhaps the most remarkable aspect of the issue is that there is no longer any widespread pressure for additional school integration in city schools. Proponents of integration now talk in regional terms. They want suburban children to be involved in shared facilities such as educational parks where resources can be pooled, new programs can be undertaken, and integration can be an outgrowth of better educational facilities. School integration in New Haven has been left hanging as part of the broader question of what can be done to improve city schools.

School integration was a noble but limited response to the challenge of helping a new generation grow up without the racial isolation and consequent fear and misunderstanding of the old generation. Its lofty purpose and crucial nature made it an issue worthy of much more than red-necked demagoguery or angry protest, but perhaps it is still not practical to anticipate otherwise. The results in New Haven, however, indicate future paths to be followed not just in this one city but in others, especially those of comparable size.

First, as a political issue racial integration was destined to failure, or at least inadequacy. Regardless of private practice, the acceptable public ethic in America runs counter to the notion of special interest, and this program virtually had special interest written right into its title. The integration plan was neither developed nor presented as an over-all education plan with clear benefits that could be perceived by a majority of New Haveners. It was a response, developed under emergency conditions, to social protest, and there were not enough votes in the house to carry it. As President Johnson has so pointedly—and, to some, offensively—made clear, Negroes are still a minority, even in the city. If civil rights progress is to be achieved according to current ground rules—the likelihood of which some leaders now challenge—then the President, who has mastered those rules, offers expert advice which when stripped of politeness boils down to the proposition that a minority can get only what is acceptable to the majority.

The second lesson which can be drawn from New Haven's experience is related to, but really more important than, the question of minority *versus* majority. This lesson is that racial integration of the schools distorts the image of the Negro student and clouds some chronic ailments of urban school systems. There is a prevalent feeling in many cities that a causal relationship exists between the increase in Negro student enrollment and decline in quality in urban schools. Of course the question of whether urban schools have slipped in quality is largely a matter of what criteria are employed. In New Haven if one were to judge school quality by the rate of school construction, teacher training, and salaries, one could say that the schools have improved in the past twenty years. If one were to judge school quality by the textbook supply, the classroom size, and the overall condition of schools, one might conclude that New Haven has slipped during this century. But the causes in this second example have nothing to do with Negro migration to the city and much to do with the austere budgetary practices of most New Haven mayors.

Perhaps the most reliable gauge of school quality is student achievement, as measured in city-wide tests. The available test scores demolish the notion that school quality is a function of the racial composition of its students. They suggest strongly that it is directly related to economic class. In October, 1963, at the time the Board began its integration study, arithmetic and reading achievement tests were given throughout the city. Five schools with 75–100 per cent Negro enrollments recorded below-grade levels on the tests. At the same time, however, five of thirteen schools with 85–100 per cent white enrollments were similarly below grade.* All the below-grade level schools were located in low-income neighborhoods.

The relationship between economic class and such matters as family composition, motivation, health, and attitudes has been and continue to be the subject of research, but the effects of the family condition on student performance and school quality are given their most practical expression by teachers. Veterans of the New Haven teaching staff state that the main difference between the city schools and the suburban schools is lack of uniformity in quality. The city schools have a greater range in school quality than the suburban schools. The "problem" schools, so the teachers suggest, are generally located in low-income neighborhoods, where parents may not be uncaring but where they simply

---

* This is for the sixth grade, using a Stanford Achievement test. The scores indicated that the Negro schools slipped below the five white schools by the time the students reached the eighth grade. In the fourth grade the scores for both the five Negro schools and the five white schools were roughly the same.

have neither the time nor the energy to police their children's schoolwork and are timid and unsure about demanding good schools. This is in contrast to middle-class parents, who are not necessarily better informed but are far more aggressive, vocal, and persistent in their demands for both good student performance and good school quality. "Where student motivation and parental interest is high, so will the school quality be" is a well-worn and true expression of the requisites of good school quality.

The problem of establishing uniformly high quality among schools in the city is largely a problem of establishing uniformly high parental interest in the schools. New Haven has a special problem here in that there has always been a large private school enrollment; this came about partly because private education preceded public education in New Haven. In 1964, Superintendent Paquin reported that 24 per cent of all school-age children attended Catholic parochial schools and private schools. Roughly a fifth of the parents in New Haven, therefore, have no direct interest in public education and, if anything, may even have a vested interest in keeping down public school expenditures. But a more urgent and practical problem is the traditionally silent poor of the city,* who on school matters have asked for little and have received less, and for whom, as with the Negro, an integration plan was developed without their participation or urging.

The third lesson of the New Haven experience is that very little will be done to overcome the gaps in the quality of city schools until Negro parents and low-income white parents get involved, learn the facts, and start speaking out. If they do not, then they will continue to endure the lethargy and mediocrity

---

* The poor have been so silent that we are not sure how many there actually are. Traditionally the crude device of income levels as they appear in census data has been used. A cross-section of annual family income based on 25 per cent of the New Haven population in 1960 showed the following major categories:

Annual Family Income	0–$3,999	$4,000–9,999	$10,000 and over
White	7,430	20,365	5,725
Non-white	2,399	2,429	221
	9,829	22,794	5,946

that are the products of a government without citizen pressure. This plea for widespread Negro involvement in the process of government is most decidedly not a plea for separate Negro action and separate Negro gains. The problems of public education are so pervasive and the challenges so great that it is impossible to perceive that the needs of Negro children and white children, particularly in the early years of schooling, are separable. On the contrary, New Haven's experience suggests strongly that parents must be united if progress is to be achieved, just as it shows that there must be an integration of interest before there is any integration of students. This presents the obvious questions of whether such an accommodation is feasible and whether the once-silent poor can speak effectively for themselves. In a preliminary way, New Haven indicates that the answer to both questions is yes.

15

Do It Yourself

There is a new political force emerging in New Haven. It is still too early to ascertain how far it will go and what it will accomplish. It can be best described as direct citizen action which deals with specific needs, is program-oriented and highly sophisticated, and produces results. It comes from low-income neighborhoods. So far, it has manifested none of the whiplash of angry protest over general conditions.

In the Scranton School area a reactivated P.T.A. organization with an ADC (Aid to Dependent Children) mother as its new leader waged a successful campaign for classroom and playground improvements. In the sprawling Hill area several ethnically diverse neighborhood groups who never dealt with each other before joined in an assault on the Park Department and the Mayor's Office to demand and receive a comprehensive summer recreation program. During the 1965 session of the Connecticut General Assembly about three hundred residents from several different neighborhoods arrived in Hartford by bus to urge passage of a bill providing state aid to local anti-poverty programs. They overwhelmed the hearings, met with Governor John Dempsey, and held a press conference. The bill was passed. A school principal in one low-income neighborhood failed to convince parents that he was anything but apathetic and uncaring. The parents demanded that the Board of Education remove him. The Board did.

Aside from the residents' impatience with present conditions and their appreciation of the old adage that if you want something done do it yourself, there are three local factors in the new movement. One is a group of Yale student activists who live in part of the Hill neighborhood and help residents to articulate their problems and organize for reform. The students play an important but limited role in the new trend, for their activities are concentrated in only one neighborhood. Moreover, Yale students have always played a role in citizen protest in New Haven, either as instigators or as the target. The second factor is Lee. Like the students, Lee is hardly a new force in the community, but his role is critical. He has been making government responsive, and without responsive government responsible citizen action is not possible.

The third factor is Community Progress, Inc., the private anti-poverty organization developed by the Lee administration in 1962. If there is one city-wide cause for the new trend in citizen action, it is CPI. A major part of its program is the stimulation of citizen interest and involvement in the process of government. In four years it has invested $1,639,574 to establish a string of neighborhood offices staffed with teams of workers who recruit for CPI's programs, provide individual counsel to residents, and strengthen and expand neighborhood organizations. CPI neighborhood workers have played key behind-the-scenes roles in most of the recent stir and action. In the Scranton School area they helped the ADC mother get other parents to meetings, they framed agenda, and they suggested ways to approach the Board of Education. For the Hill summer program, they got the splintered neighborhood groups together, pointed out areas of mutual needs, and set up meetings with the Mayor and the Park Department. To support the state legislation, they got citizens interested by showing how the bill could affect their neighborhood and then helped organize the transportation to Hartford.

Neighborhood organization is just one of a roster full of CPI activities. It works closely with thirty-four public and private agencies, helping them to coordinate their programs, making them responsive to the newly articulated needs of the poor, and finding solutions to such long-standing problems as unemployment, illiteracy, poor school achievement, and juvenile delinquency. But it does much more than merely plan and coordinate. With the original $2,500,000 million it received from the Ford Foundation, plus larger amounts of state and federal money, CPI is a funding agency which grants or channels money as an incentive to other agencies to work closely. CPI also operates programs of its own, particularly experimental projects and mainly in employment.

CPI activities and priorities are best illustrated in its dollar investments. In addition to the $1,639,574 that has gone into neighborhood organization, it has spent or channeled $5,373, 176 in employment programs, including individual on-the-job training, basic skill training, teen-age work crews, work experience projects, direct job placement, and five neighborhood employment and job-counseling centers. The public schools in New Haven have received $4,952,934 to start programs mainly for the poor, including pre-kindergarten, summer school expansion, tutoring, remedial reading, basic curriculum changes, the reduction of teacher-pupil rations, and the establishment of seven community school centers. CPI has provided $583,631 for new health programs, and it has worked with the Police Department and a local nonprofit corporation which is concerned with legal services for the poor. So far, $922,966 has been spent to establish neighborhood law offices, to help the police expand its Youth Bureau, and to provide a closer relationship between the juvenile court and other agencies in the city. In addition, $524,432 has been invested in a research program to uncover areas of social need and to measure the effectiveness of new programs.*

Quantitatively, CPI is an impressive operation. Last summer it was in a position to offer useful employment to every teen-ager in its seven target neighborhoods. Approximately 37,000 persons have been directly affected by all its programs, and almost 5,000 persons have received job training or have been placed on jobs through its employment program. The qualitative effect, however, is more difficult to assess, although intensive follow-up on those who have gone through the program produces some im-

* These expenditures are for the period from September, 1962, to June, 1966.

pressive case histories. Part of the problem of measuring the individual results of CPI programming is the invisible nature of the poor; another is that the emphasis in CPI is to develop broad opportunity programs for large segments of the population. Many CPI employees get deeply involved with special problems. An ex-businessman named David Altschuler once outfitted an entire kindergarten class with new shoes and has regularly provided personal loans to unemployed persons waiting to get into training programs or jobs. But as an organization CPI is concerned less with individuals with complex needs than it is with large numbers of the poor who will respond to programs offering self-help.

CPI is quite dissimilar to the great majority of other anti-poverty programs, and the dissimilarities count for much of its success. One big difference is that CPI is not a product of the federal anti-poverty program, although today it receives most of its funds from the Office of Economic Opportunity (OEO). CPI was a long-shot try by the Ford Foundation—but most particularly by Paul Ylvisaker—which paid off. It preceded the national program and indeed provided some of the practical experience and insights which made the national program possible.

Another distinctive characteristic of CPI is its close association with local government. In other cities anti-poverty programs chose or were forced to become anti-City Hall programs. In New Haven the program was hatched by City Hall. Since it started, Lee has not given CPI the same personal interest that he gives to urban renewal, but he understands its importance, supports its goals, and gives it his personal backing when problems arise. A third unique characteristic of CPI is the strong executive control of its programs. This was perhaps inevitable in New Haven, where executive leadership has become the style of local government and where Lee has weakened potential opponents and created a political climate in which program executives grow strong. It was also the natural result of the man who was picked to direct CPI, Mitchell Sviridoff.

Rising to the top of the pack and staying there is a recurring pattern in Mike Sviridoff's career. He was born in a poor city neighborhood, which is now one of those covered by his anti-poverty program. After high school he got a job as a welder in a Connecticut aircraft plant, where he organized the workers and became their first union president. This caught the attention of the United Auto Workers, who asked the twenty-seven-year-old Sviridoff to take a top job in their New England regional office. At twenty-eight Sviridoff became the President of the Connecticut C.I.O., and in 1957, when the Connecticut C.I.O. and A.F.L. merged, Sviridoff, at thirty-eight, became its first President. In 1954 he was one of Lee's first appointees to the Board of Education along with Maynard Mack, a Yale Professor of English. Sviridoff's wife, Doris, who had served on the Citizens for Lee Committee in the 1953 campaign recalls that "actually the Mayor's Office was calling to ask me to serve on the Board, but Mike answered the phone." By 1960, Sviridoff was President of the Board and organized and led a city-wide school-rebuilding program and a recruiting effort to replace the retiring Superintendent of Schools. Laurence Paquin was the man who was recruited. Sviridoff was a participant in the negotiations for the Ford Foundation grant and was working in the U.S. State Department when he was asked to come back to the city to head CPI. Not long ago, Sviridoff helped organize a national association of local anti-poverty program officials and, true to form, became its first President. He has recently been appointed head of New York City's anti-poverty program.

One local reporter summed up Sviridoff's public image in these terms:

"Mike can be tough and hard-driving, but when I covered Board of Education meetings, I found it a challenge to deal with him and frankly admired him. Away from the meetings I found him friendly, decent and thoroughly fair."

Like Lee and Logue, Sviridoff throws his full energy and ego into his work. Under his direction CPI became an agency of usually frantic activity, enormous growth, and one-man control. When CPI started in 1962, it had a $2,500,000 Ford grant, three employees, and a small office just one block from City Hall. Today it has received over $13,000,000 in additional public and private funds, has a staff of more than three hundred people, operates two schools, leases eleven properties, and occupies space in eighteen buildings. Sviridoff's background as a labor leader and school board president has undoubtedly affected CPI's program emphasis, which is heavily weighted toward employment and education. Close to 70 per cent of its budget is in these two areas. It is also clear that Sviridoff has not forgotten his collective-bargaining days, for CPI is reputed to have the most comprehensive employee benefit programs in the New Haven area. As Lee once remarked, "That Sviridoff—sometimes I think the main reason he took the job was to establish a model employee fringe package."

Another clear sign of Sviridoff's influence is CPI's emphasis on hiring people of varying backgrounds with little concern for their professional training. Because Sviridoff learned by doing, he is unimpressed with professionalism and has sought people whom he regards as "urban generalists." He recently explained part of his attitude when he described the role of his deputy, Howard Hallman, during the early years of CPI:

"Neither Howard nor I had any professional training to run CPI during its formative years, for the very good reason that there was no one professional road leading to this new program. What we did have was a desire to learn, a basic understanding of the problem we were dealing with, and two different, but highly compatible personal approaches. Howard was an idealist who appreciated the importance of pragmatism. I was a pragmatist who appreciated the importance of idealism."

The practical effect of Sviridoff's hiring ideas is that the top staff at CPI has included a prominent local businessman, a labor mediator, the president of the local labor council, two social workers, a former professor of sociology, two teachers, a lawyer, two former members of Logue's "Kremlin" staff, and a human relations counselor. Among those working in the neighborhoods, CPI has shown a strong preference for hiring nonprofessionals, especially residents of the neighborhoods, to whom it has given increasing program responsibility.

Perhaps the most critical Sviridoff contribution to CPI has been its pragmatic, moderate philosophy. As a labor leader, Sviridoff made his mark as a quick learner and as a politically sophisticated, skilled negotiator. He was never known as a radical, nor did he ever fit the image of a tough union boss. To put it another way, there was never the slightest possibility that Sviridoff would show up at CPI talking revolution. Rather, he demonstrated a keen sensitivity to organization and began talking about "strategies of change." An insight into CPI's strategy was given by Sviridoff in a recent speech:

"[Our] strategy is to deliberately and unashamedly court success in the early stages of the program. This means we did not attempt the impossible first. In the first round we deliberately concentrated on the majorities who have the best chance, once helped, of helping themselves. . . . The long-run hope is that the examples of such successes might make the hard core more amenable to treatment."

The strategy of courting early and dramatic success is widely employed by many public agencies. To use a parallel New Haven example, Logue picked for his first rehabilitation efforts those homes which were in the least poor condition and had owners with the steadiest incomes. The danger of the strategy is that it may become—or critics will charge that it is—a permanent approach. One member of a private social agency in New Haven has argued that "CPI has done nothing more than skim the cream off the poor, leaving the rest to us. CPI gets the credit; we get the problems." CPI's response to this charge is that in recent years it has deliberately sought out the poor. In the CPI employment program, for instance, an intensive recruiting and follow-up campaign has uncovered relatively few people who are unfit for or uninterested in its various job preparation, training, and placement programs. As of March, 1966, CPI had trained and placed 4,709 persons. This is a large catch for a labor market which once counted 6,000 unemployed persons annually. Among those who had been helped, wages had increased by 26.4 per cent. What CPI does concede is that it is not sufficiently upgrading the job skills of the poor.* Basic skills are being provided, better-paying and secure jobs are being found, but the poor are not being given enough training to help them advance in an increasingly specialized job market.

The most persistent criticism of CPI is that the poor have not been sufficiently involved in its program planning. One of the earliest critics on this point was Charles E. Silberman, who accused CPI of paternalism. Silberman based his charge on the composition of the CPI Board of Directors. After noting that it includes representatives of the Community Council, the United Fund, the Board of Education, the Redevelopment Agency, the Citizens Action Commission, Yale University, and the New Haven Foundation, Silberman charged that CPI policy makers included everybody "except the people being planned for."** There was no arguing with Silberman's charges of Board composition; it was indeed reflective of established organizations. CPI countered his and similar criticisms with the argument that "more meaningful" participation of the poor had been achieved through the establishment of strong neighborhood organizations and the hiring of large numbers of indigenous workers. In 1966, a hundred and sixty members of the CPI staff lived in the neighborhoods covered by CPI programs.

When the Office of Economic Opportunity was established in the fall of 1964 to administer the federal anti-poverty program, it adopted the principle of maximum participation of the poor on local anti-poverty boards, and aggressively and courageously insisted that local agencies would have to involve the poor in program planning before they could qualify for federal aid. So determined were many of the top OEO officials to bring new

* For a quasi-public corporation, CPI has often been remarkably forthright in discussing what it regards as its shortcomings. In its 1966 Annual Report, for instance, its employment program is described as still having "important gaps and problems." The three deficiencies which are listed are: programs to upgrade nonprofessionals to professional status (i.e., teacher aides to teachers); more skill-training programs for the poor by the State Vocational Education Division; and better methods of assessing employment trends in private business and industry.

** Charles E. Silberman, *Crisis in Black and White* (New York: Random House, 1964), p. 352.

faces into the war on poverty that they began to provide funds to brand-new local agencies which had few, if any, ties to the local political establishment. During 1964 and 1965 many U.S. mayors gradually woke up to the fact that a new local pipe line to the federal treasury passed right by their windows and led to store-front operations down the street, and they were furious. Much of their anger was generated by the open political hostility of some members of the OEO staff. In the December, 1965, issue of *Harper's Magazine,* William F. Haddad, former Assistant Director of OEO, flatly asserted:

In the Poverty Program, today's city halls and statehouses see the means to reinforce their position. If they should succeed—and the outcome is as yet by no means clear—then the Poverty Program will be a disastrous failure.

Haddad went on to portray most mayors in highly unflattering terms, and then, after pleading for the poor to have a major role in planning new programs, he wrote:

. . . It is only when the federal government—through OEO—injects itself into the local decision-making process that the poor can again have a real voice in the Poverty Program.

The great flaw in OEO policy was not in concept or purpose but in implementation. Those who were left to enforce it often displayed either indifference or ignorance toward the realities of local politics, and, like many other federal agencies, OEO was strong in proclaiming general statements of purpose but weak in carrying them out. In many cities, the hard OEO line on City Hall was really a hunting license for established "out" politicians to take on the "in" politicians with righteous declarations that they represented the poor.

In New Haven, CPI was directly affected by the OEO policy because gradually it switched its funding source from the Ford Foundation to the federal government. A group of young civil rights activists and established political enemies of Lee's used the OEO mandate about Board composition to attack CPI. Some seemed genuinely interested in getting the poor on the CPI

Board. Others were primarily interested in grabbing headlines. During an early negotiating session with Sviridoff, for example, fifteen of a group of thirty civil rights bargainers left the meeting after twenty minutes to attend a previously scheduled news conference during which they were to announce that the negotiations had failed.

Even more dismaying was the performance of an OEO inspection team which came to the city to discuss Board representation with the CPI Board. Two of the team were particularly critical of Lee's dominant role in New Haven. One Board member asked if OEO thought that Lee tried to represent the poor in his city. The OEO inspector replied:

"The problem with your mayor is that he's too far ahead of the people. He throws out these new programs before the people even ask for them. There's no room for protest. He's controlling the people."

At this point another inspector asked, "Who is the mayor in this city?" And that, of course, was in several ways an example of unforgivable ignorance.

The biggest complaint one can make against OEO is a weakness which characterizes many large bureaucracies; namely, that a highly sophisticated program philosophy becomes a crude, blundering oversimplication after it passes through hundreds of hands. It seems clear that in framing the policy of maximum feasible participation of the poor, the top staff at OEO had several areas of anti-poverty programming in mind, including neighborhood organization, neighborhood project planning, and the hiring of poor for anti-poverty projects. Yet under the management of many of its staff, this OEO policy was geared primarily toward the formal, easily identified question of Board composition. OEO's principal target in New Haven became the CPI Board, and very little attention was paid to the background of CPI employees and the quality and integrity of neighborhood groups. This was a serious mistake. A little OEO staff work might have shown that New Haven had compiled a strong recent record of winning over citizen boards to promote staff policies. There was little reason to believe that the inclusion on the CPI

Board of "indigenous types," as one OEO staffer annoyingly referred to them, would alter this trend.

All the time OEO was pushing for Board expansion Sviridoff would grumble, but tucked away in his desk drawer was a plan for Board expansion that he was waiting to produce at the right moment. He was bargaining the way he used to for the U.A.W., and the OEO bureaucrats were no match for him. In September, 1965, Sviridoff "conceded" and OEO accepted his proposal, now implemented, which called for seven additional members on the CPI Board and a resident advisory committee. OEO had played to Sviridoff's strength, and the question of the involvement of the poor in CPI programs was never raised again.

This brief recital of OEO efforts to involve the poor in the anti-poverty program of one city is meant only to indicate the frailties and limitations of bureaucratic action. Eventually the noble concept of participation of the poor was negotiated by a handful of people, the usual people, and the poor were not represented even at this bargaining table. That is not necessarily bad; it is mainly illuminating. It demonstrates one of many ways in which the federal government is too large to be responsive to different local conditions, and how its policy declarations can stimulate, but not guarantee, change. Perhaps this point is obvious to some, but it may not be to those who rely mainly on journalistic accounts to judge the effectiveness of their government. The press falls for such slogans as "war on poverty," and the war image suggests agreements on appropriations and unity of purpose. The "war on poverty" is nothing of the sort. It is much more a bargaining session among such highly conventional players as congressmen, federal administrators, local politicans, and civil rights leaders.

Implied in the account of CPI and its activities are similar human and bureaucratic frailties. The real potential of CPI to overcome poverty is often obscured by the flutter of program dollars and the intensity of its activities. The local papers have not done a good job of describing its chances of success or its actual operations. They have succumbed to their own slogans and given CPI the popular image of a "test tube" program run by "pie in the sky" liberals who have turned New Haven into a giant "laboratory." In reality CPI is a utilitarian vehicle for change which runs on a hope and a prayer. The hope is that the economy will expand; the prayer is that the poor will respond.

"I'm not going anywhere, but my kids are going to make it. My kids are going to be scrubbed, dressed, go to school, read, and get good jobs."

"I want nothing from you or any other white man—no handout, no do-gooder, no public housing. I'm going to make it on my own."

"I look at your suit, them shoes, your briefcase, and that fancy recording machine and you ask me what I want in life. . . . Man, I want your job."

The Ford Foundation and the federal government can provide the money. CPI can provide the outlets. But the three people quoted above and thousands more like them are going to have to do it themselves.

Reprise:

Election Day

It was 9:30 A.M., Election Day, November 2, 1965. The air was crisp, the sky was clear, and the activity at the polls was just beginning to slacken after the early morning rush. Richard Charles Lee was running for his seventh two-year term, his ninth try to become the Mayor of New Haven.

He had risen early, attended a 7 A.M. Mass, and, during a hearty breakfast, reflected on some of the meaning of the day's events. "You know," he had said at one point, "if I win today I become the senior U.S. mayor. Bob Wagner was, but he retired. I'm not sure that's a good distinction, but who would ever have thought I'd prove to be this durable?"

After breakfast he took his children to school and then drove with his wife to the polls, where they posed for the press and cast two sure votes for Lee. While taking his wife back to their house, Lee was unusually silent and pensive. It was not hard to imagine some of his thoughts. Here for the ninth time he was casting his future and his family's future to the wishes of voters. Lee seldom spoke of these dangers. He always seemed invigorated by, rather than fearful of, the Election Day process. It provided him with opportunities to measure his successes and failures. Later he would sift through the returns and interpret the neighborhood-by-neighborhood effect of his programs and personal appeal.

Lee was pleased and proud that the election had taken on some national significance. A few days before, the New York *Times* had endorsed him with an editorial suggesting that the differences between Lee and his Republican opponent, Joseph

223

Einhorn, accentuated the fundamental issues facing most cities. Einhorn had emerged as a candidate of those who opposed school integration. He had also criticized urban renewal and the local anti-poverty program. "Under the forceful leadership of Mayor Lee," the *Times* editorial writer said, "New Haven has in recent years become an inspiration to other cities trying to solve these problems." The writer concluded that "Mayor Lee's defeat would not only block progress for New Haven but would dishearten people working for reform and innovation in many other American cities."

Any national significance noted in this election was further emphasized by the people who came to New Haven to endorse Lee's programs, directly or indirectly. Lady Bird Johnson toured local architecture, Marian Anderson dedicated a housing project, Vice-President Humphrey held a mayors' conference at the local Jewish Community Center, and Senator Robert Kennedy came "to help Mayor Lee" because "that's what my late brother would have done."

The political pros and polls indicated that Lee was a heavy favorite, and to some the day's results were mainly a question of plurality. Lee's past performances had conditioned the city to expect that he would pull around 60 per cent of the vote—a margin of from 10,000 to 15,000, depending on the turnout. "A Mayor like me," Lee said, "has to pull big pluralities. Otherwise they're tired of me." There was a factor in this election which was hard to gauge. Einhorn was running largely on the discontent engendered by school integration, an issue which had torn the community apart in 1964. No one could say for sure how the issue would affect the election.

After Lee drove his wife back to their home, his mood changed dramatically. Now there was work to do and no time for reflection. "Let's go mine the gold," he exclaimed as he walked from his house to the family station wagon parked in front. He was followed by his driver, his brother Ray, and a few close friends who carried a various assortment of Election Day materials, including a police short-wave radio, maps, election lists, pencils, and pads. Lee was his effervescent self as he sat in the front of the car to lead the expedition through the main streets and back alleys of New Haven. He was off to tour the entire city, "to get a feel of the vote," and "to give party workers a goose."

The first stop was at nine-forty at a ward headquarters in the western part of the city which has painful memories for Lee; this was where the Democrats still claim that in 1951 a Republican moderator turned away six hundred Lee votes before the polls officially closed. Ever since, Lee has been compulsive about Election Day details, and his tour of ward headquarters was designed both to charge party workers and to check on them. As he walked into the headquarters, Lee's tone was that of an inspecting general.

"One of the cars in front has no Lee stickers on it. Why not? I have a bunch of them in the rear of my station wagon. Go get them and put them on right away."

To the woman checker working the voting list he said, "How's the ward vote compared to this time in 1963?" She replied that the turnout was about the same. "What does that mean?" he demanded. "Where's the '63 list? You don't have one? For Christ's sake," he said, turning to the ward chairman, "find this lady a '63 list so she knows what she's doing. What kind of an operation is this? Damn it, there's Lee gold in this ward. Go out and get it and know what you've got compared to '63."

"Now, look, everyone," Lee said addressing all the workers, "we've waged a positive campaign. We've shaken twenty thousand hands, we've gone to the shops, the factory gates, the press, the radio, the TV. We've campaigned as never before and it feels good—not just good, it feels great. Now it's up to you to get it out. It's there, so get it out. Get it for me, get it for us, and we'll have a victory and we'll have a celebration like never before. I'm counting on you. See you tonight." At this point the workers broke into applause. Lee shook hands and made his way to the door.

"I just can't get some of these wards to do it the way they should," he said to his brother as he got back into the car. "About the only thing I can do is goose them." One of the other passengers returned to the car with some school straw votes he had received over the phone from Lee's office downtown. In New Haven all schools have mock elections and the results indicate voting trends, particularly when matched against those of previous years which are carefully retained by Lee's staff. Reliable or not, the school votes are the first concrete indication of how an election might go and Lee meticulously analyzes any and all Election Day information.

As the car proceeded to its next destination, Lee judged that the school votes were encouraging. In the eastern section of the city, where there is a heavy Republican vote, he showed an edge in the school results. In predominantly Negro schools he was, as usual, way out in front, 90 to 1 in one of them. But, most important, in white neighborhoods which were affected by the city's school integration plan, he showed an increase over 1963.

The car was moving toward a public housing project on the extreme western edge of the city. It was nine-fifty. Lee motioned to his driver to stop at the road leading into the project next to a guard at a school crossing.

"Hey, Mary," Lee said to the guard, "How's the vote?"

"Hi, Mr. Mayor," the guard said as she leaned on the door. "Looks about the same as two years ago."

"Good."

"You know," she said quietly, "if it weren't for this uniform, I'd be helping out."

"Well, you're off now until noon, aren't you?"

"Yes."

"Well, change into something else and get out there if you want."

"Can I?"

"Sure. Go ahead."

"O.K., Mr. Mayor. Good luck."

"O.K., Mary. Come on down to the party tonight. It's at the Taft right after the returns are in."

"O.K., Mr. Mayor. See you then."

The car now pulled up in front of one of the public housing apartments, which was ward headquarters in this section of the city. There were only four people in the room.

"Where's everyone?" Lee demanded.

"They're all out driving people to the polls, Dick," a worker said.

"Good. How's the vote?"

"A little better than '63."

"Good. Where's your phone? I want to call party headquarters. The first of the absentee ballots should be counted by now."

Lee was on the phone for about one minute. As he put down the receiver, there was a smile on his face. He revealed that the absentee votes from the 15th ward, an area of controversy over school integration, showed him ahead by 52 to 23, two votes over the previous election. He concluded the ward visit with the customary pep talk and an invitation to come to the election party that night. At this point Lee and his friends transferred themselves, their charts, papers, and portable short-wave radio to a larger car—a huge black limousine borrowed from a funeral home. As Lee got in the front seat, he remarked, "It's too early to celebrate, but at least we can have some fun." He reached into the glove compartment of the borrowed car, took out a pennant marked "FUNERAL," and stuck it on top of the dashboard. "If anyone asks, we're going to a Republican wake."

It was ten-fifteen as the Mayor's party entered the heartland of traditional Lee support, six wards in the northeast of the city which included the neighborhood where Lee was born and raised. This was a largely blue-collar area, with ethnic enclaves —Irish, Polish, Negro, and some Italian. For the most part, these were "bread and butter" Democrats, the kind who probably voted for Al Smith in 1928 but couldn't understand Adlai Stevenson in 1952. The voters of this area of the city never gave strong support to urban renewal; many were generally upset by school integration. They wondered why Lee ever got involved in anti-poverty programs, and they never could take the fancy-talking young liberals he had surrounded himself with at City Hall. But they could forgive Lee these faults because he was a neighborhood boy; he spoke their language; he showed up when they needed him at wakes, confirmations, and weddings; his administration had produced jobs; and he was, after all, a good Democrat.

The strong ties between Lee and the blue-collar Democratic vote were most evident when the Mayor toured plants and shops during the campaign. His reception in the office areas was usually coolly reserved, but when he stepped into the noise and grime of the assembly lines there was warmth. At the dress shops the women mobbed him; at a wood mill a man had grabbed his hand and whispered, "Kick the hell out of this guy, Dick"; at a hardware factory there were homemade signs with "Welcome Dick Lee"; and in the individual work areas of many plants one would sometimes see pictures of the Mayor and his family tacked up side by side with family photographs.

Although there were hardly any people on the streets as the limousine pulled into one ward, Lee seemed to know those who were walking on that cool November day. From the car he yelled greetings to passersby.

"Hey, Harry, you still sober?"

"Dahelia—hey, Dahelia—how many times you voted today?"

"Hey, Jack, remember—vote early and often!"

"Hi, give my regards to your mother."

At one ward headquarters, a deserted store where Lee had received his first haircut, it was time to call for more absentee vote results. In the neighborhood where Lee was born, the vote was 112 to 9. In another blue-collar ward it was 72 to 20, in another 109 to 29, in one more 21 to 3.

Lee revealed these results to the assembled party workers, all of whom were Negro, and they applauded. "Now, look," Lee cautioned. "These results are good, but to me they mean that we have to work even harder. Who's got a list?" Someone produced a voting list which Lee examined and then said, "Most of those you haven't got are Lee votes. Now, take this street, that's an all-white street, and I don't want any Negro canvassing it. You understand?"

"We understand," said one of the Negroes, smiling. "We hired some white boys to canvass there, Mr. Mayor." "Well, where are they?" asked Lee. "We're working their tails off here right now," answered a worker, pointing to another street on the list. "But when they finish over there, we'll move them over here, don't you fear, Mr. Mayor." "O.K. boys," said Lee, "See you tonight."

The time was now eleven o'clock and the voting had reached the slowest pace of the day. The next two wards on the list were in marked contrast with the previous six. Both were located in neighborhoods populated by old-line Yankees, members of the Yale faculty, and middle-class Irish and Italian families. As opposed to the dingy store-front or back-room headquarters, the party nerve centers here were located in the finished basement of a middle-class home and on the second floor of a rather imposing Elks' lodge. The party workers were well scrubbed, neatly dressed, and politely enthusiastic. Lee's pep talk, however, was the same, although some color was removed from the language. He revealed the school vote and the first of the absentee returns, and concluded with a strong appeal to get out the vote.

The trip to the last two wards before lunch took Lee and his party back into a blue-collar area. In the first of these, the 14th ward, the party was so well organized that there was little Lee could say except to praise the workers lavishly and, as he had done in the other elections, invite his car companions in "to see what a first-rate ward organization looks like." The ward alderman, Bart Guida, had a personal organization which had worked with him during his more than twenty years on the Board of Aldermen. The 14th ward did not operate from a standard voting list but from a card file which indicated how each resident in the ward had voted over the years, how many voters there were in the family, and where each of them was on Election Day.

The last ward headquarters on the itinerary before lunch was at the back of the St. Stanislaus Church and School. Lee entered the school and was besieged by about fifty schoolboys who were on recess. They shook his hand, patted him on the back, and wished him good luck. Lee finally broke away and made his way to their teacher, whom he gave a pinch on the cheek and asked,

"Did you vote for me, Sister?" The blushing sister replied that the entire school staff had, and Lee asked her to say a prayer for him.

When he arrived at ward headquarters in the rear of the school, he joshed with the workers, urged them, of course, to get out the vote, and then worked his way past another group of shouting children to an exit.

It was now twelve noon. Election Day was half over. On the way back to City Hall, Lee discussed the morning's events:

"Well, it looks good, very good. I have worked hard on two campaigns: mine and his. I was positive, I hit my record, and I ignored him, never once mentioned his name. He had one big issue—the schools—and I took it away from him. He couldn't run on the need for an elected School Board because I turned over the entire question to the Charter Revision Commission. I gave the Board a new image by appointing a new President. He wanted to debate school integration, but I played only to my strong issues. The real question now is how much Henchel will hurt me."

On the basis of some school votes and a few absentee ballots, Lee had evidently concluded that he was winning and that school integration was not playing a major role in the election. His mention of Charles Henchel was the first time that day he had spoken of a relatively minor but nonetheless important side issue in the election. Henchel had been Town Chairman Barbieri's choice to run as the Democratic candidate for Judge of Probate, an office which had recently become vacant. His name was first among the Democratic candidates, including Lee's, on the voting machine. The mandatory party lever* on Connecticut voting machines made Henchel's candidacy important to his running mates. If he was an unpopular candidate, he could adversely affect the rest of the ticket, since voters would be

* The mandatory party automatically casts a vote for all the candidates of one party, Republican or Democrat. If one wishes to split his vote between party candidates, the lever for one of the parties must be pulled, the individual candidates of that party which one does not wish to vote for must be negated one by one, and then the individual levers of those candidates of the other party one prefers must be pulled. Party levers were made optional in 1966.

attracted to his Republican opponent and, because of the party lever, to the other Republican candidates. Conversely, if he was a strong candidate, that would be good for the other Democrats.

The judgeship Henchel sought is a legal anachronism that survives because the Judge of Probate is a dispenser of considerable patronage. All local estates go through the court, and the judge assigns appraisers to verify estate value. The appraiser jobs, and the high fees which go with them, are handed out to party faithfuls. Henchel's Republican opponent had campaigned to "reform" the court, which he claimed was corrupt. He had even charged that Henchel and Barbieri had received appraiser fees from the court in the past. Henchel had defended the court thereby minimizing the importance of any abuses which may have accompanied the court's operations. Both Barbieri and Lee were agreed that Henchel was waging a poor campaign, but they seemed privately pleased because it gave them an opportunity to test their strength. Barbieri never said it, but during the last days of the campaign he seemed to relish the idea that he had a weak candidate heading the ticket; if the party still won with a large plurality, that would be a great testimony to the pulling power of the party organization; i.e., Barbieri. Lee was equally silent about his motivations, but he appeared anxious to show that he could outdraw an organization candidate who headed the ticket, and that Democratic voters might split against Henchel but would not split against Lee. A friendly game of power politics was under way between Lee the Mayor and Barbieri the political leader.

Lee's observations on the election, and particularly on his votes in relation to Henchel's, stopped as the limousine approached the rear of the *Register* building, where one of the workmen loading the afternoon edition walked over to Lee's car, handed him a paper marked "office copy," and wished him good luck. During the short drive from the *Register* building to City Hall, Lee skimmed the paper, which was filled with the usual Election Day background stories. It was shortly after noon when the limousine arrived at City Hall. Lee and his coterie quickly got out and went up the steps, into the faded main corridor, up the rickety elevator, and out into Lee's second-floor office. Telephoning immediately to Democratic Headquarters, Lee asked, "What's the absentee count? . . . What do you mean you don't have them all? The damned things were counted a half hour ago. Get a full rundown and call me right back."

Five minutes later a party worker called with a full tabulation of the absentee votes. They were encouraging as far as Lee's re-election was concerned, but inconclusive on the question of how well he would draw compared to Henchel. But now, at midday, Lee had all the election information available until the polls closed. There was a chance that later in the afternoon Lee would learn of some direct voting booth results. These insights were not provided by machine breakdowns, as is commonly believed, but were evidently derived by having a worker stationed in front of voting booths where the curtains did not close tightly. According to political legend in New Haven, there were—and perhaps still are—voting machines placed in the lobbies of large buildings where a worker located on a balcony or stairway over the lobby could, with the use of binoculars, get a clear picture of the action in the voting booth. The reliability of these accounts of poll watching is open to some question, for as far as one can tell, the management of voting processes in New Haven appears to be scrupulously honest. Certainly it was not Lee's plan to receive voting data throughout the rest of the day. In fact he was now anxiously pacing his office wondering how to keep fully occupied.

"Mike," Lee said to his driver, who had just entered the room with a sandwich for him, "I think we'll squeeze some wakes in this afternoon. Let me see that paper again." Lee turned to the obituary page and, while munching on his sandwich, studied the list of the deceased. One of his secretaries then informed him that McQueeney, the Managing Editor of the *Register,* was on the phone wanting to know what time would be convenient the next morning to take a victory picture of Lee and his family. "Guess Charlie thinks we're in," said Lee as he picked up the phone.

"Hello, Charlie, what do you hear?" Lee kept reading the paper as McQueeney told him what he had heard. "Is that so?"

Lee replied automatically. "Say, Charlie, should I go to this
——— wake? Do I know anyone in that family? . . . No sur-
vivors? Well, I'll say a prayer for him instead on my way to the
tenth ward. . . . Oh, yeah? Well, send the photographer to the
house around eight-thirty tomorrow morning. We'll be ready for
him. O.K., Charlie. I'll see you."

It was now twelve-thirty. As one of the Mayor's secretaries
brought in some more sandwiches, Lee's party gathered around
the office conference table for lunch. Someone remarked that if
Lee's conference table could talk it could tell some harrowing
tales. It was part of the refurnishing job Lee gave the Mayor's
Office in 1954, and since then it has been the scene of most
major administration decisions, heartbreaks, and successes. Irate
businessmen have bled on it, unhappy politicians have pounded
on it, civil rights leaders have presented ideas over it, labor
leaders have negotiated on it, developers have laid plans on it,
and Lee has always sat at the head of it. It was here that developer Roger Stevens decided to work with the city in rebuilding downtown New Haven, and it was here that the Stevens'
project fell apart and was patched together more times than
anyone wanted to remember. It was here that highway officials
were told where to build their highways, that businessmen were
told where to invest their money, that federal officials were told
where to grant their funds, and that contractors were told where
to stick their bribes. It was here that Macy's announced it would
build in New Haven, and it was here that it was announced that
the Ford Foundation would grant the city $2,500,000 to begin a
pilot anti-poverty program. But if there was that moment to
think of the past, there was no time to linger on it. "Let's get
going," said Lee.

The first stop of the afternoon was a restaurant in the Wooster
Square area, an Italian neighborhood. As the car stopped, Lee
turned to one of his friends and said, "Go in the back to the
kitchen, and if Ranger is there find out what the line is on the
election." Ranger is the name of a New Haven bookmaker who
has a good reputation for predicting the outcome of local elections and a bankroll to prove it. In about three minutes the

friend returned, saying, "Ranger says a plurality for Lee of 16,800 votes." "What did he say about Henchel?" asked Lee. "Ranger said nothing," the friend replied.

The limousine maneuvered through the narrow streets of the Wooster Square neighborhood, past a new cooperative housing development, a handsome new retail area, and a row of rehabilitated houses, and then, on Lee's request, stopped briefly in front of a new community school. "You see the senior citizens center, right there?" Lee was pointing at one part of the school complex which includes four buildings—a library, an auditorium, a classroom building, and the senior center. "Well, ever since we built this complex three years ago, the old folks have had my picture hanging in their recreation area. In the last election one of the Republican candidates came and tried to take it down. We had to get the police down here to save him from being lynched."

As the car proceeded farther down the street, Lee observed, "Fifteen people were killed in a factory fire on that school site eight years ago. I've done more for this neighborhood than any other in the city. Yet the Italians here have always gone Republican. Damn it all, would I like to win it this time!"

The car stopped at the end of the street in front of ward headquarters. Lee hurried inside. "How's it going?" he asked the ward chairman. "Pretty good," replied the chairman through a bite of huge sandwich dripping with lettuce, ham, salami, onion rings, and sliced olives. The chairman waved at a table in the center of the room. "Help yourself to some pasta, Dick." "Damn you paisanos," replied the Mayor. "If I ate all the time like you do, I wouldn't have half a stomach left, I'd have none at all. How's the vote?" "Pretty good, Dick," said the chairman, taking another bite from his magnificent sandwich.

"There are sixty-seven votes in the convent across the street. Did all the sisters vote yet?"

"Umph," said the chairman, nodding his head. He waved his sandwich in the direction of a young girl who was sitting at a desk marking the voting sheet. "Dick, I want you to meet Mrs. ———, who is working with us for the first time this year."

"I know your husband," Lee said, looking at the girl. "He

played for Hillhouse a few years back, didn't he?" The girl nodded. "Well, it's a pleasure to meet his wife. Give him my regards." He turned to the ward chairman. "Now, look, I think we can get this ward. Are you getting out the Lee vote?" "Sure, Dick, sure," said the chairman as he wiped his mouth with a handkerchief. "Well, you'd better." Lee turned to the other workers. "See you tonight at headquarters. Keep up the good work." There was applause as the Mayor left the building. "Maybe this is the year this ward will do something right," he said, getting back into the car, "but my friend in there won't have anything to do with it."

The Mayor's party headed along Grand Avenue to the Fair Haven district. "Stop the car up here," Lee said to his driver. "I want to razz my friend." Pointing to a heavy-set policeman directing traffic ahead, Lee yelled out the window, "Damn it, ————, if you get any fatter I'll have to make this a one-way street!" "Ah, Mayor," replied the cop, "I've lost two pounds since you were last here." "Where, in your head? The least you can do is not stand sideways when you're moving traffic." "O.K., Mayor," said the cop, with a smile.

While touring ten more ward headquarters between one-thirty and three-thirty, Lee chastised a policeman for not correctly guarding a street excavation, made a quick inspection of a new industrial area, lectured a truck driver who was driving carelessly, noted a construction site where he wanted the Redevelopment Agency to be careful about how the developer landscaped his property, and exchanged family information with the wife of a former Republican mayoral candidate.

At three-forty-five, during visits to the five final wards in the Hill area of New Haven, the Mayor's party met Democratic Town Chairman Barbieri's party, which consisted of Judge of Probate candidate Henchel, Congressman Robert Giaimo, and one of Giaimo's campaign staff from the preceding year. While Henchel remained in Barbieri's car and Giaimo disappeared into the nearby ward headquarters, Lee and Barbieri exchanged Election Day information on the sidewalk. During the conversation Lee heard that party polling booth sources had reported that he was way ahead of his Republican opponent and that Henchel, too, was winning but trailing Lee by an indefinite number.

It was now four o'clock, the beginning of the city's big Democratic vote as the shops and factories released their workers to the early dusk of November. It is between four and six—the time of the homeward-bound factory vote—that Democrats are normally elected. There was no more that Lee could do.

Quite accidentally but symbolically the Mayor's limousine headed back downtown from the Hill area on a street crowded on both sides with run-down brick tenements and garbage-strewn alleys. But to the right, visible through the lots that spaced the tenements, was the outline of the $4,000,000 Saarinen-designed Hill High School. And in front, rising from the road ahead, was the city's new skyline, bordered in front by heavy expressway traffic, on the side by Paul Rudolph's parking garage, and topped by the bare steel of a new office tower which caught the last rays of the low November sun. A director could not have staged it more aptly; no one view could better have shown what the Lee years in New Haven were all about.

Lee instructed his driver to take him through the downtown area to the Yale Gym, where, after a steam bath, he would pick up his wife and children and then travel to the neighborhood where he was born and receive the final voting results. As the car passed the construction site for a new hotel and office tower, Lee asked his driver to stop for a moment. He got out, looked up at the buildings, took in the sight of it all, and got back in and sighed. "Well, whatever happens, it's been worth it," he said. As one of the car's passengers looked up at the steel frame of the office tower, he could clearly see what the setting sun was catching at the top of the building. On the highest beam one of the steelworkers had chalked, "VOTE FOR DICK LEE."

At five-forty that afternoon there was unusual activity in front of a deserted store on Shelton Avenue in the Newhallville section. Three police cars and a row of motorcycles were stationed at the curb, engines running, emergency lights blinking. Farther down the street, seven black limousines were double-parked, engines set at idling speed.

The two hundred or so people from the neighborhood who had been attracted to the excitement were standing in a crowd shaped like an hourglass, with a large group milling around the sidewalk in front, a line two abreast squeezing to get through the door, and another large group crammed inside. At the far end of the room were a battered desk with a telephone on top and ten empty wooden chairs.

Since 1951 this shabby store had been Mayor Lee's personal headquarters on Election Night. This was the neighborhood of his birth; the crowds were his neighbors of many years, and this was the place where they would share the returns.

At exactly five-fifty-six, Lee, his wife, two of their three children, his mother, brother, sister, and their immediate families arrived in front of the store and filed inside. The crowd, knowing their roles well by now, politely made a path, applauded enthusiastically, and merged again as soon as the family had passed.

Lee and his family took their customary seats at the end of the hall, Lee in front of his desk with his young son, David, on his lap. Mrs. Lee sat to his right, their daughter Sally stood between them, and the remainder of the family fanned out in and behind the chairs on both sides of the desk. While Lee's brother Ray established the telephone connection with Democratic Headquarters, the Mayor nodded smilingly to faces in the crowd. At one minute after six Ray Lee handed the phone to his brother, and Lee handed his son to his wife. The results of the election were now coming in.

This store on Shelton Avenue may be the only place in America where an observer can learn second-by-second election returns from one of the candidates, for as Lee scribbled down the results he received on the phone and passed them to his wife, who in addition to minding their son was now compiling a master list, he would call out highlights to the crowd.

"Twenty-fourth ward—993 for Einhorn, 1,367 for Lee." There was applause and Lee waved the crowd quiet.

"Fourteenth ward—524 for Einhorn, 984 for Lee." Again the crowd applauded and again Lee hushed them.

"Seventeenth ward—1,210 for Lee, 197 for Einhorn." The

applause was heavy, and Lee let the crowd carry on, for they were cheering the results from their own neighborhood. Then, for forty seconds of silence, Lee jotted down results. The only way people in the room could judge what was happening was by the expression on his face, which gradually broadened from intense, nervous interest to a grin, and he suddenly exploded with wild delight.

"Yowee! Tenth ward—363 for Lee and 116 for Einhorn!" For the first time Lee had carried the Italians in Wooster Square, and now he joined in the jubilant applause.

A landslide was in the making. Lee quickly got back to the phone to enjoy every detail of it. There was a long period of silence broken finally by Lee's exuberant announcement that he had carried every district through the 29th ward, except the 19th, which had delayed in reporting because, Lee quipped, "Somebody must have tried to vote Republican."

Thirty seconds later he announced that he had carried every ward in the city. His over-all victory was 33,392 to 17,099. He had received a record-setting 66 per cent of the vote. What he diplomatically chose not to reveal was that he had run far ahead of the organization candidate for Judge of Probate, Charles Henchel. Henchel had received only 29,662 votes. After making a short impromptu speech to the neighbors in his "clubhouse," Lee and his family and friends got into the limousines out front, and with motorcycles and police cars leading the way, the Lee victory caravan cut through the evening darkness for the celebration downtown.

Lee left the victory parties early. By 11:00 P.M. he was home, lounging in his slippers and pajamas, smoking his pipe, and enjoying the quiet of his study. During the past two years he has spent many of his evening hours in this room which he designed himself and enjoys as the fulfillment of one of his boyhood dreams. For privacy was a luxury in the neighborhood where he was born and raised.

He seemed relaxed and refreshed despite the hectic activities of the day. He also seemed sad, but this may have been because of the setting, for the study was filled with reminders of the past.

He was alone; the house and neighborhood were quiet. Un-
characteristically, he was doing nothing more than sitting and
gazing at the ceiling.

On the wall across from him hung two pictures of his good
friend, Whit Griswold. One showed the late Yale President
awarding Lee his cherished honorary degree. The other was of
Griswold, alone, playing his flute. Near these was a picture of
another important figure in Lee's life, Carl Lohmann, and Lohmann, too, was gone. Across the room were books and memen-
toes which, like the pictures, recalled major events in his life or
people who were special to him. Some of them recalled the joy
and the sadness he has known. There was an album with pictures
of the young men of "the Kremlin," of Logue, and of the old and
new city. There were the records of his ill-fated 1951 campaign.
There were books by and about the late John F. Kennedy.

All of these memories must have been in Lee's thoughts in the
solitude of Election Day night. How he regarded the memories—
with regret, sadness or pleasure—was impossible for even him to
say, but perhaps a clue is given in a conversation he had in this
same room a few weeks earlier. A former colleague had visited
him and during their conversation Lee was asked whether he had
regretted letting opportunities such as the United States Senate
nomination in 1958 pass by, or if he felt cheated as he saw some
of his former aides achieve national acclaim while he remained
the Mayor of New Haven, Connecticut.

"Sure," he had said, "every once in a while I have my regrets,
but then I think I still have a lot of living to do, and I've already
done something that few men will ever do—I've rebuilt a city,
not just any city, mind you, but a city I love."

The next morning he arrived at his office at nine-thirty. He accepted with delight the congratulations of the elevator men,
secretaries, and staff, and then made his first call, to the *Register*
to find out what kind of editorial they would run. Next he dictated
some letters, reprimanded a young secretary for misspelling a
name, and asked that his Development Administrator, Melvin
Adams, be reached on the phone. After receiving several congratulatory calls, he glanced over the agenda for the Board of

Finance, struck one item, asked that his Director of Administration be summoned to his office, and then picked up the phone to speak to Adams. "Mel," he said, "bring over that State Street model right away. One of the banks called me and wants to get into the project."

The Mayor's game was by no means over. He had just been given another turn.

Appendix

CHRONOLOGY OF MAJOR EVENTS

1941

June   The City Plan Department is established.

1942

July   The master plan is approved in principle, subject to any detailed changes necessary in the future.

1949

July   The Housing Act of 1949 is signed by President Truman, providing federal aid to communities for slum clearance and new housing.

November   New Haven Mayor William Celentano defeats his Democratic opponent, Richard Lee, an alderman:

Celentano	34,923
Lee	34,211

1950

June   New Haven signifies its intention to seek aid under the Housing Act of 1949 through an aldermanic resolution.

August   Mayor Celentano creates a Redevelopment Agency upon the urging of the City Plan Department.

October   A. Whitney Griswold inaugurated as President of Yale University.

November   Norris Andrews is made Director of the City Plan Department.

241

1951

May Maurice Rotival is appointed as a consultant to develop project outlines according to the city master plan.

October Andrews and the Executive Director of the Redevelopment Agency, Samuel Spielvogel, begin negotiations with the State Highway Department on the alignment of the Connecticut Turnpike, the Oak Street connector, and relocated Route 5 (eventually Interstate 91).

November Mayor Celentano again beats his Democratic opponent, Richard Lee:

Celentano	34,303
Lee	34,287

A court later rules that Celentano won by just two votes.

December Planning begins on the Oak Street Project.

1952

March Mayor Celentano appoints a relocation commission to develop plans and policies for displacement caused by the Connecticut Turnpike and possible redevelopment action.

1953

June Rotival and the city planners make their recommendations for highway placements; negotiations are under way with the Highway Department.

July Congress declares that before a city can qualify for redevelopment aid, it must have adequate codes and an enforcement program. New Haven moves to update its codes and pass a comprehensive Housing Code.

August Mayor Celentano joins in the negotiations with the Highway Department.

November Mayor Celentano loses to Richard Lee in the mayoral race:

Lee	39,526
Celentano	35,944

Mayor Celentano announces that the State Highway Department has agreed to shift Interstate 91 alignment

(Route 5) to save Wooster Square, has approved in principle the need for the Oak Street connector, and has agreed with the city's proposals for the Connecticut Turnpike. Construction proceeds on the Turnpike.

December   Lee has persuaded Logue to join him; the two are mapping the outlines of the redevelopment program Lee has promised in his campaign.

1954

January   1   Lee is inaugurated for his first term as Mayor of New Haven.

2   Lee appoints Arthur T. Barbieri, the Democratic Town Chairman, as Public Works Director and George Crawford as Corporation Counsel. He also sets up a fourteen-member Economy Committee, holds his first cabinet meeting, announces his intention to centralize purchasing and to eliminate individual department telephones.

4   Lee meets with the Police Board, overrules its choice for Assistant Police Chief, successfully pushes his own man.

5   Lee meets with the Fire Commissioners, announces a freeze on Fire Department salaries, refuses to back proposed promotions, raises the Fire Chief's salary.

7   Lee meets with the Board of Finance, removes the Personnel Officer from the meeting, starts assuming control of the fiscal machinery.

18   Lee announces a freeze on all city hiring. No employees can be hired without his personal approval.

February   1   Lee delivers his first State of the City Message to the Board of Aldermen; he stresses economy and a strong mayor's role in city government.

March   19   Barbieri fires fifty-two Public Works employees.

25   Lee proposes that a private consultant recommend reorganization of parking and traffic functions. Wilbur Smith & Associates are hired.

April   13   Lee holds his first meeting in New Haven with Highway Commissioner G. Albert Hill on the Oak Street connector. Conflicting views expressed by city officials impress Lee with the need for a single voice in negotiations and a reorganization of development functions. Smaller meetings continue with Hill on the connector.

May   6   Lee hires Fred A. Schuckman as his fiscal aide in dealing with the Board of Finance and municipal reorganization.

          16   Lee reorganizes office space for city departments.

          17   The U.S. Supreme Court rules that racial segregation in public schools is unconstitutional.

June   3   Lee appoints his mentor, Carl A. Lohmann, former Secretary of Yale University, to the Park Board. Lee appoints a Charter Revision Commission, thus beginning his first unsuccessful attempt at basic municipal reorganization. Behind the scenes, Lee is desperately trying to find someone to become Chairman of the Citizens Action Commission, which he had promised would be operating by June.

           5   Lee announces that the city will now function under a performance-type budget; Logue begins his budget rounds.

           6   The head of the city employees' union threatens litigation over the firing of fifty-two Public Works employees and other personnel practices of the new administration. He is reassigned as a milk inspector.

July   1   Wilbur Smith & Associates privately submit to Lee recommendations on the reorganization of traffic and parking functions. The consultants propose that traffic planning be taken out of the Police Department and placed in a new city department. Lee begins to line up support.

          24   Lee opens the first of twelve new neighborhood playgrounds.

August   2   President Eisenhower signs the Housing Act of 1954, with its broad provisions for urban renewal, planning, and rehabilitation.

          19   Maurice Rotival is hired by the city to do detailed redevelopment planning under the master plan. His staff reports to Lee and Logue.

29   The Wilbur Smith & Associates study on reorganization is made public. The consultants have now been ordered to devise a one-way street system for the city.

September 21   Lee appoints Mitchell Sviridoff, Assistant Regional Director of the C.I.O., and Maynard Mack, a Yale Professor of English, to the Board of Education.

26   Lee finally has his CAC Chairman, Carl G. Freese, a local bank president. The CAC is announced at a luncheon at the New Haven Lawn Club. Merritt W. Vanderbilt, a local manufacturer, and A. Whitney Griswold, President of Yale University, are Vice-Chairmen. Griswold and Lee are now beginning to develop their idea of Yale's purchasing three old high schools.

October   19   Lee and Highway Commissioner Hill agree on the Oak Street connector. Lee is now negotiating with the Southern New England Telephone Company to get them to abandon their plans for a new headquarters building which is in the right of way and to build, instead, in the Oak Street Project.

22   The Board of Finance recommends and the Board of Aldermen accepts Lee's first budget. His proposed 1955 program includes:

$17,806,875 for General Fund operating expenses,

400,000 for a Capital Improvement Fund,

2,200,000 in bonding for capital improvements, and

430,000 in estimated surplus from previous budget which Lee proposes to hold as a reserve fund.

The most significant part of Lee's first budget was that $1,405,000 more in taxes had been collected than was originally anticipated under the budget he inherited. Rather than use this to decrease taxes, Lee plowed the money into capital improvements and increases in the operating budgets of key city departments such as City Planning.

24   The new one-way street system is introduced.

November   2   Abraham Ribicoff defeats Republican incumbent John Lodge in the race for Governor of Connecticut.

18   H. Gordon Sweet becomes Executive Director of the Citizens Action Commission.

24   Lee consolidates the police districts.

December   10   William R. McGrath is appointed by Lee as director of a new city department of traffic and parking, with the first assignment of implementing the proposed one-way street system.

1955

January   17   Lee announces the appointment of a new Police Chief, Francis C. McManus.

21   The Executive Director of the Redevelopment Agency, Samuel Spielvogel, submits his resignation after a series of private clashes with Lee and Logue.

February   1   Nicholas deB. Katzenbach and Stephen Carroll, of Maurice Rotival's office, submit private reorganization proposals for the Redevelopment Agency pending action on the proposals being drafted by the Charter Revision Commission appointed by Lee the preceding June. This private report, which is circulated by Lee, recommends the appointment of a coordinator of all physical development activities. It recommends Logue for the job.

7   Lee gives his second State of the City Message, which deals mainly with routine matters and barely hints at the frantic behind-the-scenes reorganization and planning that he and Logue are engaged in on the renewal program.

10   Lee leads a large delegation composed of CAC members, top city bureaucrats, and representatives of the Chamber of Commerce on a tour of Philadelphia's urban renewal program and its renewal organization, including the post of Housing Coordinator for Philadelphia's program.

	24	Upon the recommendation of a special committee of the Board of Finance, Lee issues an executive order creating the post of Development Administrator and appoints Logue to fill it. He also makes Logue the Acting Director of the Redevelopment Agency.
	25	Fred A. Schuckman resigns as Lee's fiscal aide to become Governor Ribicoff's Budget Director.
	28	In his last act in office, Highway Commissioner Hill signs the agreement for the Oak Street connector.
March	3	A consultant hired by the Rotival office at Lee's request suggests that the city scrap all previous redevelopment planning and administration and start afresh. The consultant applauds Logue's appointment as a good first step. Logue is rushing to complete a final project report for the Oak Street area.
	9	The first approach is made to Roger L. Stevens to see if he would be interested in joining with the city in developing new commercial facilities downtown. Stevens is already involved in discussions with the University on a joint housing development proposal. Stevens indicates interest in commercial development, and throughout 1955 he joins with Lee and Logue in exploring the possibilities of strictly private development in the downtown area with no urban renewal assistance.
May	11	Logue characterizes New Haven as a "dying" city and begins a front-page fight with Malley's and other leading stores. Unknown to most people is that the basis for Logue's statement is a Louis Harris survey of shoppers who express criticism of many of the stores and a preference for the suburban shopping centers.
June	21	Public hearings begin on the proposals of the Charter Revision Commission. The Commission recommendations include a four-year term for mayor, the creation of a department of planning and development, and a department of finance.
	26	Lee opens a new animal shelter and goes on television to find homes for dogs and cats.

30   H. Ralph Taylor is appointed the new Executive Director of the Redevelopment Agency. Later, Harold Grabino and L. Thomas Appleby join the Redevelopment Agency and round out the top executive staff.

July   6   Lee unveils the proposal for Yale to buy three city high schools, the purchase price to be used to build two new high schools. He seeks and obtains approval by the Board of Aldermen and the Board of Education.

11   The Board of Aldermen authorizes the Redevelopment Agency to proceed with urban renewal planning in the Wooster Square neighborhood and an area vaguely described as the "wholesale market–Church Street extension area." Apparently no one reads the boundary description for this second area, for it includes the heart of the retail section downtown. By this time Stevens and his two new friends are beginning to realize that large-scale commercial development is impossible without urban renewal assistance.

September 11   The Board of Aldermen approves the sale of the high schools to Yale and a contract is later signed with the University. Under this contract the city is committed to vacate two of the high schools by June, 1957, and the third by June, 1958.

October   5   Philip E. Mancini, Jr., is nominated by the Republicans to run against Lee. He adopts a campaign critical of the sale of the high schools to Yale and portrays Lee as a sinister agent of the University.

20   Lee submits his budget for 1956. It includes:

$19,184,047 for General Fund operating expenses,

250,000 for a Capital Improvement Fund,

2,655,000 in bonding for capital improvements, and

545,700 as a surplus from 1955 which Lee proposes to use as a reserve fund.

The tax rate of 35.5 mills is maintained. The budget is accepted by the Board of Aldermen.

November 8 The municipal election returns are:

Mayor		Aldermen
Lee	43,847	31 Democrats
Mancini	23,039	2 Republicans

The proposed charter revision fails to pass.

December 8 Lee undergoes an operation for the removal of a stomach ulcer.

16 The Board of Aldermen authorizes the Redevelopment Agency to contract with the federal government to receive funds and begin the first renewal project, Oak Street.

1956

January 1 Lee is inaugurated for his second term.

26 Heman B. Averill is appointed by Lee as his Director of Administration, a new post created by executive order.

February 7 Lee presents his State of the City Message. Increasing emphasis is placed on urban renewal, planning for the future, but no details.

Lee's message provides a tone for the eleven months ahead. Publicly very little appears to be happening, but Stevens and the city are doing detailed planning, negotiations have started for Yale to build apartment buildings in the Oak Street Project, and the framework for the urban renewal program has been established.

March 5 The aldermen give final approval to the Oak Street Project and it begins.

April 2 The aldermen authorize the Redevelopment Agency to begin planning on a fourth urban renewal project, Dixwell.

May 7 The aldermen authorize the Redevelopment Agency to start detailed planning on the "wholesale market–Church Street extension area." No one, including the press, seems yet to have read the boundary description, which includes the heart of the retail section. By now the Church Street Project is taking shape.

June   29   President Eisenhower signs the Interstate Highway Act.

July   26   The federal government authorizes planning money for the Dixwell Project. Church Street plans are well under way.

August   28   The first controversy breaks out over the alignment of Interstate 91. The State Highway Department reveals its preliminary proposal to cut the road to the west of East Rock, through a park, and into suburban residential areas. Suburban protest starts.

September   4   The Highway Department suddenly announces five proposals for the interstate route. Controversy mounts. Ribicoff assures the towns that the proposals are tentative.

              10   The aldermen authorize the Redevelopment Agency to begin planning on a fifth urban renewal project, State Street. Again no one reads the boundary description, which includes much of the remainder of downtown New Haven.

              10   Lee calls a meeting of suburban officials to suggest a unified approach to the Highway Department on the alignment of Interstate 91. He suggests a regional planning agency to propose alignment on behalf of area towns. This leads to the creation of the Quinnipiac Valley Development Corporation (QVDC).

              16   Lee announces that the Southern New England Telephone Company will be the first developer in the Oak Street Project. The Board of Aldermen goes on to approve the land disposition contract.

October   19   The Board of Aldermen receives and accepts Lee's proposed 1957 budget, which includes:

$19,661,407 for General Fund operating expenses,

250,000 for a Capital Improvement Fund,

4,775,000 in bonding for capital improvements, and

642,500 in estimated surplus from the 1956 budget which will go into a reserve fund.

The tax rate of 35.5 mills is maintained.

1957

January   21   Lee leads a contingent from the CAC, city department heads, and representatives from the Chamber of Commerce to tour downtown urban renewal in Pittsburgh.

25   A factory fire in Wooster Square kills fifteen persons. Lee vows to clear old lofts under urban renewal.

February   4   In his annual message Lee dwells on the need for urban renewal.

13   Stevens submits a formal letter of intent to act as the major developer in Church Street.

March   3   Lee directs rat-eradication program in the Oak Street slums; 4,000 rodents killed.

4   Work finally starts on the city's two new high schools. Logue has pared the costs to meet available funds.

5   The Redevelopment Agency starts work on a light industrial park to house displaced business from the Oak Street Project.

10   Lee meets with Griswold to request that the city continue to use the old high schools Yale now owns beyond the agreed-upon dates. He asks that Yale not request $120,000 in interest that it is entitled to under the contract. Griswold agrees. Griswold is now having problems on the new hockey rink.

19   Lee announces that relocation is complete in the Oak Street Project. Demolition is now under way.

April   7   A shortage of federal urban renewal money threatens the funding of the Church Street Project and others New Haven has planned. Lee joins with seven other mayors in a meeting with President Eisenhower.

30   Yale and Roger Stevens announce that they will participate in an auction for land in the Oak Street

Project. The bidding will be for a housing development.

May   1 Albert M. Cole, Administrator of the Housing and Home Finance Agency, tours the New Haven projects, praises the scope of the program, pledges that New Haven will get funds for its projects.

        8 The Oak Street land auction is held. Yale loses to a Boston outfit.

     10 Construction starts on the first major redevelopment improvement, the new headquarters of the Southern New England Telephone Company.

     19 Carl A. Lohmann dies.

June   12 The Church Street Project and Stevens' participation are annnounced by Lee.

A bill creating the Quinnipiac Valley Development Corporation is passed by the Connecticut General Assembly. Logue becomes its Director, and it begins planning a new alignment for Interstate 91.

     25 Edith V. Cook, a state representative, is nominated by the Republicans to run against Lee. She is critical of Barbieri's management of Public Works, "reckless" spending, and high rents in the city.

September 3 The aldermen approve the Church Street Project. The Central Civic Association, Savitt, and the Hotel Taft start litigation against the project.

October 24 The aldermen receive and accept the administration budget for 1958, which includes:

        $21,165,482 for General Fund operating expenses,

             250,000 for the Capital Improvement Fund,

          3,435,000 in bonding for capital improvements, and

            366,500 in estimated surplus from the 1957 budget which will go into a reserve fund.

The tax rate of 35.5 mills is maintained.

November 5 The municipal election returns are:

	Mayor		*Aldermen*
Lee	41,694	32	Democrats
Cook	18,363	1	Republican

6   Newspaper stories speculate that Lee is the next Democratic nominee for the 1958 senatorial election.

December   12   The federal government approves the Church Street Project.

1958

January   1   Lee is inaugurated for his third term.

2   The Connecticut Turnpike is completed and opened to traffic. Work is now under way on the Oak Street connector.

16   Golden says Lee has the Democratic nomination for U.S. Senator if he wants it. Pressure is mounting on Lee to declare.

February   3   In his annual message, Lee introduces "human problems" of the slums and the need for help.

13   Lee says he will not run for the U.S. Senate.

March   14   Governor Ribicoff opens a special session of the General Assembly to consider anti-recession legislation. Throughout the nation 5,100,000 people are unemployed.

April   13   Stevens signs a contract with the city in which he agrees to purchase Church Street Project land at $18.69 a square foot for 230,274 square feet, or for approximately $4,300,000. Stevens is to take title to all the land the following May 1st.

18   Acquisition and relocation begin in the Church Street Project.

The special session of the General Assembly adjourns. Among the bills passed are Public Act 8 (state aid to industrial redevelopment projects) and Public Act 24 (state aid to urban renewal through the state payment of half of the local one-third share of the project cost).

May   5   A Charter Revision Commission is formed in Lee's second attempt to achieve basic municipal reorganization.

June	6	The state approves Wooster Square as the first project to receive aid under Public Act 24.
	10	Savitt temporarily stops his suit against the city on the Church Street Project.
	17	The Central Civic Association drops its case.
July	7	The Charter Revision Commission makes its recommendations, which include a four-year term for mayor and a new development department. The Quinnipiac Valley Development Corporation begins its alignment negotiations with the State Highway Department.
September	9	The two new high schools open for classes although they are not yet completed.
October	14	Since attempts at negotiation with Savitt have failed, the Redevelopment Agency goes to the Connecticut Superior Court to acquire his property through condemnation proceedings. Savitt challenges; the court rules in favor of the Agency. Savitt appeals to the Connecticut Supreme Court.
	23	The Board of Aldermen receives and approves Lee's budget for 1959, which includes:

$22,232,710 for General Fund operating expenses,
139,000 for a Capital Improvement Fund,
4,438,000 in bonding for capital improvements, and no surplus from 1958.

The tax rate of 35.5 is maintained.

	30	The aldermen approve the Long Wharf Redevelopment Project, which is designed to keep Sargent & Co., a hardware plant, in New Haven. The project, the city's sixth and the third to go into execution, proceeds.
November	5	Governor Ribicoff is re-elected. Thomas Dodd is elected to the U.S. Senate. The proposed new charter is defeated.
December	10	A survey reported in the newspapers shows that only 12 of the 355 CAC members knew that the CAC was taking a stand on the proposed charter.

23   City bond counsel rules that for bonding purposes the autonomous 32nd ward of New Haven will have to be annexed.

1959

| January | 5 | The Hotel Taft loses its appeal in its suit against the Church Street Project. |

January 5   The Hotel Taft loses its appeal in its suit against the Church Street Project.

21   Lee submits a bill to the General Assembly to annex the 32nd Ward. A huge protest ensues.

February 2   Lee's annual message is devoted primarily to urban renewal.

The aldermen give final approval to the Wooster Square Project. It becomes the fourth urban renewal project in execution.

March 4   H. Ralph Taylor announces his resignation as Executive Director of the Redevelopment Agency. Appleby is later picked as his successor.

17   The Connecticut Supreme Court of Errors orders a retrial of the Savitt case. This places the city in default of its agreement with Stevens, who is supposed to take title to his land in May.

18   Stevens announces he will stay in the project. He is now working to get Malley's into the project and to acquire the site of the First New Haven National Bank's proposed new headquarters building.

April 20   The Savitt case is settled out of court.

30   H. Gordon Sweet resigns as Executive Director of the CAC to become Director of the Long Wharf Project.

May 6   The General Assembly passes legislation under which the city annexes the 32nd ward.

June 17   The State Highway Department announces its alignment for Interstate 91. It follows most of the proposed QVDC alignment.

August 10   James J. Valenti, principal of a junior high school, becomes the Republican nominee to oppose Lee in the fall election. Valenti charges scandal in assessments, links them to Barbieri, attacks the Church Street Project, hits the rising city budget.

24 The First New Haven National Bank announces merger with another local bank and says it will quit the Church Street Project. Lee receives news while on a cruise wooing businessmen.

25 Stevens, in a New Haven speech, admits that the Church Street Project is in "a fluid state."

27 The CAC, in its first meeting in four months, selects Merritt W. Vanderbilt to succeed Lucius Rowe, who has resigned suddenly.

September 17 The President of the Chamber of Commerce criticizes the Lee administration for its handling of the Church Street Project.

27 Lee announces that Stevens is swapping sites with the Malley Estate and will build a new Malley store in the project. The roundup of Estate heirs begins.

October 13 Republicans charge that the Board of Assessors has made illegal reductions in assessments for friends and relatives of Barbieri.

16 The U.S. Attorney General rules that the proposed bank merger violates anti-trust laws. Bank is back in the construction business.

22 The Board of Aldermen receives and accepts Lee's budget for 1960, which includes:

$23,675,317 for General Fund operating expenses,
138,500 for a Capital Improvement Fund,
5,940,000 in bonding for capital improvements, and no surplus.

The tax rate of 35.5 mills is maintained.

26 The aldermen approve a new land contract for Stevens, enabling him to buy project land in four steps.

30 Stevens buys his first parcel of land in the project, the site for the new Malley store, for $1,281,573. He starts paying taxes and interest even though the building is still a year from construction.

The Oak Street connector is opened for traffic.

November 3 The results of the municipal election are:

	Mayor		*Alderman*
	Lee	36,694	27 Democrats
	Valenti	22,710	6 Republicans

	7	McGrath unveils a new one-way street system.
	12	Barbieri resigns as Public Works Director.
	30	A final alignment for Interstate 91 is settled upon.
December	1	Lee removes one of the members of the Board of Assessors and announces he will replace the Board with a single assessor with professional qualifications.

1960

January	1	Lee is inaugurated for his fourth term.
	2	John F. Kennedy announces he will run for President.
February	1	During his annual message Lee announces he will appoint a single assessor and improve assessment practices.
	19	Logue announces that he will accept an offer to direct the Boston urban renewal program. He will divide his time between Boston and New Haven until the end of the year.
May	18	Census data are released, showing a sharp increase in Negro population and a net decrease in over-all population.
	25	Ground is broken for Malley's store, although agreement with the Estate is still not final.
June	18	Progress Pavilion is erected on vacant Church Street Project.
July	14	Kennedy gets the Democratic nomination for President. Lee, who served on the Democratic Advisory Council, becomes adviser on urban problems.
	28	Lee urges Negroes to sit out on streets, block traffic, make homeward-bound suburbanites see their housing problems.
August	1	The Redevelopment Agency begins detailed planning for a huge General Neighborhood Renewal Plan in the southwest area of the city.

September 30 The Malley agreement is finally approved by the Estate and the court; construction begins on the new Malley store.

October   10 Lee is Chairman of the Urban Affairs Conference in Pittsburgh, during which Kennedy makes a major-issues statement on cities.

          24 The aldermen receive and approve Lee's proposed 1961 budget, which includes:

> $26,549,582 for General Fund operating expenses,
>   86,500 for a Capital Improvement Fund,
>   5,765,000 in bonding for capital improvements, and no surplus.

A tax-rate increase, Lee's first, of 3.75 mills to 39.25 mills.

          27 The aldermen authorize the Redevelopment Agency to receive funds for and begin the Dixwell Urban Renewal Project. Dixwell becomes the fifth project in execution.

November   8 John F. Kennedy is elected President.

December 21 George Crawford resigns as Corporation Counsel.

1961

February   4 Stevens' construction of the new Malley store stops; Stevens has run out of money. An effort to get Yale backing is under way.

           9 L. Thomas Appleby succeeds Logue as Development Administrator. Harold Grabino becomes Executive Director of the Redevelopment Agency.

May   22 The Board of Education adopts a school construction proposal to replace roughly one-third of the city's school plant.

The State Highway Department begins acquisition and relocation preliminary to the construction of Interstate 91.

June   1 The Redevelopment Agency staff is preparing an anti-poverty program for Ford Foundation support.

           6 Justin L. O'Brien retires as Superintendent of Schools.

12 Lee receives an honorary degree from Yale University.

July   6 The aldermen authorize the Redevelopment Agency to accept federal funds for a comprehensive review of existing urban renewal projects and a determination of what other action is necessary. This community renewal plan study is to provide a basis for further urban renewal programs.

August   7 The Board of Aldermen passes the school construction program.

13 Republicans nominate Henry H. Townshend, an alderman from the 32nd ward, to run against Lee. He campaigns against the delays in the Church Street Project, the rise in assessments, and the increasing size of city budgets.

October   23 The Aldermen receive and accept Lee's proposed 1962 budget, which includes:

$26,986,957 for General Fund operating expenses,

106,000 for a Capital Improvement Fund, and

6,805,000 in bonding for capital improvements.

The tax rate is 39.25 mills.

November   7 The results of the municipal election are:

	Mayor	*Aldermen*
Lee	30,638	23 Democrats
Townshend	26,638	10 Republicans

1962

January   1 Lee is inaugurated for his fifth term.

March   15 Yale University has agreed to provide loan commitment to Stevens. A new financing and disposition agreement is presented to the Board of Aldermen.

16 Edward L. Friend succeeds Norris Andrews, who has resigned as City Planning Director.

April	2	The aldermen approve the new Stevens pact and Yale support.
	4	Edward L. Friend dies.
	8	Laurence Q. Paquin agrees to succeed Justin O'Brien as Superintendent of Schools.
	12	The Ford Foundation gives New Haven $2,500,000 for a pilot anti-poverty program. Mitchell Sviridoff becomes Executive Director of newly formed Community Progress, Inc.
	13	Lee meets with J. Richardson Dilworth and gains entry to Macy's.
May	1	Lee meets with Macy officials and starts negotiations for a new store.
	28	Grabino announces his resignation as Executive Director of the Redevelopment Agency and is succeeded by Melvin J. Adams.
June	11	John F. Kennedy receives an honorary degree from Yale.
July	16	Lee becomes President of the United States Conference of Mayors.
September	17	Lee announces Macy's is going to build in the Church Street Project.
October	23	Lee's proposed 1963 budget includes:

$28,812,876 for General Fund operating expenses,

  3,820,000 in bonding for capital improvements, and

an increase in the tax rate to 41.25 mills.

	25	Malley's store opens.
November	13	The city's zoning laws are overhauled and modernized.
December	19	Macy's announces it is going to build in the Church Street Project.

1963

April	19	A. Whitney Griswold dies.
May	3	Dogs and fire hoses used against demonstrating Negroes in Birmingham, Alabama.

6   The Board of Aldermen approves the Dwight Renewal Project, which becomes the sixth project in execution.

7   Lee unveils his model of New Haven.

14   The Board of Aldermen authorizes planning and early land purchase for the Fair Haven Project, the city's seventh.

27   The U.S. Supreme Court rules against unwarranted delay in school integration.

29   McGrath announces his resignation. He goes to Boston.

June   9   Kennedy appears at annual meeting of the U.S. Conference of Mayors in Hawaii. He appeals for help from the mayors in dealing with civil rights problems.

12   Medgar W. Evers is murdered in Jackson, Mississippi.

17   The Board of Aldermen gives final approval to the Hill High School Project, the city's eighth.
The U.S. Supreme Court rules that no state or locality may require recitation of the Lord's Prayer in public schools.

18   Lee establishes a Human Rights Committee to investigate minority group problems and make recommendations.

30   CPI gets a $300,000 grant from the U.S. Department of Labor to provide job training for youth.

July   10   Negroes enter white schools in Birmingham, Tuskegee, and Mobile after Kennedy federalizes the Alabama National Guard.

August   19   The New Haven School Board meets with NAACP leaders on school integration.

20   Henry H. Townshend, Jr. is renominated to run against Lee in the fall election.

28   Civil Rights March on Washington.

September   8   The New Haven School Board bans prayers in the public schools.

15   Five children are killed in the bombing of a Negro church in Birmingham, Alabama.

19 Lee says Governor George Wallace of Alabama is "officially unwelcome" in New Haven. Yale students have invited the Governor to speak. Controversy ensues.

23 The Board of Education resolves to implement a plan to overcome racial segregation in the New Haven schools.

October 13 Kingman Brewster, Jr., is named to succeed Griswold as President of Yale.

18 New Haven receives a $800,000 federal grant to combat juvenile delinquency. This is the first such grant given, and a ceremony is held in the White House.

21 The Board of Aldermen receives and approves Lee's 1964 budget, which includes:

$30,337,993 for General Fund operating expenses,
6,516,500 in bonding for capital improvements, and
a tax rate of 41.00 mills, a reduction of .25 mills.

November 3 The results of the municipal election are:

Mayor		Aldermen
Lee	33,150	30 Democrats
Townshend	21,805	3 Republicans

9 The Board of Aldermen authorizes the Redevelopment Agency to proceed with early land acquisition under the Newhallville Renewal Project, the city's ninth.

November 22 President Kennedy is killed in Dallas.

1964

January 1 Lee is inaugurated for his sixth term.
April 11 Kingman Brewster, Jr., is inaugurated as President of Yale.

12 The connector from Interstate 91 through East Rock Park is announced by State Highway Department. Controversy follows.

May	14	The Human Rights Committee recommendation for a strong local anti-discrimination ordinance is passed by the Board of Aldermen.
	27	Stevens' development obligations are transferred to the Gilbane Building Company, John McShain, and the Fusco-Amatruda Company. Yale loan commitment is liquidated.
June	3	The Board of Education's proposed racial integration plan becomes public knowledge; controversy follows.
July	2	President Johnson signs the Civil Rights Act of 1964.
July	8	The Board of Education adopts a racial integration plan for the fall term. Taxpayer groups attempt an injunction.
	17	Barry Goldwater is nominated to run for President.
	18	Racial violence erupts in Harlem, spreads to other cities.
	19	The Connecticut Superior Court denies the injunction against the integration plan.
August	2	President Johnson signs the Civil Rights Act of 1964.
	27	Paquin announces he will resign to become Superintendent of Baltimore Public Schools the following year.
	30	President Johnson signs the Economic Opportunity Act of 1964.
October	22	Lee's proposed 1965 budget is accepted by the Board of Aldermen. It includes:

$32,278,497 for General Fund operating expenses, and
4,963,000 in bonding for capital improvements.

The tax rate is increased to 44.75 mills.

November	3	President Johnson is elected.
	9	The Board of Aldermen approves early land acquisition for the Newhallville Renewal Project.
	25	CPI becomes one of the first local anti-poverty agencies to receive an OEO grant. It receives $430,000.

1965

January   10   Lee appoints former Mayor Celentano to be the Chairman of the Equal Opportunities Commission, which is set up under the anti-discrimination ordinance.

February   27   L. Thomas Appleby resigns as Development Administrator to become Executive Director of the Washington, D.C., Redevelopment Land Agency. He is succeeded by Melvin J. Adams.

March   31   The Ford Foundation awards CPI another $2,500,000 grant.

June   30   In his last act as Superintendent, Paquin suspends a high-school principal for poor record-keeping in college transcripts. George Kennedy succeeds Paquin as Superintendent.

August   16   Joseph Einhorn, a furniture salesman and chairman of a citizen's group protesting the integration plan, becomes the Republican candidate for Mayor.

October   20   Lee's proposed 1966 budget includes:

$34,897,154 in General Fund operating expenses, and
5,405,000 in bonding for capital improvements.

The tax rate remains 44.75 mills.

November   2   The results of the municipal election are:

Mayor		*Aldermen*
Lee	33,392	33 Democrats
Einhorn	17,099	0 Republicans

1966

January   1   Lee is inaugurated for his seventh term as Mayor of New Haven.

Index